Meeting the
Tree of Life

Meeting the Tree of Life

A Teacher's Path

JOHN TALLMADGE

University of Utah Press
Salt Lake City

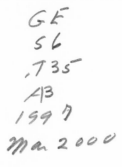
©1997 by the University of Utah Press
All rights reserved
Design: Mary Shapiro
Cover Illustration: Ann Zwinger

Library of Congress Cataloging-in-Publication Data
Tallmadge, John.
Meeting the tree of life : a teachers' path / John Tallmadge.
p. cm.
Includes bibliographical references.
ISBN 0–87480–530–9 (cloth : alk. paper).
ISBN 0–87480–531–7 (paper : alk. paper)
1. Tallmadge, John—Journeys—United States. 2. Environmentalism.
3. Wilderness areas—Environmental aspects—United States.
4. Environmentalists—United States—Biography.
I. Title.
GE56. T35A3   1997
508' .092—dc20   96–42234

Permission to reprint portions of this work is gratefully acknowledged.
Previous versions of "The John Muir Trail," "Into the Deeps," and "In the Mazes of
Quetico" appeared in *Orion* magazine. "A Home in the Winds," "The Great Divide,"
and "Moving to Minnesota" originally appeared in *North Dakota Quarterly.*
"Meeting the Tree of Life" first appeared in *Witness.*

Permission is gratefully acknowledged to quote lyrics from "Wayward Wind"
by Stan Lebowsky and Herbert Newman,
Copyright ©1955 PolyGram International Publishing, Inc.
Copyright renewed. Used by permission. All rights reserved.

For Howard and Kate Tallmadge

Contents

Preface

Imagine a map of North America drawn from your memory instead of from the atlas. It is made of strong places stitched together by the vivid threads of transforming journeys. It contains all the things you learned from the land and shows where you learned them. It reveals your home range as a creature of body and soul.

Think of this map as a living thing, not a chart but a tissue of stories that grows half-consciously with each experience. It tells where and who you are with respect to the earth, and in times of stress or disorientation it gives you the bearings you need in order to move on. We all carry such maps within us as sentient and reflective beings, and we depend upon them unthinkingly, as we do upon language or thought. For the land is part of us no matter what we believe or where we happen to live. And it is a part of wisdom, to consider this ecological aspect of our identity, so that we can become better teachers and storytellers and stewards of the earth.

This book offers a glimpse of how such a map can grow. It draws on my experiences in the wilderness and the university from the time I left the army as a young man of twenty-six until I left the classroom as a seasoned teacher of forty. During this period I was learning my craft, seeking a home, and exploring both inner and outer landscapes under the influence of great nature writers, whom I regarded not just as artists and scientists, but as guides for the conduct of life. My outer landscape consisted of cities and colleges and some of America's most remote and beautiful places. My inner landscape consisted of memory, desire, great books, and a soaring idealism shared by all those who came of age in the 1960s. We were all inspired by the movements for peace, civil rights, women's liberation, and nature, though some expressed themselves more flamboyantly than others.

Although the stories in this book are drawn from experience, the fact that they happened to me matters less than the common process they reveal. Memoirs are usually produced by celebrities, but there must be as much wisdom and miracle in the events of anyone's life, and even more, if we only took time to look. That grace abounds has long been known but is somehow quickly forgotten. With respect to danger, endurance, and heroism in general, these journeys will hardly seem melodramatic. Anyone can go to the wilderness, after all—it's one of our country's most democratic endowments—and a modicum of attention will always yield valuable lessons. As for speaking in the first person, Thoreau proclaimed that he would not talk so much about himself if there were anyone else whom he knew as well. But writing, I think, can serve just as well for discovery as it does for exposition, and minister to ignorance as well as to knowledge. More often than not, I have written to find out.

Nor does the book aspire to autobiography, that is, to a comprehensive account of the writer's life. For one thing, life consists of many concurrent stories, braided like colored yarn. Slice through it on a given day, and you get what appears to be a complex mosaic of events. The writer's task is to follow the colors, to tease out those episodes that belong to the story at hand. For another thing, my career as a scholar and teacher went on after the catastrophic events recalled in the final chapter. I became a husband and father, a householder, a dean. I moved to another part of the country and took a position at a new kind of university. I found that one can enact a vocation in rich and productive ways never before imagined. But all that belongs to another story.

This book is written for all those who have tried to pursue their personal, professional, and ecological lives with dignity. I hope it will speak especially to students and teachers drawn to the wisdom and beauty of the land. They have been my closest companions on the journeys herein described, and for them a short bibliographic essay has been appended.

No book like this comes to light under one person's hands alone. An author's last pleasure is to offer a bow of gratitude to all those who have helped with the work. I owe deep and profound thanks to my family: to my parents, Howard and Kate Tallmadge, who taught me to love adventure and care for the land; to my brother and sister, Allin Tallmadge and Mary Kate Holden, who accompanied me on my earliest travels at Lake Waramaug; to my wife, Pam Bach, whose love, constancy, and good sense have sustained all my life and work for more than ten years; and to my daughters, Rosalind and Elizabeth, who remind me each day that exuberance is beauty.

I have been blessed with wonderful teachers during my growth as a writer and scholar. My undergraduate mentor, Peter Bien of Dartmouth College, helped launch my teaching career and has sustained me with friendship, wisdom, and critical insights for more than twenty-five years. The late A. B. Giamatti and Peter Demetz of Yale University provided models of humane and rigorous scholarship combined with first-rate teaching. The late Ken Eble of the University of Utah and Wayne Carver and Bill Woehrlin of Carleton College affirmed my faith in the academy as a community of teachers. Sherman Paul, of the University of Iowa and Wolf Lake, Minnesota, jump-started my scholarly career with an invitation to write on John Muir; he improved this book immeasurably with heady draughts of encouragement and tough-minded critique through a correspondence that continued, with heroic generosity, into the final months of his life.

Much of whatever literary quality these stories possess is due to the counsel of wise and perceptive editors. Aina Niemela, George Russell, and the late Olivia Gilliam first brought my wilderness writing to light in *Orion* magazine; without them, this book would never have been born. Barbara Dean saw the potential in these early articles and solicited the germinal proposal, then offered priceless wisdom and encouragement during the long years of gestation. Ed Lueders of the University of Utah has been an invaluable mentor, colleague, hiking companion, and editor; to him I owe particular gratitude for my understanding of personal narrative, for astute stylistic suggestions, and for recommending this book to the University of Utah Press. Thanks to Peter Stine and Thomas J. Lyon, who commissioned the title essay for a special issue of *Witness*, and to Robert W. Lewis for publishing three chapters in *North Dakota Quarterly*. And particular thanks to Mick Duffy and the staff at Utah for investing so much faith, imagination, and effort in bringing this book into the world.

I am grateful to the companions, named and unnamed, who made each wilderness journey so much more than a lonely pilgrimage. I am particularly thankful to Vern Bailey and Bob Tisdale for introducing me to the Boundary Waters and Quetico. Thanks to my students at Yale, Dartmouth, the University of Utah, and Carleton College for helping me learn the art, craft, and humility of teaching. Thanks to the learners, faculty, staff, and administrative colleagues at the Union Institute who provided intellectual and professional support during the final years of composition. And special thanks to the Orion Society and the Association for the Study of Literature and Environment for creating opportunities for dialogue and fellowship on a national scale.

Many companions in the nature writing community have nurtured my work over the years. John Elder of Middlebury College has been a constant friend and inspiration during our long shared journeys in education, literature, family life, and the way of the spirit. Parker Huber has been a vessel of light. Ann Zwinger has strengthened me with her wisdom and her art, especially her lovely gift of a jack pine bough used in the design. Many others read portions of the manuscript, offering counsel that strengthened my resolve and improved my prose. Particular thanks in this regard to Scott Russell Sanders and Mitch Thomashow, who reviewed the manuscript for Utah; to Mike Branch, Scott Slovic, and Cheryll Glotfelty of ASLE; to John Calderazzo, Tom Fleischner, Ed Grumbine, Bill Howarth, Torsten Kjellstrand, Barry Lopez, Tom Lyon, Joe Meeker, John Miles, Sy Montgomery, Gary Nabhan, Dick Nelson, Michael Patton, Fred Taylor, Steve Trimble, and Terry Tempest Williams. You inspire me by your example and challenge me with your regard. You teach me the meaning of grace.

Meeting the
Tree of Life

CHAPTER ONE

On the Road

REPRESENTATIVE MEN

They say a thousand-mile journey begins with a single step. Today that step is usually into a car.

The car I stepped into one hot July afternoon in 1973 was a Volkswagen beetle, folk vehicle of the Vietnam era. It was parked in a Philadelphia suburb shaded by trees so dense that moss had grown up through the cracks in the pavement. After three years in the army, its owner and I were about to set off for California. We intended to hike the John Muir Trail from Mt. Whitney north to Yosemite Valley, following the crest of the High Sierra. Two hundred miles of backpacking at altitude, with several peaks thrown in, seemed a good way to purge ourselves of the toxins of military life. After that we could return with a free will to graduate school and resume the long climb toward careers in college teaching.

My friend hugged his parents and slipped behind the wheel. As we backed into the street, I felt our journey begin as smoothly as the launching of a canoe. We glided past large, elegant homes that showed no inclination to move—for in this town the money was as old as the trees—and entered a thoroughfare clogged with rush-hour traffic. It was an unobtrusive beginning. The maze opened without a sound, and we entered intent on the path ahead, never imagining which turns would eventually give our journey its true shape. Movement was freedom, and freedom burned on my tongue like cinnamon after three years of numbing routine. I began to watch for the blue and red signs of the interstate highway that would carry us west toward a new life of adventure.

What we had planned was nothing special, of course. Americans have always gone into the wilderness. Young Indians on the threshold of manhood went off to fast and dream in the mountains, seeking visions. White settlers, less attuned to the spirits of place, just filled the powder horn and hopped the back fence. Genteel explorers like Francis Parkman and Henry Thoreau used the railroad or the steamship to reach their jumping-off places. For all of these people, an obvious frontier still bounded the civilized world. But for us, living late in the twentieth century, frontier had always been more an internal sense than a geographic fact. Because we had grown up far from wilderness, in cities and suburbs whose land had been shaped to our needs, adventure always seemed to begin with a drive on some interstate highway. The road plucked us bodily from a seething indoor life, but it also imposed a passive interval that prepared us, like meditation, for the second step of the journey, the one that leads out of the car and onto the trail.

Up on I-76 the traffic was rushing westward, and we accelerated to join the flow. I watched Philadelphia shrink to a smudge in the mirror as suburbs whizzed by and thinned to farmland and woods. The sun poured a long, mellow light on the road as my mind relaxed to familiar highway sounds: the roar of the engine, the hum of tires, the thumps of the wheels riding over the pavement joints. After a while I ceased to notice these sounds; they became background noise, like my heartbeat or breathing. In the exhilaration of departure, I fancied the road would bear us to California in no time. I ceased to remark the small towns we passed—Ephrata, Carlisle— and fell into memories released by the sounds of the road.

During the Vietnam War, a man with a low draft number had three choices: report for duty when called, enlist with a training option, or flee the country. My number had come up during my first year in graduate school, and I had enlisted for Russian training at the Defense Language Institute in Monterey, California. For a scholar, this was pretty soft duty, more like a college than a military post, but my friends and I still felt like political prisoners. I remember craving freedom and authenticity during that winter in California. After class there was nothing to do on base except bowl, watch movies, or drink beer. But off-base lay the grand seascapes of Big Sur. Each Saturday I would hitchhike down the coast, admiring the gaunt cliffs edged with surf, the silver fog, the calligraphic cypresses, the gray light sparkling on the sea below. In a bookstore on Cannery Row I found thin volumes of Robinson Jeffers, whose bitter verses reflected the alienation and wonder that I had felt. More important, I found John Muir's guide to Yosemite. Written in the serenity of age, it captured the passion of a young man's first encounter with mountains. Muir had turned to nature at a time of despair. After nearly losing his sight in a factory accident, he had given up engineering and disappeared into the Sierra Nevada. There he had lived like a tramp for six years, exploring, collecting, tracing the ancient glaciers. Muir had discovered beauty and grace in the most rugged and inaccessible places. In the midst of solitude he had found joy. His words awakened the hope of an inner freedom won through strenuous encounters with wilderness. Perhaps the Sierra could offer a healing joy to counteract the dead days of the army.

By May the coastal counties were already turning brown, but snow still lay waist-deep on the rim of Yosemite Valley. One Friday evening I left the barracks with a couple of friends and drove eastward away from the sea toward the Coast Range hills. We stopped on Pacheco Pass to look out across the Central Valley as Muir had done, but instead of his sea of wildflowers we saw only the colored grids of industrial farming. The road cut through baked fields reeking of dust and fertilizer, past small towns of pink stucco houses surrounded by almond and fig plantations beyond which tall orange clouds rose over the mountains. At dusk the city of Merced appeared like a smear of lights, and the road began climbing through foothill pastures where slabs of eroded slate stuck up like tombstones. Behind us night filled the valley with blue haze; ahead the black, crystalline silhouettes of pines appeared. Cool air poured into the car, fragrant with sage. The road twisted into the night, and I soon lost all sense of direction apart from the glowing center line. Eventually we began to descend, cutting back and forth until the road suddenly leveled off, and I heard beyond the roar of our engine the glorious, liquid rumble of mountain water. This was the Merced, John Muir's "River of Mercy." We stopped and got out to listen, inhaling its clean, effervescent, and scentless fragrance, feeling through our soles the thud of boulders shifting in its bed. Perhaps it was only the accumulated distaste of months of army life, or my dreamy mood after three hours of driving, but as I gazed at that tumbling water, glowing faint blue in the starlit air, it seemed less like a geological phenomenon than a living creature. I felt an inclination to bow, to thank it for greeting me. But instead I shivered and got back into the car.

The road burrowed into the mountains, following the Merced Canyon. At one point it passed under a boulder that had slipped from the wall above. A toll booth appeared, built out of logs, and a sleepy ranger waved us through. Huge trees loomed in the headlights, crowding the road. We could no longer hear the river, but we felt the canyon widen as if its walls had suddenly swung back. A white glow broke through the trees on our left. We pulled over and stepped outside. Beyond the trees rose an immense rock wall. A full moon had risen, and the rock glowed under its light like marble. This was my first view of El Capitan. I could not see the top without tilting back far enough to endanger my balance. Yet strangely enough, I felt neither shock nor fear. It was as if a great wave had lifted me up and left me gently but permanently displaced.

Next morning we hiked up the Merced toward the high country, following the first few miles of the John Muir Trail. Gazing at Vernal and Nevada falls, I felt all the lover's emotions: excitement, wonder, breathless anticipation, even a deep ache in the chest. I hardly noticed the cars and tourists in the valley, or the paving that had been slapped incongruously on the first mile of trail. All that seemed parenthetical, of less consequence amid Yosemite's flooding beauty than dead leaves scattered on a stream. That night we camped at Nevada Fall and watched a bear try to steal our food. The next morning we climbed the shoulder of Half Dome and gazed off toward the head of the valley, where other domes sloped as gracefully as sculptures into a toy forest three thousand feet below. At the sky's edge rose the peaks of the High Sierra, gray as aluminum and streaked with snow. The Merced wound in among them and disappeared. I wanted to follow it to the regions of rock and ice from which all the life in the valley seemed to flow. I could feel those high peaks beckoning me. I knew that I had to come back here as often as possible. I had to know this place. Like the pilgrim whose soul once felt the force of overmastering love, I had to behold its spirit face to face.

From that moment I understood Muir's extravagant desire. But unlike him my friends and I were forced to make trips on weekends. The road made it possible for us to lead double lives. Weekdays we reported for duty, taciturn, uniformed, and obedient. Weekends we followed rivers to their sources in glacial ice. We cooked over campfires and made our beds under the sky. And when we returned, exhilarated and overtired after five hours of driving, we slept lightly and took up our duties next day with the buoyant deliberation of sleepwalkers. Our uniforms were a perfect disguise; they made us invisible to the eyes of authority. No one could hurt us, because our souls were elsewhere: as we lay on our bunks in the hours before dawn, we could still feel them leaping upon the mountains.

The wilderness gave us a sense of authenticity. At times I felt guilty about having so much fun, even while other GIs were wasting their weekends in beer joints or topless bars. When I watched news clips from Vietnam or read about someone burning his draft card, I wondered if my friends and I were living in bad faith. But as Yosemite sank more deeply into my mind, I began to see that these weekend excursions were part of a great turning toward nature that had engaged our entire generation. We had not been acting solely for ourselves, but as what Emerson had called "representative men." Our journeys were quests for a durable scale of values, explorations of moral as well as physical landscapes.

That was why we needed wilderness, not the tamed and well-groomed nature of gardens and parks but nature in its most elemental and inhuman form. Our generation was struggling to form an identity based on romantic principles: deep feelings, artistic intuition, the worship of nature, and the politics of rebellion. Like Protestant reformers, we sought to go back to a purer life by rebuilding our institutions upon the foundation of nature. It was not just bored GIs, but a whole generation that felt this hunger for authenticity. Raised in a time of prosperity and technical marvels, we had come to believe that all things would be possible for us, that nothing would be denied. Yet as we came of age, we had discovered how much this good life depended on cheap minority labor, the despoliation of land, and a military-industrial complex that required human sacrifice in the form of wars in remote, "expendable" countries. We saw in the wilderness, with its healthy and interdependent communities, a model for just and sustainable human societies.

The wilderness also provided models for individual life. Compared to us, who felt torn by conflicting loyalties, wild creatures seemed to be living with perfect integrity. We admired the resolution with which they pursued their lives, the faith they kept with ancestral patterns, the fierce attachment they showed for their native ground. Especially we honored them for refusing to be intimidated. When civilization moved in, they generally died or moved on. Unlike us, who had put on uniforms, they never accepted domestication. In this sense they seemed more virtuous and heroic.

Our generation had also turned to the wilderness out of a deep nostalgia for possibility. The swarming cities in which we lived only reminded us that nature had once stretched pure and clean for thousands of miles to the west. Thomas Jefferson's dream of yeoman citizens living at peace with the land had seemed possible then. Perhaps in the remnants of timeless, Edenic wilderness we could rediscover the seeds of that dream and learn how to transcend the depredations of history. Perhaps we could reach back to a time when the world was young, or if not, at least pay homage to an ideal.

Finally, we had gone to the wilderness because we yearned for power. Like all young people, we experienced the world as a mass of congealed and suffocating demands. We took to heart Emerson's claim that society conspired against the manhood of every one of its members. To our restless eyes, the older generation seemed hopelessly compromised, even diseased. We did not want to become like them! And so, after rejecting their values and institutions, we sought to reconstitute our moral lives through direct encounters with nature. We viewed the hardships of the trail as a discipline that would open our souls to the totemic spirits of place. We felt that our purity of heart, intensity of desire, and willingness to suffer would win from nature the power to prophesy and change our people's angle of vision.

Such was the mood in which I encountered the High Sierra. In retrospect, it all seems clear, but of course I hardly thought of these things at the time. I did not even think of them, consciously, on the first night of this new cross-country journey, as our Volkswagen soared and plunged through the folds of the Appalachians. All I felt was an inarticulate purpose, as if I were riding a wave that was rolling west through the hearts and minds of our generation. Even the interstate seemed to serve our desire, as it bored through the darkness beyond our headlights. For almost two centuries these mountains had kept the Europeans at bay. Daniel Boone had grown up in their shadow and dedicated his life to the lands beyond. The range was a labyrinth, a Gordian knot of ridges, canyons, and twisted streams, but the road took no heed. It cut through the landscape as rudely as Alexander's sword. In one stroke it canceled the geography of the past.

Perhaps we should have realized how much of America we were leaving behind, how much these aspirations carried an ominous strain of denial. But we were confident in the intensity and purity of our desire. We had faith that nature would empower us to live without the past. And so we hardly thought of these things as we rushed down that smooth and luminous road through the twisted mountains into the American night.

A RHYTHM IN THE BLOOD

Next morning we woke in a motel near Cambridge, Ohio. The sun rose, blond and steaming, beyond fields that stretched in all directions. At 6:30 A.M. the radio carried commodity prices, bluegrass music, and the Reverend Ike exhorting his listeners to "Use your mind *power* to get what *you* want!"

The interstate headed west, as straight as a furrow. Beyond its fenced corridor county roads ran off at right angles toward the horizon. We had left the Appalachians and entered the central lowlands of Ohio. This was pioneer country, and these farms had fulfilled Daniel Boone's American dream. Neat and prosperous, they breathed an air of solid contentment. It was hard to imagine the land so thickly forested that a squirrel, as they said, could run all the way to the Mississippi without ever touching the ground. Where these houses and barns now stood, there were once only log cabins whose owners lived on potatoes planted among the stumps of five-acre clearings.

Still, the present landscape was more benign than Philadelphia. Nature felt closer, and after a day of driving the road had become familiar. Because of the uniform scenery, we seemed to be moving more slowly, as if we were drifting in green sargasso. I felt my mind sink toward deeper memories. I knew our journeys were representative, though they had not been conceived as political gestures. But what were our personal motivations?

During the 1950s my hometown was a crowded place. With fifty thousand inhabitants and an area of two square miles, East Orange, New Jersey, was more densely populated than Calcutta. I remember it as a dusky maze of stores, apartment buildings, and old Victorian houses shaded by spreading trees. The city seemed to go on for hundreds of blocks in all directions. I knew I could not get out on foot or bicycle, and a bus would only have taken me into the next town, indistinguishable except in name. On rainy days, when the wind came from the east, I could smell the sea mixed with odors of sulfur and tar from the Bayway refineries. On sunny days I might climb a huge beech tree that grew in our neighbors' yard, trying to see the New York skyline. I would come down smudged with the soot that clung to its bark like a permanent shadow.

These cities had grown up on a red sandstone plain between ancient basalt escarpments: the Palisades of the Hudson to the east and Watchung Mountain to the west, a low ridge that culminated at a point called Eagle Rock. This was the only place from which one could look out over the country, and my father would sometimes take me there on Sunday afternoons. Although the city now stretched beyond the horizon, he explained that Dutch settlers had farmed there three hundred years before. In the center of the basin, three rivers met to form a great estuary, the Jersey Meadows, where acres of man-high cattails had once sheltered muskrats, and sinuous channels attracted migrating geese. But after the Civil War, cities had replaced the farms on the edge of the Meadows. They had begun to use the marsh for a dumping ground, and industry, attracted by such cheap land, had begun to build factories on top of the fill.

After World War II, my father had gone to work in a Meadows plant that employed fourteen thousand people to make telephone cable and switchboards. One Saturday when I was old enough, he took me to see the huge furnaces and machines. But what I remember most was the awful drive. East of our home the neighborhoods thickened to slums, their narrow streets littered with broken glass. We passed burned-out tenements and vacant lots dense with *Ailanthus*, a tree known in China as the "tree of Heaven." On the far side of Newark the Meadows opened out, and the road leapfrogged across them on struts of corroded steel. I could see patches of cattails standing in thick, green pools, but no birds alit there now. Instead, small roads cut straight across, leading to chemical dumps and power plants. Piles of black coal and yellow sulfur clustered around the smokestacks. Nearby, waste oil shimmered in pits. On the horizon Manhattan skyscrapers loomed over the slums of Secaucus, while to the south, Newark Bay glinted like dusty foil. Looking back I could see the land rising toward the dark silhouette of Watchung Mountain. Sharp as a pottery rim, it seemed to be holding us in, as if civilization itself were a kind of toxic waste.

From this Dantean landscape the road offered periodic release. My family owned a lake house in Connecticut where we spent weekends and summer vacations. Each Friday after supper we would pack the car and slip onto the Garden State Parkway, heading north. As a child I used to doze in the back, charmed by the patterns of light that would swoop through the windows and glide like fantastic moths across the upholstery. On rainy nights I would press my face to the glass, lost in the bright kaleidoscope of a single drop. More often than not, my parents would carry me into the house asleep, and the next morning I would wake up to a green world fresh with the smell of water.

Like the children who walked through a wardrobe into a magic kingdom, I felt as if I had discovered a second home. Our cottage was set on a hillside. In early spring we could see the lake glittering below, but in summer we had to walk through dense woods to the shore. There the water would open out in serene and majestic light, as if a curtain had been withdrawn. I loved to approach it that way. The lake offered clarity and expansiveness after the dusky maze of the city. Its perfect flatness made it seem like a shard of some ideal world, cupped, as in a hand, by the creased, grandmotherly hills.

Lake Waramaug had been formed when a glacial moraine had blocked an ancient valley. Great boulders lined its shores. On our wading beach I would often find pebbles of granite or hornblende that the ice had plucked from exposures far to the north. Here the soils were not red and sandy like those of New Jersey, but gray and brown, heavy with clay and sparkling with flecks of mica. Thousands of years ago the ice had scoured this land to bedrock, and the country still breathed an aboriginal freshness. The stones, cool to the touch even in summer, kept an arctic dignity. Before I learned the truth about glaciers, I used to dream of a mile-high wall of ice advancing, crushing forests, looming over the hills like a tidal wave in suspense. The ice had carried these stones on an epic journey. To me they were like the words of a great, lost poem.

It was at the lake that I grew to love adventure. Behind our house the woods stretched unbroken to the top of the hill. Halfway up was an old wagon road overhung with maples and ceding its bed to jewelweed, moss, and enchanter's nightshade. My little cousins and I often followed that road to the end of the lake, where it met the old logging trail from Pinnacle, the highest hill around. In summer that was a good hill to climb for blueberries. On its bare, domed summit the glacier had dropped a boulder as big as a car, with room enough for a half-dozen kids on top. I loved to get up there and look out over the green hills to the west. From this height the lake seemed to lie at our feet like a slab of stone. Except for a few cottages and the lakeshore road, we could see no marks of civilization. The view made us feel like explorers, like mountain men.

Wildlife, too, came close to us in those days. Sometimes on our way to the old road we would start deer from their day beds in the wild grape arbors. Afternoons we fished for the bream that swam, glinting like Mexican tiles, among the dull rocks of the shore. Evenings we fed the wild geese that stopped at our lake to rest from their long migration. They plucked old bread crusts delicately from our hands, and at dusk they would fly in formation over the house, honking to one another. Sometimes I would wave to them as they passed. I loved their fierce cries, their spirit of aspiration.

I came to associate the country with all that was healthy, alive, and free, and the city with all that was trapped, artificial, and unclean. The country meant solitude and a life of adventure and contemplation. The city meant work, school, people, and institutions. It was exciting—it offered success and honor—but without the lake, I think it would have consumed me. Riding back late on Sunday nights, I would see a river of lights flowing to meet us: thousands of weekend vacationers returning to New York City. They seemed to be carrying torches, like celebrants in a triumphal procession. And next morning I would wake up again in our old Victorian house with rain streaking the window after a night disturbed by sirens. In the gray dawn I would hear the rumble and buzz of traffic stirring, a reminder that the road would always be there to take me away.

So I grew up with two homes, and the road stretched between them like a vibrating string. Its sounds and rhythms were in my blood; they comforted me the way rocking comforts a child. I grew used to these long trips, and the longer seasonal rhythm of swinging back and forth between city and country, so that at last the road itself came to seem like a third home. I could not imagine staying in one place for more than three months, much less a whole year. I could not imagine living just one kind of life. I was always restless, no matter where I was. I could not relax unless I was moving on. Perhaps it was like this for others too. After all, our whole generation had grown up with the road.

Shortly past noon, the interstate crossed the Illinois border, which was marked by a thick red line on the map and a big green sign by the roadside. But neither the road nor the landscape showed any change. Square, immaculate farms still stretched to a horizon as smooth as green felt and randomly pegged by a barn or a silo. We were supposed to be in the heart of the country, but it did not feel that way to me. These fields were planted right up to the fences. Except for an occasional woodlot, the only trees grew in the tangled creek bottoms. There were no lakes, no glaciated rocks, no hilltops, no old roads disappearing into the woods. What wildness remained had been squeezed onto ribbons of ground too steep to cultivate by machine. Eight-wheeled tractors hulked in the barnyards, bigger than self-propelled howitzers. Steel silos clustered behind farmhouses bristling with TV antennas. Occasionally we passed a feed mixer that towered on struts like some kind of spacecraft. Here in the heartland city and country seemed hopelessly intermeshed. Where, then, could the road be taking us?

By midafternoon our fuel was low and most stations along the interstate had closed. We decided to buy gas cans as a precaution against running out of fuel on the Great Plains, where shortages had been reported. At Effingham, Illinois, we stopped at a farm co-op and bought gas from a short-haired kid in a "Pioneer Seed Corn" cap. The walls of the building were sandbagged with sacks of fertilizer; white, submarine-shaped tanks of anhydrous ammonia were lined up out back. The co-op had no gas cans, but the kid directed us to an implement dealership down the road. We found it easily enough; out front stood a squad of payloaders, buckets raised and extended as if in prayer. Inside we wandered through rows of huge, mysterious parts until we finally stood, clutching our gas cans, behind a crew-cut farmer buying a pipe that looked like a piece of sculpture. On the wall nearby was a rack of wrenches with sockets as big as coffee mugs. We felt as if we had stumbled into a factory.

But outside the air smelled of pollen and cut grass. I was curious to get a close look at the corn, so while the gas cans were being filled, I walked off into one of the fields. The plants were already head-high, and their leathery, dark green leaves rattled quietly in the breeze. Gazing down the endless, uniform rows made me feel uneasy. There was just enough space for a person to walk, but I could go in only a few yards before succumbing to claustrophobia. It was eerily quiet in there. The stalks, stiff as bamboo, seemed to have been thrust upright into the ground. Between them, swirls of sand marked runoff channels. There was no sign of animal life, nor, indeed, of any other plants. This was no Thoreauvian beanfield, hoed for its instant and immeasurable crop. Nor was it anything like the green world of my youth. This cornfield was just another industrial product. It seemed as natural as astroturf.

Back on the highway, we sped toward St. Louis. After so many hours of driving, I felt irritable and confused. My body ached from sitting in one position, and my mind tossed and turned in a welter of memory. Small, identical towns whizzed by and vanished. In the dissolving heat, the landscape began to blur. I was starting to think that the road might have betrayed me. Where was it leading? This was no land for adventure and contemplation. Its neat farms reminded me too much of the army, where human beings were sown, cultivated, and cut down. I wanted a wider landscape redolent of freedom. Like Huck Finn, I wanted to light out for the territory.

St. Louis, the jumping-off place of the mountain men, appeared first as a name on a green sign, then as a halo of suburbs, and finally as a smudge in the haze that crystallized into skyscrapers. Unhappily we had arrived at rush hour and were soon engulfed. We crept across the Mississippi, which I, raised in the East, had always imagined as the boundary between the old and new worlds of America. I guess I had expected the Great Plains to begin at once. But after we passed the famous Gateway Arch, which seemed to fasten the city to the earth like a giant staple, all we found were more pastel suburbs with chainlink fences and swimming pools. We might have been back in Pennsylvania! And beyond the suburbs were only more farms with corn growing right up to the road. What had become of the Plains? Huck would have had to travel a long way to get to the territory.

Three hours later the sun finally sank like a red disc into the Kansas haze. Above its orange afterglow, we saw a jet plane falling toward the horizon. Its fuselage sparkled, and its vapor trail glowed like a comet's tail. It was heading west and seemed to be beckoning. Would Emerson, had he lived in our time, have asked us to hitch our wagon to such a star?

Near midnight I awoke somewhere on the Plains. We had turned off to find a motel, any motel; there was supposed to be a town about ten miles away. That was fine with me; I was too disoriented to complain. No lights were visible on the land. To my dazed eyes, the sky seemed prickly with stars. The road heaved and plunged in hypnotic swells. Finally, far ahead, we saw a violet glow that we thought must come from the town. But when we topped an intervening rise, all we found was a single mercury flood-light. It was mounted on a telephone pole inside a fenced enclosure of raked gravel with a large concrete slab in the center and black, winged pipes sticking up in the corners. The barbed wire gate was marked with a series of letters and numbers. I had never seen such an installation, but it took only a moment to figure out what it was.

We stopped the car, shivering in the unaccustomed silence. The enclosure was fascinating, but neither of us dared to venture across the road. We felt naked, moist, and pitifully exposed, even though there was no one around. The only sign of life was the faint, electric hum of the mercury lamp. Yet somewhere beneath us soldiers were seated at consoles taking messages, checking procedures, and testing the launch systems, all in an environment as prophylactic and self-contained as a space station. Up here, surrounded by ghostly, regimental corn, the place looked as weird and barren as a piece of the moon. It gave just a hint of what that missile could do.

We slunk back to the car and drove on. What else was there to do? Perhaps no escape of any kind was possible in a nuclear age. We had lit out for the territory and driven far into the night, only to find this. Yet somehow it made a crazy kind of sense. For in our time this was where civilization came to an end. This was the New Frontier.

BLUE REMOTENESS

I woke up staring at a white cinderblock wall. From outside came a horrible rasping whine, like a chainsaw striking a nail. I stumbled to the window and looked out, but no one was there. The lady at the desk said it was just locusts eating the shrubbery.

As we loaded the car, the locusts whizzed and clattered all around us. They were ugly monsters, pitch brown and fat as cigars. If one struck the car, it would tumble off and stand for a moment as if stunned, then launch itself with a snap. These locusts looked built to last. They had a robot angularity, like the farm machines we had seen in Illinois. Perhaps it was just a case of parallel evolution. In any event, they were more likely to survive a nuclear war than we were.

Back on the interstate, we passed through Salina and Russell, famed in the days of the great cattle drives. Just west of WaKeeney we crossed the hundredth meridian, where geographers say that the West really begins. The mixed hardwoods of Illinois and Missouri had given way to cottonwoods clustered in creek bottoms. On the gravel shoulders, blue chicory and yellow sunflowers now grew with the ragweed and dandelions, but all the plants had a dusty, bleached appearance, as if they were made of paper. Beyond the highway, shorn wheat fields rolled to the horizon, along which we could see white cumuli starting to build. The light was overpoweringly intense, with a mineral edge we had not felt before. Under it the land seemed to stand forth in its essence. The swelling bosses of cloud looked as solid as polished granite, and the stubbled fields, cut ankle-high, glowed with the saffron color and close-grained textures of pinewood bleached at high altitude. This was the land some had called the Floor of the Sky, where Cabeza de Vaca and Francis Parkman had seen the horizon under the bellies of buffalo. Through our open windows, the wind carried an odor of straw, spices, and baked clay. The dry air sucked at our pores. For the first time since leaving the East, I caught the unmistakable tang of remoteness.

It was more than ten years since I had crossed the Great Plains. I was fifteen then, and the lake had become a small, familiar world. Its forest trails were worn deep, like the path between Thoreau's cabin and Walden Pond. When I was ten, Pinnacle had seemed like a magic mountain, but five years later it was just a hill, a place to go on a family outing with women and children. Even the long drive from the city had become boring and familiar; the road no longer meant escape and adventure, but only a brief change of scene, like walking into another room. Everywhere I went was "home" and afflicted me with the suffocation all adolescents feel, no matter what their circumstances may be.

In those days I listened eagerly to my father's tales of his own teenage adventures: fishing for muskellunge with his dad on Georgian Bay, or canoeing six hundred miles with Indian guides through the woods of northern Ontario. On one trip high water had forced them to paddle all the way to James Bay. When they ran out of food, they ate wild blueberries and fish; at times the mosquitos were so thick that when he slapped his arm his hand would be smeared with blood. By the time he and his friends had reached the Hudson's Bay Company post at Moose Factory, their canoes were as scuffed and pliant as old shoes, and the big stick of pitch they used for repairs had shrunk to the size of a golf ball.

All this sounded wonderful to me. I wanted to experience real wilderness in the company of men. I knew that somewhere out West there were lakes with no houses or motorboats, no access roads, even no names. I knew there were mountains with real pinnacles, naked cliffs, and snowfields that lasted through the summer. They lay beyond the folded Appalachians, which seemed to bind me as they had once bound Daniel Boone. My father understood my frustration and arranged to send me into the wilderness—not with Indian guides, for we still lived in urban New Jersey, but with the Boy Scouts. I went to northeastern New Mexico for two weeks of backpacking at Philmont Scout Ranch. It was then that I first crossed the Plains and came face to face with real mountains.

I remember my father taking me to the train station, dressed in his business suit. He said, "I wish I were going with you." I remember him handing me on board and watching as the train pulled away, though he says I never looked back. I remember changing trains in Chicago at midnight and waking up in the yellow hills of Kansas with the sky flooding in and not a tree to be seen anywhere. It was my first experience of a sharp horizon. I saw then, as now, a line of enormous cumuli ranged at the planet's rim. I saw dust devils spinning across the plain. I saw tumbleweeds as big as umbrellas caught in fences. And eventually, far in the distance, I saw the Rocky Mountains materialize, dull as lead, below rain plumes that swept from the domed white clouds above.

At first the mountains seemed insignificant, rounded like the hills I knew. I was disappointed. But as we approached, they seemed to recede, gathering themselves into an awful reserve. An hour later, they filled our view, massed like an overhanging wave of stone, like the glaciers of which I had dreamed as a child. I could see three separate storms breaking over them, cleft by wedges of dazzling blue. Hail clattered against the windows, then ceased as the sun poured in. A few minutes later we plunged into heavy rain and lost our view, only to emerge as quickly as if we had just run through a waterfall. Fascinated, I realized that these mountains were making weather. Back east, storms came and went; the lakes and hills passively received them. But out here the land expressed itself in storms. It was dynamic, spirited. It was alive.

I didn't tell anyone about these feelings, of course. I was too busy trying to act like a man. At ranch headquarters in Cimarron, we camped in a tent city and listened to lean, bronzed staff explain how to backpack the Boy Scout way. I kept looking off toward the foothills, lion yellow and speckled with pine, where dry arroyos emptied onto the plain. Through a notch in the ridge I saw a white pyramid thrusting skyward: the Tooth of Time. That was a real pinnacle. I guessed that from up there I would be able to see not only our whole encampment, but also the town of Cimarron and even the plain beyond.

But the Tooth of Time was not on our itinerary. Instead we spent ten days marching through foothill canyons, camping at sites where counselors met us with planned activities: archaeology, gold panning, marksmanship, natural history. It felt too much like Scout camp for me; worse, it felt like a summer at the lake. I preferred the long hikes between camps, where a ridgetop view would disclose the distant peaks, or evening free time, when I could scramble up the slopes looking for fossils in the shale, hoping to spy a rattler asleep on a ledge or discover a yucca lifting its dried, extravagant spire. I loved the scrub oaks, skinny like me, with their stiff, sharp leaves and dense wood that made good coals. I loved the air, so dry it caked my nostrils. I loved the smell of resin and pine duff in the air.

Nevertheless, Philmont was hardly wild. Thousands of Scouts went through each summer, and the place had a trampled, sanitary look. After a week I began to despair of finding real wilderness. But fortunately the staff at our last camp offered to take us up Baldy Peak, a mountain just outside the ranch. At 12,549 feet it was the third highest peak in New Mexico.

We rose at dawn, something that I had never done, but our guide said we must if we wanted to get back by dark. The jeep trail we had taken to camp ran up the canyon until it came to a barbed wire fence. Beyond, a footpath snaked into aspen woods thick with larkspur. This was the ranch boundary. As I ducked the fence, I felt as if I were entering someone's garden, the edge of the wilderness was that finely drawn. The trail followed a stream that gradually steepened, clogged with watercress in places. We passed an old beaver dam with a tuft of lilies growing at one end. In the pond behind it were two trout as big as my arm. They just lay there in the sun, unconcerned by the twigs we tossed in to frighten them.

The trail climbed through meadows, where we found old cabins or corrals and once a rusted pail with a columbine growing up through the bottom. As we gained altitude, the forest began to change. By late morning the aspen had given way to pines and firs interspersed with rocks. White puffs appeared in the sky, then began darkening and clumping together. The air grew cool and moist. Soon we could look back and see the tops of the foothills. We could hear the stream rushing and tumbling beside us, screened by the dark trees.

And then, all at once, the forest opened, and the path stopped at the edge of a vast circular meadow. A blue-green herb like clover grew everywhere, calf-deep and so level it might have been mowed. Here and there a rusting hunk of machinery poked through. On the far side a fan of white tailings spilled from an abandoned mine. Beyond the trees, bare slopes rose into the mist. We could see the diagonal trace of an old road creeping across them. There was no wind at all; the mist swirled and coiled as if moved by an unseen hand.

Though no more superstitious than the average group of Scouts, we decided to stop for lunch before crossing this meadow. It looked too much like somebody's grave, and besides, we were spooked by the writhing mists. But an hour later, full stomachs and curiosity overcame our fear of enchanted ground. We skirted the meadow, reached the old road, and soon gained the upper slopes. Where the road crossed our stream, we struck off uphill, scrambling over lichen-encrusted rocks that looked ready to slide, though in fact they were tightly wedged. Strangely, the mist rose with us, perhaps a sign that we had not offended the gods. Before long we reached the head of the ravine, where our stream issued from a bank of rose-tinted snow. Amazed, we sucked handfuls, then pelted each other.

From the top of the snow we could see the summit ridge, a gray barrier over which torn clouds were rushing. We scrambled upward, breathing hard. At the top the wind roared into us. We could lean forward and not fall over! Whenever the mists blew apart, we could look down on wooded ravines where the storm clouds were gathering like smoke. We could see our stream, the ghostly meadow, and the dark crease of the canyon that led to camp. We could see the foothills tapering off into slopes of light green sage, and beyond them the plains disappearing under a silver surf of cloud.

From this height the maze of canyons through which we had wandered stood forth in maplike clarity. I could trace our route exactly, down the arroyos, past the Tooth of Time, out the ranch gate, and onto the plain. For a moment I even seemed to see the railroad stretching east like a shining nerve to connect our old Victorian house, my father with his stories, Eagle Rock, and the tame green world of the lake where I had first known unspoiled nature. It was as if the land and my life had suddenly come into phase, like superimposed images that lock into clarity. The past lay flat, like an open page, like a story that climaxed at this point. But I could also look westward into the future, where wave after wave of blue peaks broke against the horizon. In the rushing wind, I felt a dizzying sense of power. If there were gods, this must be how they saw the world: not just each life, but all history set forth in vast, geometric elegance. I knew then that for me the path would always lead west, toward blue remoteness. But then the clouds swept in and cut off the view.

All this had happened when I was fifteen. Now, speeding through eastern Colorado again, after ten years of climbing and backpacking, I realized that the present journey had really begun on the top of Baldy Peak. Each trip had been one more attempt to regain that summit high. But so many things had changed in the world since then. I had grown up with a sense of boundless, imperishable nature. I had believed in the West as a refuge of sacred ground. But the road, which I had supposed would take us into the heart of that country, had led instead to farmlands drenched in pesticides, grotesque machines, and rows of cloned, industrial corn. It had led, at midnight, to a floodlit enclosure beneath which the death of the earth itself lay wrapped in a steel cocoon. The road still flung us westward, but what did it mean? What could the wilderness journey possibly mean in a nuclear age?

And yet there was still that old ache to be gone, to step onto the trail, to climb the streams to their sources in rock and snow. It was as if some momentum in the adventurous life were carrying me, like the speeding car itself, toward an unforeseeable end. As we turned off the interstate toward Colorado Springs, the land began rising beneath us. Far ahead thunderclouds were massing over the Rockies. The Plains began to tuck and rumple, gathering to low ridges spotted with pines. Blue peaks appeared, dusted with rain. I felt an aching rush, as if coming home. And yet I knew that inside one of those mountains flanking Pikes Peak, the air force had built its nuclear command center. The mountains that drew me would also draw Soviet missiles. So much for the spirits of the earth. No place was sacred anymore.

Why travel, then? I hardly knew. I was tired of the Plains and oppressed by memories and dreams. I wanted more than anything else to get out of that car and take the second step onto the trail. I hardly cared where the journey might end. The road offered no escape, just paradox. But the mountains still beckoned, and the mountains had never let me down.

CHAPTER TWO

The John Muir Trail

I stepped out of the car in a parking lot ringed by huge white boulders. It was four o'clock in the afternoon, but the sun had already gone down behind the shoulder of Mt. Whitney. At 9,000 feet, the air had a chill that was sharpened by scents of resin and sage. After a week on the road and three days of packing food in L.A., I felt both exhilarated and scared to be in the mountains at last. The trail began as a dusty track that wound through tall pines toward a granite cliff. It looked like the threshold of a labyrinth.

We locked the car and climbed toward a bivouac site at 10,000 feet. From there, ninety-seven switchbacks would lead us to the summit of Mt. Whitney, 14,450 feet above sea level and the highest point in the lower forty-eight states. Beyond that the Muir Trail would thread its way north to Yosemite Valley, crossing the spurs and canyons that run westward off the High Sierra crest. The trail rarely dips below the alpine zone, where spring and summer last a mere eight weeks. It is not what the early explorers would have called a practical route. Much of the country remains as rugged and remote as it was in the days of John Muir and Clarence King, and parts were not mapped until just before World War II. Having tasted the High Sierra above Yosemite and Kings Canyon, I imagined the whole route as a feast of sublimity.

My friends and I had planned an adventure that was meant to be part vacation and part rite of passage. We did not expect that five weeks on the trail would teach us profoundly new lessons in woodcraft, persistence, and personal transformation. But we discovered that backpacking pursued with deliberate imagination could become a kind of spiritual discipline. Months later, immersed in graduate school, I realized that we had grown through awareness in five stages that seemed clear enough when viewed from a distance but blurred at the edges, like seasons, when seen from inside. The trip had worked on us unawares. Its lessons harmonized with the thought of American prophets like Emerson, Thoreau, and Muir, western mystics like Martin Buber, and even Zen masters like Shunryu Suzuki. I came to believe that anyone who goes on the trail for more than a week will return with a deeper sense of personhood, a more intimate and respectful regard for the lives of other beings, and a stronger love for the planet that nurtures all of us, even amid the dryness and darkness of a nuclear age.

This process of growth had begun inconspicuously. Six months before our discharge the East had been sunk in a soggy winter. The external world reflected our state of mind. The brass gave "short timers" nothing important to do, and the army soon wearied us with its blind routines. We began living on memory and desire, dreaming of knife-edged crests from which we could see blue peaks breaking in waves. We thought of trout rising in the green pools of the Tuolumne River, fed by glaciers we had climbed two years before. We remembered the sunlight slanting through cedars beside the Merced, making the smoke of our campfire solid in the dawn. We could smell the pine duff, dry as cinnamon, the ice-cream fragrance of melting snow. It would be good to return as pilgrims to a land that had nurtured us in the past. We began reading guidebooks, gazing at maps and slides, digging out journals from previous trips. As summer neared we reported each day for duty, uniformed and obedient. But in the evenings we gabbed for hours, comparing plans, or buried ourselves in the works of the wilderness writers, eager to imitate their adventures and share their visions. We were sick of the human world, which the army seemed to epitomize. We felt like conspirators working underground.

So began a long period of preparation, during which we studied the route and considered what food and equipment we would need for a hike of 211 miles. All domestic routines were now called into question. Like Thoreau we had to consider the "necessaries of life." For physical and mental comfort in the Sierra we needed warmth, dryness, food, water, and, always, a sense of location. Figuring out how to meet these needs imposed a rigorous discipline. "Simplify, simplify!" Thoreau had urged, but we found it was not so easy. Should we bring a tent, or would a tarp do? The difference was five pounds (we took the tarp). What food would provide the most nutrition and calories for the least weight and volume? (Peanut butter—we took a lot). Our normal, richly provisioned lives had accustomed us to the luxury of not having to make such decisions, but the trail was more strict and would force more self-reliance. Packing consumed many days and made us very deliberate. At times we felt like middle-aged people gazing sadly at their own fat in the mirror. Complex emotions of alienation, self-consciousness, and longing marked the real start of our expedition.

And the mood carried over into that first night on the trail. I hardly slept, giddy with altitude and expectation. The mountains felt both familiar and alien. I was eager to get moving yet fearful of the long climb ahead. And next morning, as I sweated and groaned up the switchbacks, I realized just how out of shape I was. My pack, stuffed with food for a week, felt like a bag of cement. My hips and shoulders creaked; my head throbbed from the altitude; the ultraviolet sun burned my indoor skin. Glaciers had quarried the land into a maze of towers, cirques, and frozen lake basins, but I hardly noticed its stark, inhuman beauty. By the time I reached the top, I was taking one breath for every step and saw only smears of color where the view was supposed to be. But I never let myself wonder, "What am I doing here?" It was only the second day out, with two hundred miles to go.

For the next five days I hiked alone, while my companion went down to nurse an injured foot. After Mt. Whitney the going got easier, but my mood swung between excitement and depression. Walking along the rim of the Kern River Canyon, I could gaze off toward the alpine peaks of the Great Western Divide, drink from snowmelt streams pouring down from the Whitney Range, or picnic in glacial meadows alive with penstemon, paintbrush, or mountain aster. The hot, young California sun beamed from a flawless sky, reminding me that I really was here in John Muir's Range of Light. But I found myself walking faster than necessary, always thinking about the next stop, whether it was a view, a stream, a lunch spot, or a campsite. And when I wasn't walking, I was busy fixing the pack, adjusting a boot, stoking the fire, checking the map, or making notes in my journal. Whenever I had an empty moment, I would start missing civilized comforts like fresh fruit, bedsheets, or cheap novels.

Naturally I repressed this shameful homesickness, but then I would start to worry about other things. Suppose my companion did not arrive with the food, or suppose one of us got hurt? Suppose we came down with giardiasis? Suppose a bear got into our packs? Yosemite seemed a very long way off. I began to dream about the end of the trip, wishing, perversely, that it was already done. I imagined showing my slides to admiring friends gathered in an East Coast parlor with a fire crackling in the grate. I imagined the brass clock on the mantel, the smoked almonds and sherry, the end table with copies of the *New Yorker*. Then I'd get depressed and go to bed, only to dream about sex, my family, my fruit trees (would they get sprayed?), my old school, my commanding officer. I'd wake up hating myself, wondering if John Muir had ever worried like this.

Of course, these conflicts were just withdrawal symptoms. My body resisted its new regimen by stiffening, aching, blistering, and refusing to sleep, while my mind reacted by clinging desperately to its old concerns. The environment had shocked me into an unaccustomed awareness, and I felt like an adolescent, racked by self-consciousness and growing pains. I was breaking old habits, and it hurt.

But after the first week these symptoms began to subside. By the time my friend arrived with fresh food and a healed foot—on schedule, of course—I was sleeping soundly and my hips no longer chafed. I could look across a snowfield without squinting and pick out the trail on the other side. My heels were too tough for blisters and my sunburn had gone to tan. I ate like a starving coyote and even licked the plate, for I had lost all excess fat and now burned off everything I consumed. My sinuses had dried up, and my stools were as firm as elk pellets. All my senses had sharpened, particularly hearing and smell.

As we headed north, the passes seemed to come more easily. The ground grew perceptibly softer at night, and we began to tell time by the positions of the sun and the moon. The land, still awesomely beautiful, grew more familiar. We noticed patterns of weather, topography, and vegetation; soon we could predict where the best campsites would be. It was good to arrive at the end of the day and prepare our meal with Sierra water, then sit back with a cup of tea to gaze at the home galaxy, which really did seem like a stream of heavenly milk as it foamed with numberless stars. We stopped worrying about the state of the world or the end of the trip and started paying attention to what was happening at the moment. Everything around us had begun to seem very interesting. We felt ourselves growing curious and alert, like ranging animals; we had awakened to our new environment and were beginning to explore.

With this awakening came curious reversals of perception. One night we were camped on a ledge near Twin Lakes, below Pinchot Pass. As I lay in my sleeping bag looking up at the sky, I suddenly felt as if I were looking *down* into an abyss filled with floating lights. I panicked, but was instantly comforted by the solid feel of the earth itself gently pulling me close, holding me back from that terrifying, vertiginous emptiness. In the same way, I came to see the mountains as home, and the human world I had left as a prison. All the comforts I had missed during the first week now seemed like debasements: thinking of them brought only scorn and revulsion. How could we have lived for so long with the rudeness of telephones, the lusts of advertising, the fatigue of news, the wheedling hypocrisy of politicians, the danger of nuclear power, the madness of freeways, hamburgers, television, college, money, drugs, taxes, war? Wild and fierce in our self-reliance, we felt proud to be strong and free and seeking visions in the wilderness. We looked down on other hikers if they only seemed to be out for the weekend.

But it was not long before the mountains brought us up short. Near the middle of the trip, we were crossing Muir Pass, on the northern edge of Kings Canyon National Park, when a lightning storm trapped us above treeline. After several hours, we managed to escape into the next valley, pelted by sleet and racing against hypothermia. On the way down we crossed an alpine meadow where aster and penstemon still bloomed under the cold blasts. I remember looking at them with rueful wonder. The weather threatened my life but not theirs. Suddenly I realized how alien they were; this was their home, but I was a transient, good for only one season at best and not making much of a show as I shivered in my clinging poncho, colder and hungrier than I had ever been in my life. The storm was pounding all of us, but these flowers did not even close their blooms! I felt a sudden surge of respect. If I had not been trying so hard to keep warm, I might actually have bowed to them or at least nodded a greeting.

Thus began the fourth phase of our journey, and a new way of seeing our bodies, our culture, and the land. I call it "encounter," to borrow a phrase from Martin Buber, whose writings helped me to understand this stage. By now we had been out for three weeks, and our bodies were as hard and tough as they would ever be. We no longer strained to cross the high passes. Our backpacks seemed to have become extensions of our torsos, no longer "dead weight" but living organs. Our equipment now worked like a semipermeable membrane that put us in touch with the land while shielding us from its extremes. Our biological cycles had swung into phase with the diurnal rhythms of the planet. Sierran elements now permeated our body chemistry: the water of melting snow, the proteins of trout, the nitrogen and silica of wild onions. We were largely adapted now and moved through the land as easily as fish moving within the tides.

We had also acquired new habits in bending to life on the trail, but these were different from our civilized routines. We knew just what to do when making camp or preparing a meal, and we worked as efficiently and as surely as carpenters who can drive a nail with one stroke. At the same time, we realized the deep satisfaction of ministering to our basic needs. Eating, drinking, preparing a hearth, or making a bed took on a ceremonial air; we looked forward to them and used them to celebrate the day. In the process, our basic needs were sanctified and our human nature was affirmed; they were perfectly ordinary, but we had never appreciated them so much.

After the trip I discovered that Zen practitioners, too, have long recognized the spiritual value of simple routines and physical work. To them even something as ordinary as sweeping a floor or brewing a cup of tea can center the mind in the universe and bring it into peaceful and vital accord with its true nature, thus bringing grace into every aspect of life. Writing of the plain habit of sitting, for instance, Shunryu Suzuki says, "If you continue this simple practice every day, you will obtain a wonderful power. Before you attain it, it is something wonderful, but after you obtain it, it is nothing special. It is just you yourself, nothing special."

Likewise we backpackers found ourselves working in accord with our basic nature, relaxed, confident, and receptive. After the anxiety of withdrawal and the fierce alertness of awakening, we moved into a state of poise, feeling as centered and ready as concert musicians waiting for their cue. In such a state we were ripe to encounter beings in nature on their own terms, not as objects but as unique identities, almost as persons (though certainly not *human* persons). By chance a stone, a plant, or an animal would arrest our attention and stand forth as something hard, stubbornly different, vigorously alive, and worthy of respect. Once after a long day, I sat in a high meadow watching the sun cast a pale, clear light on the pine trees growing nearby. Pavements of ice-polished granite swelled through the sod, strewn with erratic boulders. We needed a fireplace, and I noticed some flat stones that would do, but I suddenly thought, "If I move them, no one will know where the glacier left them. I'll be stealing their history." All at once they were no longer lumps of raw matter, but beings with a past. They had rested there since before people learned to write, and their arrangement suggested a kind of eloquence. When Jesus walked, they had been resting ten thousand years. I felt that it would be rude to disturb them. So I built our fire in the sand.

Another time I met a pine tree growing around a rock. It was a lodge-pole with the distinctive scaly bark bleached golden by high-altitude sun. Its top was broken about fifteen feet up, as if it had been torn by an avalanche. Its roots flowed around the rock like tentacles, sinuous as taffy and seamed by years of exposure. The tree looked like a cripple, but its needles were green, and its side branches had turned upward to the sun. I admired its stubborn persistence. I realized that if I kicked it, it would not respond. I wondered what it would do if I cut into it with a chain saw. Then I realized that nothing I could do would intimidate that tree; it would go on pursuing its ultimate concerns until I killed it. Even in a nuclear blast, it would persist to the last second before going up in smoke. It was rooted in place, committed absolutely to this piece of rock, these mountains, this niche in time. It was a living creature with an irreplaceable history manifest in its very shape, its size, its bleached and twisted roots, its broken crown. The tree bodied itself forth in front of me, speaking with its whole being. I felt suddenly addressed. There was no question of cutting this tree. I reached out and pressed my palm against it. I felt the sharp scales of its bark, the stiff resistance of the wood inside.

Days later I was cooking dinner at our camp above Lake Ediza, in the Minaret Range just south of Yosemite. I was squatting by the fire, motionless as a stone and thinking of nothing at all, for by now we had grown laconic in all ways and moved as frugally as Indians. To an outsider we might have seemed stolid and rude, but that evening there was no one around. Suddenly, for no apparent reason, I glanced toward the rocks above camp. There was a small creature that looked like a cross between a fox and a cat. How long had it been watching me? I had only a moment to gaze into its glittering, intelligent eyes before it vanished. It was a pine marten, a rare companion for people hiking the John Muir Trail at the end of the twentieth century.

Moments like these cast their light over the whole rest of the trip, but it was only later, as I was reading Martin Buber's *I and Thou*, that I began to understand why. Buber says that our life consists of relationships; at any particular time, a human being can stand in one of two modes of relation to the world. The first mode Buber calls "I-It," when the perceiving subject or ego looks out upon the world as a collection of ends and means. The second he calls "I-Thou," when the human being confronts another being as a "person," with its own identity and concerns not measurable in human terms alone. The "I" in each case is different, so that human beings also define themselves when they take a stand in one mode of relation or the other. The "I" of "I-It" is habitually manipulative, self-embracing, and consuming; Buber says that of course this is necessary to life, but insists that it is not the whole of our life. In contrast, the "I" of "I-Thou" is nurturing, respectful, and whole, capable of affirming another being's intrinsic nature without diminishing its own. The "I-Thou" relation, so infrequent, so unforeseeable, is nevertheless essential to our spiritual life: from it spring love, growth, joy, creativity, and forgiveness. Anyone who passes most of life in the realm of It gradually feels the world narrowing as all things become "resources" to be used. In reducing the world to an extension of our needs, we dehumanize ourselves. But when we open to Thou, we feel the world expand and brighten as we enter into a larger and larger community of creatures. For the duration of that encounter, when we greet another being across the abyss of differing ultimate concerns, the "I" which we habitually recognize is changed; by affirming the personhood of another, our own personhood is also affirmed, including character, past, culture, and body. For a moment we stand encompassed by that relation, and the whole world is suddenly seen in a new light—not altered, but transfigured, as when a cloud parts to light up a January hillside, or when a lonely man walking along the street suddenly realizes that he is in love. "When I confront a human being as my Thou," Buber writes, "then he is no thing among things nor does he consist of things. . . . Neighborless and seamless, he is Thou and fills the firmament; not as if there were nothing but he, but everything shines in *his* light."

Buber goes on to insist that "relation is reciprocity," yet how can you answer another being who, as it were, cannot speak your language? I remember responding in two ways to these encounters while on the trail. First came a rush of joy, purely visceral and inarticulate, and then a ceremonial gesture of recognition, like the deep bow a Zen archer would make before his target. I did not think of such analogues at the time, of course, but some formal acknowledgment seemed to be in order. Often it was no more than a glance, a nod, or a small movement of the hands, such as we sometimes see in old paintings. To an outsider, I suppose, it would have seemed quite whimsical, but at the time I felt it was the least I could do.

In any case, such moments of encounter and recognition left us feeling buoyant and free, as if we had received a wonderful power. It was almost embarrassing that we couldn't attach it to anything more dramatic than stones, trees, or small animals. Perhaps, like Emerson, we had finally come to see the miraculous in the common. In a similar vein, Suzuki cites a famous Chinese poem: "I went and I returned. It was nothing special. Rozan famous for its misty mountains; Sekko for its water." And Buber, near the end of his book, exclaims, "What is greater for us than all enigmatic webs at the margins of being is the central actuality of an everyday hour on earth, with a streak of sunshine on a maple twig and an intimation of the eternal Thou."

Meanwhile, as we approached Yosemite, we felt the season beginning to turn toward fall. The nights grew cold, and one morning we woke to find white stars of frost on our sleeping bags. Six days before the end, we crossed into the watershed of the Tuolumne River, and it was then that we really began to think about coming home. Of course we did not want to go back, and we now began, ironically, to feel the pains of withdrawal once more. We had fallen in love with these mountains, which had cleansed, enlightened, and sustained us, and the thought of leaving hurt as much as losing a parent or a loved one.

So we tried to ignore the thought, and in the last days we moved very carefully, savoring everything. We camped unobtrusively and left no traces. We felt like gardeners who have been entrusted with a vast and precious estate; every plant was exotic, every rock a sculpture, every fair day a gift of light and warmth. Meanwhile, whenever we met other hikers, we found ourselves telling stories, suggesting ways to avoid steep snow, recommending climbs, views, campsites, places to find wild onions, hot springs, aspen groves, good fishing. We felt proprietary about these mountains and liked the idea of passing our knowledge along. Though we did not realize it, we were becoming stewards.

This phase of returning brought tension, fear, anxiety, and a determination not to let go of the mountains, even if we did have to go back. Swinging close to the road at Tuolumne Meadows, we got a disturbing foretaste of civilization. The groves were full of recreational vehicles that looked like bread boxes on wheels. We passed two men sitting on a picnic table beside an open cooler, throwing knives at a tree. A kid raced by on a purple bike with a foxtail streaming behind. A middle-aged couple was trying to photograph a squirrel as it nibbled a crust of bread. A ranger drove by in a patrol car with a rotating red flasher. Everyone had Yosemite T-shirts. We bought some peanut butter in the store and left in a hurry.

Two days later we climbed Half Dome to spend our last night on the trail. We watched the peaks of the High Sierra beckoning in the dusk, rosy with alpenglow, and then looked down on the swarming cars and restaurants of the valley, already darkened and sparkling with electric light. The human world was pulling us toward family, friends, and graduate school, but the mountains were home, and we sat on the threshold racked with longing and frustration. We felt we could walk forever now, following the Tahoe Trail and then continuing on to Lassen, Oregon, or even the North Cascades. This was not the triumphant end we had dreamt of. Instead of returning heroes, we felt like exiles.

The next day we strode grimly into the valley and fought through the crowds to our first restaurant in over a month. We had dreamt of fresh food as civilization's most redeeming feature, but that night we threw up most of our meal by the roadside. Readjusting was not so easy. For the next month we paced like caged beasts, brooding and sullen but ready to talk obsessively about the Sierras. The human world seemed unclean, artificial, and frenzied to us. Most of our friends thought we were crazy.

Returning marked the fifth stage in our growth, and it extended far beyond the moment of arrival in civilization. As the shock of reentry wore off, I found my imagination returning to the mountains. We had received truths that it was now our duty to share. True conservation, we realized, meant more than simply fencing off wilderness (though that was certainly important); it meant conserving and nurturing people's capacity to encounter the land in all its radiant personhood. True stewardship meant thought and reading, teaching and storytelling, all of which would have to begin at home. "I left the woods for as good a reason as I went there," Thoreau had written. "Perhaps it seemed to me that I had several more lives to live, and could not spare any more time for that one." He had closed up his cabin so that he could put it into a book, thereby opening it forever to the minds of his readers. Shunryu Suzuki had left the monastery to become a teacher, thereby taking the monastery with him into the world. John Muir had left Yosemite to marry and raise a family, but he had also labored to raise the consciousness of his readers to the same High Sierras he had reached himself. We realized that it had taken strength and endurance to climb his mountains, but it would take as much or more to carry them with us into civilization.

In later years each of us would return to the wilderness. We went, variously, to teach, learn, escape the quotidian, or fulfill an obscure sense of obligation. Whatever the initial motivation, I found that these five stages of awareness would almost always repeat themselves. Some variation might come with the size of the group, the places visited, the personalities involved, or the length of the trip, but I would usually pass through the alienation and excitement of preparation, the pain of withdrawal, the fierce alertness of awakening, the poise and grace of encounter, and the bittersweet resolution of returning. I would come back feeling healthier and more alive, affirmed in my humanness, more attuned to the lives of other sentient beings.

For sensitive backpackers the spiritual life need not require extraordinary measures—no vows, no renunciation, no sacred texts, no ascetic mortifications. Such a life grows underfoot, as close as grass, as familiar as eating, drinking, or opening your eyes. After many days on the trail, you discover the ordinary world shot through with flashes of grace. In a spoon-ful of peanut butter, in a cup of water so cold your throat aches when you drink it, in a friend's hug on top of a brutal pass you find the answer to any conceivable question. You see your friend's hand reaching down to assist you, tanned and cracked as an old shoe from days at high altitude. The nails are worn down to the quick, the palms chafed by rock and snow. You reach out. The hand is unexpectedly warm and strong. You start to laugh. The pass lifts you into the sky. On the far horizon blue waves of peaks are breaking. You feel a wonderful power. You laugh again. You know it is nothing special.

CHAPTER THREE

The Fortress and the Monastery

A CITY ON A HILL

Even on the best days New Haven, Connecticut, does not look much like a college town. It is hard to imagine a campus nestled beneath its dark, industrial skyline. In the heat of August, when the blacktop sticks to your shoes, the air smells of dust, brine, and diesel exhaust. Even the town's famous elms droop listlessly over its streets, as if they were worn out from trying to protect them.

Walking toward the Yale graduate school again, fresh from the army and the High Sierras, I struggled to orient myself in a place that seemed both strange and familiar. Like other New England towns, New Haven had been laid out around a common, or "green," from which spokelike avenues led to the countryside. Along the Green stood large public buildings, the courthouse, the post office, the library, various churches, and the campus itself, which spread north and west toward the industrial slums surrounding the Olin Matheson plant (where, rumor had it, bullets and claymore mines were produced). Between the slums and the university ran borderline streets where the cheap housing had attracted graduate students. People traveled in pairs and came home before dark; no one would think of walking, or even driving, a mere two blocks west into the desperate housing projects, where abandoned cars and the fierce stares of young men standing in broken doorways told of the failures of the Great Society.

Things had been different when New Haven was founded, during the seventeenth century. Its charter lists Robert and Thomas Talmage of Southampton, Long Island, as "original proprietors," merchants and seamen who saw commercial possibilities in a natural harbor surrounded by arable land. When Yale was established in 1701, as a training center for clergy, the frontier was still only a few townships away in western Connecticut, where famous chiefs like Waramaug still ruled large Indian populations. Whites were a minority on the continent then, and those arriving from Europe had been outcasts and minorities back home as well. To their yearning eyes the shores of America had appeared ambiguously as a promised land rich with timber and game but also a wilderness peopled by devil-worshipping savages. Unaware that such impressions arose from contradictions within their inherited myths, these Europeans had set about building cities and farms. They had believed, half-consciously, that transforming the wilderness into a garden might somehow undo the evils of history, reverse the effects of the Fall, and return society to a state of grace. New Haven had been part of that experiment, and Yale had been founded as a city on a hill, dedicated to "light and truth."

But in the heat of August 1973, Yale bore little resemblance to the Edenic community envisioned by its creators. As I walked toward campus past the Grove Street Cemetery, where my ancestors were buried, I was struck once more by the dramatic incongruity of the architecture. A neighborhood of compact, wood-frame houses had given way to a world of gothic towers and hewn stone. It felt like stumbling into Europe, but this was no Disney reconstruction; the stone was real. So were the arched porticos, the tall, leaded windows, the doors of studded oak, the steep slate roofs. Darkened with soot, the buildings appeared to have stood for centuries. One could imagine the search for knowledge proceeding in reverent, medieval silence. Yet out on the streets, with traffic blaring and kids begging change for slum churches three blocks away, there was no escaping the twentieth century.

As Yale had matured into a center of liberal education and doctoral research, New Haven had grown into a center of commerce and industry. Like other coastal towns, it had attracted poor immigrants, chiefly Irish and Italians, and later, southern Blacks fleeing slavery or Jim Crow. While Yale had immured itself in learning and privilege, educating the men who would explore, carve up, and rule the American West, New Haven had spawned a multicultural working class shot through with ethnic rivalries and desperate for any kind of work. Not surprisingly, many of its citizens had ended up sweeping the floors, mowing the lawns, or dishing out meals at the university.

Although local labor had always proved cheap and convenient, Yale did not consider itself responsible for the social ills of New Haven. Over the years it had sought to safeguard its privileged business of research and education. One method was large yearly payments to the city in lieu of taxes. Another was one graduate's thoughtful gift of $20 million, which enabled Yale to make over its campus in Gothic style during the Great Depression. Residential colleges like those of Oxford and Cambridge were laid out, Italian masons and sculptors were brought in to dress the stone, and artificial soot was applied to make the buildings look old. But the architects were also concerned for security, and so each college was separated from the street by a chest-high wall and a dry moat one story deep. Ground-level windows were barred with ornamental iron. The quads had iron gates and the buildings had heavy wooden doors. Coming upon Yale from the countryside, or even from town, you felt as if you were approaching a fortress under siege.

As I entered the campus, still buoyant with memories of the John Muir Trail, I could not shake off an impression of muted conflict. I was oppressed by a sense that universities and armies had something in common. Perhaps this was just culture shock, the last stage of withdrawal from wilderness travel. Perhaps it was merely the anxiety of beginning a new life, projected onto the crowds, the buildings, and the streets. Or perhaps it was my last persistent memory of these streets, filled with demonstrators and lined with National Guard troops on a cool spring day at the height of the Vietnam War.

A Long Weekend in May

I had entered Yale in the fall of 1969, with a Danforth fellowship and a low draft number. Ever since the sixth grade I had dreamed of becoming a teacher, first in chemistry and then, after meeting a wonderful pair of mentors, in literature. I had been awed by the power of poetry to exalt the mind and clarify the affections. I could hardly imagine a more delightful job than helping students appreciate great books. Moreover, a teaching life had seemed consonant with the spirit of the age, which was calling for social justice and personal liberation. So many of the current mass movements—women's liberation, environmentalism, peace, and civil rights—seemed to be active on campus that many professors and students believed that the university could model justice and wisdom for the culture at large. Teaching appeared as a noble, even prophetic, vocation, not just a refuge for "those who can't do" but a form of social action itself. Such a vision appealed strongly to those of us who preferred reading and writing to marching and picketing yet also felt caught up in the urgent idealism of the times.

To teach in college one needed a Ph.D., and Yale had the finest comparative literature department in the world. I was interested in Christian epic and medieval romance, which exposed the deepest religious and mythic themes of our culture. At the time I had no thoughts of irrelevance, even while pondering the more esoteric portions of Dante or Chrétien de Troyes. As long as it enhanced teaching, scholarship was bound to promote social change. I imagined that personal transformation in the classroom would have a catalytic effect on the world outside. To teach was to plant the seeds of value and belief that would nourish an ideal society.

So deeply was I imbued with these notions that it came as a genuine shock when deferments for teachers and graduate students were abolished. No sooner did the local draft board hear of my move to Yale than they ordered me in for a physical examination and reclassified me as 1-A, "available for service." I could finish out the school year, they said, thanks to a recent executive order.

I weighed the options: burn my draft card and risk arrest, escape to exile in Canada, take my chances with the draft, or enlist for an extra year with some form of training guaranteed. A friend, who was also a veteran, advised me to read the recruitment regulations, and there I discovered that one could study Russian at the language school for a year and finish up with two years in military intelligence. This seemed like a promising venture. The army would be crazy to send me to Vietnam after such an investment—though such things had been known to happen—but if they did, I could always refuse the orders. At that point, I told myself, I would be ready to go to jail.

Having made up my mind, I went down to see the recruiters. But joining the army proved surprisingly complicated. The sergeant fixed me with a glittering eye. Officer Candidate School was the obvious choice: prestige, authority, good pay and perks, "the best opportunity for a college graduate like yourself." But all he could offer was infantry or armor, and the life expectancy of second lieutenants in Vietnam was rumored to be about two weeks. Next he suggested the Army Security Agency: four years in Germany eavesdropping on Warsaw Pact maneuvers, good quarters, civilian clothes, high tech equipment, top secret clearance. But I didn't want any access to secrets, and four years was as long as a college career. What about a three-year program in Russian and military intelligence? The sergeant denied there was any such thing, until I showed him the regulations. Okay, he admitted, but I would have to take tests; he would have to find me a slot; it could take months. I said taking tests was right in my line, but he would have to come up with something by June. The sergeant sighed and handed me the forms. A three-year body was better than no body at all.

So I returned to class, intending to finish in good form. But the times were hardly propitious for medieval studies. Cries of protest for peace, the environment, and civil rights were intensifying all over the land. Paranoid and defensive, the Nixon administration castigated the protestors and the media, while Vietnam continued to devour young men at a horrifying rate. Both the antiwar and civil rights movements had spun off radical factions given to violent confrontation. Groups like the Weather Underground had been planting bombs, one of which had blown up a research lab at the University of Wisconsin. In California the Black Panther Party was staging militant, stylized demonstrations where charismatic leaders like Huey Newton and Eldridge Cleaver wielded a rhetoric of sexualized political violence that thrilled and terrified the White middle class. On such confused ground it was hard to keep one's moral or intellectual balance. The academy could no longer maintain an apolitical posture. And scholars like me, who had turned to literature in search of wisdom, found their profession under siege as it groped for answers to the most basic political questions. It was hard to concentrate on Old French romance, when, outside the leaded-glass windows of seminar rooms, the fear and injustice of decades were prowling the streets.

The spring before I had entered Yale, two fisherman had found a body in a creek north of New Haven. It belonged to a Black Panther named Alex Rackley, whom police alleged was an FBI informer. The Panthers claimed that the police had murdered Rackley, but the police charged that Bobby Seale, the Panthers' national chairman, had suspected him of being an agent and had ordered his execution. Seale had been indicted along with thirteen other party members, and had been brought to New Haven with eight of them to stand trial in May 1970.

Reaction to the arrests had been building all winter. Leftist leaders, including the Chicago Seven, were calling for mass demonstrations on May Day to free Bobby and burn down Yale, the training ground for the pig ruling class. In Washington Vice President Spiro Agnew and Attorney General John Mitchell had warned that the government would use any means necessary to preserve law and order. The governor of Connecticut had assured reporters that he would send in battalions of state police and, if necessary, call out the National Guard.

In New Haven people were terrified, not just of the demonstrators, but of another race riot like the one that had burned whole neighborhoods during the "long, hot summer" of 1967. At that time Yale had been spared; now it would be a primary target. By mid-April, teach-ins and rallies had focused campus attention on the upcoming trial and, by extension, on all the ways in which the university had walled itself off from New Haven. On April 15 a group of several hundred students called for a three-day suspension of classes and a $500,000 donation to the Panther Defense Fund. On April 21 a coalition of Black student groups, faculty, and community leaders called for a general strike at Yale, demanding fundamental and particular changes in the university's relation to its surrounding neighborhoods. By April 23 the residential colleges had voted to strike and had formed a steering committee. They were followed soon after by the faculty, before whom President Kingman Brewster had stated his opinion that a Black revolutionary could not get a fair trial in this country.

With classes suspended, people threw themselves into the effort to save not just the New Haven Nine, but New Haven itself. Teach-ins were held every day. Undergraduates fanned out into the neighborhoods, meeting with local Panthers, police, church groups, city council members, civil rights organizations—anyone at all who would talk, listen, or get involved. They carried fact sheets on the trial prepared by law students as well as reports on the strike and the events at Yale. Their aim was to counter inflammatory news stories and extremist propaganda from both sides. As the Strike Steering Committee put it, "The destruction of Yale and destruction in New Haven have no place in our program."

As the canvassers reported back, it became clear that New Haven's ethnic, political, and economic factions had begun to make common cause. Everyone knew that outsiders, whatever their politics, would have nothing to lose by starting a riot. They might think of New Haven as a battleground, a trophy, or even a shot at history, but in no sense would it ever be their home. And so, while some students came back with tales of being snubbed or ridiculed, many more told of being welcomed, heard, and encouraged. My friends and I caught a whiff of something new in the air, sweeter than sage. While the outsiders prepared for war, peace had begun to bloom on our very own streets.

Meanwhile, the Strike Committee had organized a defense of the campus. Everyone knew that walls and bars could not keep out firebombs. If Yale chose to barricade itself, it would just invite an attack: it would confirm its demonized image as a bastion of privilege and power. So the Strike Committee proposed that Yale open its doors. The residential colleges, with their dining halls and enclosed quads, were perfectly suited to draw crowds off the streets. If the demonstrators could be fed, housed, and entertained in small, intimate groups, they would be much less likely to coalesce into a mob. So while downtown businesses boarded up their windows, Yale began planning teach-ins, rock concerts, and food lines. A corps of student marshals was formed to help manage the crowds. They were instructed to deal only with individuals and to use no force. As agents of peace, they had to avoid taking sides. They were given yellow arm bands and told to wear ordinary clothes.

As May Day approached, a carnival mood spread over the campus. A strike newspaper began to appear each morning, complete with articles, announcements, and even a comic strip. The strip showed furry munchkins of gentle aspect responding wistfully to the crisis. One watches a frisbee land in his lap, then can't muster the energy to throw it back. "Now that I'm politicized," he laments, "the sport of frisbee loses its meaning."

Though many identified with these sentiments, everyone found some way to pitch in. In times of crisis strange talents and abilities come to the fore. At the Hall of Graduate Studies an insomniac Slavist took charge of security patrols. I followed, incredulous, as he led a group through steam tunnels and basement corridors where the dust lay thick as felt, demonstrating with a rolled-up essay how bombs could be hidden among the pipes. He showed us where he had dusted the attic stairs with flour to catch the footprints of saboteurs. He had taped a tray of aluminum foil to the inside of his threshold, in case someone tried to pour lighted gasoline under his door. It was easy to think of him prowling the midnight halls, his brain crackling with precepts from Bakhtin or Shklovsky.

Off-campus, people had begun stockpiling candles and food, adding locks to their doors, or inviting themselves to visit friends in the country. Anxious parents urged their daughters and sons to come home for the weekend. But home was the last place anyone wanted to be. Events were moving swiftly. On Tuesday, April 28, police raided a house three blocks from campus and arrested two youths for possession of smoke grenades and explosives. That same day the governor put the National Guard on alert, and Vice President Agnew called on Yale to replace Kingman Brewster with a "more mature and responsible person." The next day, three thousand students signed a petition supporting Brewster. And in the evening my parents called to say that my draft notice had arrived in the mail.

That night I had no stomach for politics, or even for Old French poetry. I phoned the recruiter first thing in the morning. There was no word yet on my application, he said; he would have to call the Pentagon. I walked to campus, hardly conscious of where I was going. The buildings, the elm trees, even the cars in the streets appeared wavering and insubstantial, as if the campus were flickering in heat. At the Hall of Graduate Studies, I signed up for security patrol and a lecture on coping with tear gas. At noon I called the recruiter, who congratulated me on obtaining a slot in the Russian program at Monterey. The course would begin in September, and I could defer basic training until July, but I would have to enlist formally within five days or forfeit the slot. He added that the office would be closed on Friday—it was half a block from the courthouse—but he hoped to be open on Monday. I said I would think it over and get back to him.

That afternoon the National Guard began to arrive at armories in and around New Haven. Word went out that four thousand federal troops had also been ordered to stand by at bases in Rhode Island and Massachusetts, ready for instant airlift to New Haven. And that evening, President Nixon announced on national TV that the United States had invaded Cambodia.

Within hours strikes and demonstrations had erupted on campuses all over the country. Suddenly New Haven was no longer just a provincial town with a civil rights problem. New Haven was everywhere. To those of us gathered in the lounge of the Hall of Graduate Studies, listening to the news as we sat cross-legged on oriental rugs, it was as if Yale and its neighborhoods had been caught in a glare of floodlights. The actions and gestures of even the humblest players were magnified to heroic size. A kitchen worker on food stamps in need of day care, a campus drugstore that had suddenly lost its insurance, a would-be teacher caught like a pinned frog by the draft—these found themselves shadowed by vast archetypes as May Day approached. The weekend loomed as a confluence of history and myth from which there could be no escape.

On Friday morning the first of more than twelve thousand protestors began to arrive in cars and buses. They disembarked on neighborhood streets and began streaming down the avenues toward the Green. Some carried placards and banners; many wore motorcycle helmets or hard hats, with bandannas and long-sleeved shirts—they, too, had been trained for gas. Approaching the Green, they had to pass through campus, where they were greeted by student marshals carrying armloads of strike newspapers. In tabloid form with red and black covers announcing "May Day in New Haven," the papers contained twelve pages of strike history, maps, first aid and legal advice, activity schedules, and political statements. One group, called View from the Bottom, wrote:

"We say come to New Haven: pressure the pigs of the power structure!

"This week we feel so strongly the sense of our community. We love our people, the people of New Haven with all our untogetherness and promise . . .

"Our goal is above all to get the Panthers out of jail. And if you like it here stick around. (The people will still be here struggling)."

All morning the crowds grew on the Green. A plywood stage had been set up in front of the courthouse, where a squad of soldiers guarded the lower steps. Except for an occasional jeep on patrol, there was no other sign of the Guard, though word had gone out that they were fully deployed in the side streets. A press conference was held, followed by folksingers and rock bands. The day grew sunny and warm. People sat in clusters, swaying to the music and sharing food. Guitars appeared. Here and there one caught a whiff of marijuana. The student marshals were working the crowd, chatting, laughing, inconspicuous in their arm bands and casual clothes.

The main rally got under way with hot speeches by Abbie Hoffman, David Dellinger, Kenneth Keniston, and various Panthers. Yet despite bursts of chanting and applause, no one seemed eager to start a fight. The soldiers and police kept out of the way, and the morning's festive mood seemed sure to prevail. After the last speech, around seven in the evening, people began moving toward campus with its promise of free food, entertainment, and places to sleep. By seven-thirty the Green was deserted. Yale had sucked up the crowd like a gigantic sponge. May Day had passed in peace, or so it seemed to the tired but elated marshals reporting back to the Hall of Graduate Studies, where my friends and I had been keeping watch.

At nine I finally called my parents. They had been very worried, having seen the crowds on the evening news and heard clips from some of the more ferocious speeches. Surely I would be safer in New Jersey! But just as I was reassuring them that peace had prevailed, shouting erupted in the street below. A steel door clanged. I hung up and rushed outside. Two Guard trucks had pulled up in front of the library and were discharging soldiers in full riot gear. I watched, fascinated, as they lined up beside the library wall, their backs turned on our culture's collected wisdom. These were young men like me, but how changed! In their black combat boots and steel helmets, armed with gas masks and M-16 rifles, they looked like invaders from outer space. Yet soon I too might be learning to use such weapons. I felt a sudden urge to reach out to these men. As I started toward them, a sergeant yelled, "Get back! Off the street!" He brandished his rifle and I stumbled, catching the eyes of a young soldier who was just climbing down from the truck. His face was dead white. I felt the hair rise up on the back of my neck. Suddenly, I knew these were very dangerous men.

Down the block people were pouring out of the colleges. A confused roar came from the direction of the Green. I started toward Elm Street, the most direct way to the courthouse, but just then a wedge of helmeted protestors drove through the center of the crowd, chanting slogans and waving a Viet Cong flag. Dozens of people began streaming after them. The roaring intensified. Soon I heard dull popping sounds, then screams. The Guard troops had not moved, but they had put on gas masks and stood in formation, ready to march.

Seized by curiosity and fear, I felt an overpowering urge to act. Yet there was clearly no point in going down to the Green. Because this was a one-way street, several cars turning in had already jammed up behind the Guard trucks, which were olive drab and hard to see in the dark. My friends and I decided to do our bit for peace by directing traffic away from the Guard. We grabbed yellow arm bands and, with such frail tokens of authority, managed to get the cars turned around and out of the street. Thereafter, I stood at the corner, waving oncoming traffic away.

There was no one out on that side of campus, which faced the Grove Street cemetery. The cooling air grew thick with haze; the roar of the crowds on the Green seemed to rise and fall with the breeze. Streamers of mist soon began drifting across the gothic towers of Yale, and the street lamps burned through the haze like violet moons. It was a romantic sight, yet the first wisps brought a stinging, peppery scent. I tied a wet bandanna across my face and rolled down my sleeves. Soon my eyes were streaming. The backs of my hands and neck began to prickle from the gas.

After that, events took a phantasmagoric turn. A white Cadillac pulled up across the intersection, idling furiously. When the light changed, the driver gunned it. I dove out of the way as it slammed into a Guard truck and crumpled like a beer can. Four men in white suits stumbled out and staggered off into the crowd. As I picked myself up from the gutter, a kid with a Brooklyn accent came by, wanting to know where the demonstration was. He had a bandanna tied over his face and carried a baseball bat. "I got here late," he explained, "I want to bust some heads." Shortly thereafter I flagged down a taxi, but instead of turning away it pulled up to the curb. A bearded man in a trench coat got out, clutching a briefcase. It was Leslie Fiedler, the literary critic, who had given a fiery, politicized lecture a few weeks before. He asked the way to Calhoun College, which was right next to the Green, and demurred when I warned him away. I had admired his lecture; now I helped him button his trench coat and gave him a spare handkerchief, well-soaked. He thanked me and walked off holding it to his face. I watched his back-lit figure disappear, hunched and ironic, into the stinging clouds.

By two in the morning, the streets were empty. Only confused rumors had reached the Hall of Graduate Studies, but next day we heard the full story. After the rally the crowds had dispersed to the residential colleges for hot meals, folk music, and teach-ins. A rock concert began in the hockey rink on the edge of campus. At nine, in a planned provocation, people had run onto the stages and grabbed the microphones, shouting that the Guard had arrested some Panthers down on the Green. Instantly crowds began pouring into the streets, motivated as much by curiosity as by politics. Squads of radicals from a group known as Youth Against War and Fascism were waiting to draw them down to the Green; it was their banner and chanting I had seen. But the student marshals were prepared for such tactics. They had formed a human chain, confronting individual protestors and urging them to go back to campus. They had succeeded in turning most of the crowd away, but several squads did break through, drawing more than five hundred people with them. As they converged on the courthouse, where anxious troops stood guard, a couple of homemade smoke bombs went off. Someone yelled "Gas!" and the crowd surged forward, away from the smoke. The soldiers thought they were being attacked and began firing real tear gas. The crowd began retreating toward campus, where they ran into people still coming down from the more distant colleges and the rock concert, which had ended early because of the uproar. Shortly thereafter a time bomb went off in the hockey rink, blowing out windows and doors but injuring only one person slightly. Had the concert proceeded as planned, hundreds might well have been hurt. Although the Guard used more than five hundred gas grenades, no bullets were fired. Several people had been treated for gas inhalation, but none were seriously injured. The first-aid stations had spent a quiet night. No fires had been set. At dawn the air was clear, and New Haven was still intact.

Saturday brought more of the same: rallies, speeches, concerts, a festive mood. Much smaller crowds tried to provoke the Guard that night, and only a few rounds of tear gas were fired. By Sunday morning most of the demonstrators had packed up and gone; they were followed shortly by the Guard. To those of us who gathered to trade stories, giddy from lack of sleep, the morning sun had never shone more brightly nor had the salt air ever smelled fresher or more full of hope. As we swept up the torn placards and broken glass, we knew in our bones the deep satisfaction of peacemakers. New Haven, strangled for years by hate and injustice, seemed overnight to have blossomed into community. And we had been blessed to be part of that process. We felt like children of God.

Then, less than twenty-four hours later, word came that four students— students like us—had been shot dead by Guard troops at Kent State University. So the war had come home at last. And on Tuesday morning, because my enlistment option was due to expire, I found myself at the army recruiting station, taking an oath to defend the Constitution of the United States and obey the orders of the commander-in-chief, Richard Nixon.

Two months later I turned in my last term paper, shaved my beard, and bid farewell to my garden and fruit trees. My father, who had served in North Africa and India during World War II, drove me from Lake Waramaug to the New Haven recruiting station. "I wish I were going with you," he said. I kissed him. Three weeks later I found myself crouched in a foxhole, firing an M-16. I learned to use bayonets and hand grenades. I watched an M-60 machine gun cut a Jeep chassis in half. And, one August afternoon, I hurriedly soaked my handkerchief as the drill sergeant marched us into a band of mist that had settled across the trail near the tear gas range. In the hacking chaos that followed, I was the only one still on his feet, but I got no credit for that. I had no idea then that these were only the first weird steps on a journey that would take me far from the war and the university, up to Yosemite, the High Sierra, and the John Muir Trail. And later, gazing over the human world from those splendid heights, I had no idea that greater challenges would come from the thick stone walls and bitter streets of Yale, where, three years later, nothing appeared to have changed.

THE UNDERGROUND LIBRARY

Now the campus kept a preternatural calm, like a battlefield shimmering with ghosts. Professors and students strolled on the shaded streets, absorbed in talk. Outside the colleges well-dressed families were unloading station wagons. Inside the dining halls people of color stood behind steam tables, dishing out food to students who, in 1970, had been freshmen in high school. Against the library wall, where I had first encountered the army, people stood reading, sipping drinks, waiting insouciantly for the shuttle bus.

Inside the library was cool and dry, suffused with a dim, ecclesiastical light. Thick stone walls muffled the noise from the street. As I walked toward the checkout desk, which here took the place of an altar, I noticed graduate students hunched in the alcoves on either side, picking their way through the card catalog. Above the desk was a wooden canopy carved in the gothic style and above that a mural depicting the gifts of learning. In the Main Reading Room, where the reference section was housed, pale scholars sat at long heavy tables, surrounded by stacks of books. They glanced up furtively whenever someone entered. In my dissociated state, they looked like sentries crouched in foxholes, as crazed and sleepless from the intellectual wars as they might have been from actual combat. On all sides carved wooden shelves held atlases, bibliographies, concordances, dictionaries, encyclopedias. Above them, fluted pillars arched to the ceiling, supporting canopied niches that, in a real cathedral, would have held the effigies of saints. The air smelled not of incense or candle smoke, but of dried glues and crumbling bisulfite paper, an acrid, clinging scent that breathed up from the card catalog and got into your hair and clothes. It reminded me of the odor of old pew hassocks. Here some trappings of religion were preserved, as if to sanctify learning in an otherwise secular institution. From the outside Yale might have presented itself as a fortress, but from the inside it looked like a monastery, a monastery from which the spirit had disappeared like the saints from their niches on the walls.

As fall term progressed, I began to see the fortress and monastery reflecting each other. Both the army and the university were conservative institutions, worshipping discipline and hierarchy, obsessed with order, and devoted to the pursuit and maintenance of power—physical power on one side and power of mind on the other. Both valued ritual, pageantry, and public displays, infatuated with their own imagery. Both valued asceticism and self-denial, exacting a lifetime of loyalty in return for their richest rewards. Both promulgated mythologies placing themselves at a point where all values converged, so that their devotees could hardly imagine another kind of life. So each institution wrapped itself in Edenic myths, claiming to rest at the center of the world. I remembered talking with one old sergeant during the McGovern-Nixon campaign; he was six feet tall, with a slight stoop and yellow, reptilian eyes.

"Tallmadge," he said, "the army is not now—nor has it ever been—a democracy. No matter who you elect, the army will still be there." And, after Nixon won, he had asked, "Tallmadge, when you gonna re-up?"

"No way, Sarge. I'm short."

"That's what they all say," he sneered. "You'll be back."

In fact I had re-upped at Yale on a fellowship and the GI Bill. I had come back because I loved language and believed in the wisdom that literature could convey, because I aspired to a life of prophetic teaching and needed the union card of a Ph.D. These were not things the army had prized. Yet here I found types as vividly caricatured as any military lifer. It was as if each institution had set physical marks on its servants, outward signatures of the qualities of mind it required. I remembered the top sergeants with fat cheeks and beady eyes, beer guts straining against their fatigues— these were real men—or the lean and hungry-looking majors at headquarters, hair shaved to an eighth of an inch and khakis creased to a cutting edge. They had pale, metallic eyes, not like those of the young men I had seen piling out of the National Guard trucks.

The scholars of Yale also bore such distinctive features. Here, to be sure, everyone was brilliant and learned. But so many people seemed prematurely gray, disheveled, and bent from poring over texts. It was hard to make eye contact, particularly on the street. People looked over or through you, as if their minds were outside their bodies, far up in the ether pursuing transcendent ideas. They dressed with what someone called "studied unconcern," yet the effect was rarely bohemian. Instead one sensed unhealthiness and a Faustian self-denial. I noticed especially the hands, soft, gentle, and pale as wax. These were hands more accustomed to paper than rock, not hands to help you over a pass. They were indoor hands, attached to bodies that had been kept too long out of the sun. I thought, fantastically, of cave crickets and sightless fish—pale, translucent creatures adapted to limestone waters far underground, swimming in pure thought—or termites digesting wood fiber, tunneling toward the definitive formulation, yet pale, blind, and intolerant of light, producing sawdust and methane.

These impressions made it seem fitting that, while I had been off defending the country, Yale had been building an underground library. Though the main stacks held some eight million volumes, only about ten thousand were regularly used. It made sense to concentrate these in a central location with lots of study space. During my first year at Yale, the plaza in front of the library had been fenced off and excavated, and when I returned, the place was paved and sodded and dotted with sunbathers. Three stories below lay the monastery's twentieth-century avatar, a gleaming Bauhaus environment of tan formica, stainless steel, and fluorescent lights. One entered via stairs from the plaza above, or from the main library down a sloping tunnel, beneath whose thin, synthetic carpet you felt the hardness of poured concrete. People glanced up, checking you out. The air smelled of vinyl, books, and sexual perspiration. The study spaces were small and rarely vacant, especially on the first floor, where wells from the plaza let in the only natural light. It was a pressurized environment, built for security, like a hospital or a bunker. I sometimes wondered what kind of attack it had been built to withstand.

In those days literary discourse at Yale was dominated by questions of theory and interpretation. Although the school had long been secularized, it retained the style of medieval universities in both its architecture and its intellectual life. Nowhere was this more evident than in the literature departments, where techniques of exegesis refined over four thousand years of Judeo-Christian thought were now being applied not just to scripture but to any text. Mind was the religion taught here, and especially mind as intellect. Shortly before World War II, a group of professors calling themselves New Critics had begun to revolutionize the study and teaching of literature by asserting that only the text of a work really mattered. Parameters such as culture, context, or intention must be discounted; the work of art should be thought of as an icon composed of words, a concrete object for contemplation, a "well-wrought urn."

The New Critics employed close reading as their primary tool, and by the 1960s their approach had become the dominant paradigm. A decade later attention had shifted from surface features to the deep structures of texts, using methods borrowed from linguistics and anthropology. Below the forms of texts lay the fundamental ordering of grammar, syntax, and mythic archetypes. Language itself emerged as the ultimate object of study, the foundation of all thought and culture. Even the external world, and nature itself, could only be known through language and so presented themselves as inherently textual. But language, according to thinkers like Saussure, Jakobson, and Derrida, was merely a system of signs created not by essential meanings but rather by arbitrary distinctions. So in the end, there was no absolute signification or truth but only a play of difference that ended in circularity, paradox, *aporia*. You could reach that point through a process called deconstruction, which used close reading of microscopic intensity to turn even the most obdurate text to a handful of dust.

These ideas were presented in arcane terms that exuded miracle, mystery, and authority. Yet I did not find their fruits to be increased wisdom or delight. The path of deconstruction did not seem to lead to Andrew Marvell's wondrous garden of thought, but only to a wasteland of shifting dunes. Yet in the hermetic world of the underground library, it was easy to think of words as the only reality. At times the whole place seemed to me like a modernistic defense against nature. I was tempted to forget the taste of snowmelt, the roughness of lodgepole bark, the burn of high-altitude sun. There was no place in this world for storytelling or the mystery of I-Thou encounter. Everyone here seemed preoccupied, bent to the task. The books showed wear; some were heavily underlined, and occasionally I would even find pages missing, razored out by someone intent on beating the competition in seminar. It depressed me to think that the teaching profession must now begin in places like this. The life of the mind for which we were being trained seemed so far removed from the experiences that had first taught me to love books and mountains.

So once more I found myself in disguise, going underground in two senses this time. I found that in the monastery one also had to live by one's wits, no less than in the fortress of armed service. So I became a shapeshifter, a scholar by day and a storyteller by night. In a sense I was still trying to return from the Muir Trail; becoming a storyteller was part of withdrawal from wilderness into the fallen world of professional life. It was not long before I discovered others with problems like mine—for disguise wears thin to a seeing eye—and we began hanging out in the neighborhood bars and cafes. There was a mountaineer from Seattle, bearded like Moses, who studied the history of quantum physics, and a student of German who also farmed wheat just west of the hundredth meridian; his other life was betrayed by wide, chafed palms and a countenance like fired clay. We all went to lectures with titles like "Battering the Object: The Ontological Approach." And afterwards we sat in bars or on living room floors, telling stories of expeditions and harvests and great encounters with the land. It was a ritual of orientation, like finding the north star.

Sometime that winter I also discovered the Mountaineering Collection, which had been placed in the underground library by someone with either a strong sense of irony or a subversive intent. It sat in the first stack; heading back toward romantic poetry or nineteenth-century fiction, I had always missed it before, yet here were the great stories of Annapurna, Denali, Everest, and the Eiger. I found Clarence King's *Mountaineering in the Sierra Nevada* and John Muir's *The Mountains of California*. Ranged on the tan, steel shelves, of uneven height, the books presented a profile that mocked the Euclidean world of the library; it looked like a western skyline, fractal, chaotic, inviting. Stories are like that, I thought, challenging, abrupt, and full of deceptions. They fascinate us with ambiguities and tease us with false summits or melting paradox, yet they also reward us with moments of vision in which the world seems to radiate from the point upon which we stand. How different this was from the planar world of theory! I began to sense that scholarship might be redeemed by a proper object and that storytelling, rather than the crises of politics or the forced disciplines of the military or the academy, might hold the real keys to community.

FINDING THE BOOK OF NATURE

Community, landscape, and language were all on the mind of Ralph Waldo Emerson when he published his first book, *Nature*, in 1836. I studied him that spring in a seminar on American Romanticism—for my travels in California had drawn me away from medieval studies—and was intrigued to discover that he, too, had suffered from alienation. Emerson's America had seemed possessed by material greed. The government was ambitious for war. Religion wavered between evangelical passion and Bostonian rectitude. In theology, music, and art people still turned to Europe, for America had as yet no high culture of its own. As a nation, we might have been young and strong, but we appeared hopelessly unsophisticated and countrified next to England, France, and Germany. Compared to them we had virtually no history. All we had were five million square miles of wilderness.

Wrestling with his sense of belatedness, Emerson turned to ideas he had gained from the English and German romantics, who saw nature as a mystical wellspring of virtue and inspiration. To them unmediated contact with nature could engender art, eloquence, heroism, and even prophecy. Just so, reasoned Emerson, the Homeric Age had begun, and the same thing was happening on the American frontier. Far from being opposed to civilization, as Renaissance and Enlightenment thinkers had held, nature was really the basis of civilization, and wilderness was the most natural nature of all. So Americans should no longer envy the culture of Europe: everything we needed was right here at home. Our social and cultural problems arose because we could not see clearly. Our "axis of vision" did not coincide with the axis of things.

As a corrective lens, Emerson offered transcendental philosophy. We could reach the divine by studying language and nature. Words, he said, were signs of natural facts, but natural facts were signs of spiritual truths. Nature presented itself as a great code, an extended metaphor for the mind of God. One could read it directly, like a book, and so dispense with seminaries and priests. This "Book of Nature" was an ancient idea, teased from the writings of St. Paul and developed in medieval times by Aquinas and Dante, whom Emerson had read. Galileo had used it to argue before the Inquisition, and Jonathan Edwards, that pious naturalist, had brought it across the sea to New England. But Emerson gave it a Kantian spin. "When a faithful thinker, resolute to detach every object from personal relations and see it in the light of thought, shall, at the same time, kindle science with the fire of the holiest affections," he declared, "then will God go forth anew into the creation."

Even though Emerson had not chosen to read the Book of Nature himself, he had articulated a mighty dream, one that I sensed was still alive in America. Even the deconstructionists had heard of the Book of Nature, though they were more interested in dissecting Emerson's text (nature itself being, perhaps, too hard). And certainly Emerson had inspired many in Europe and America, including Nietzsche, Melville, Thoreau, and, a generation later, John Muir. That spring it appeared to me that Emerson's thought had sprung up into a garden of forking paths, some of which led to mazes of hermeneutics and deconstruction, while others led down equally mysterious avenues of storytelling. Which paths led to the gate in the monastery wall, the trapdoor out of the underground library?

Emerson had many disciples. First came Thoreau, who put all things to the proof in action. He had settled at Walden Pond to write, believing that life in the woods would keep him closer to sources of inspiration. But Walden was not very wild, especially compared to the Berkshires, Monadnock, or Mount Washington, which he had already climbed. So that first summer he went to the most remote place he could find, Mount Katahdin in northern Maine, seeking visionary experiences of the sort that Emerson had promised. At first things seemed to go well. Thoreau found heroic woodsmen homesteading northwest of Old Town. On the upper reaches of the Penobscot River, he found views recalling the English Lake Country. But Katahdin itself proved far more challenging. Thoreau's first attempt on the summit brought him alone to a forest of stunted firs and thence to a rocky tableland high above treeline. Nature here seemed "vast, titanic, and such as man never inhabits." It reminded the literary Thoreau of epic and tragedy; Homer and Aeschylus, he thought, must surely have been inspired by places like this. The next day he once more pulled ahead of his companions, climbing onto the Tableland and into the clouds that swirled continually about the summit. This time he felt a Promethean thrill, as if he were offending the gods—he compared himself to Milton's Satan voyaging heroically through Chaos. At the high point Nature seemed to order him off, confronting him like an angry goddess. But that was just his writer's mind playing tricks. Only on the way down, far from the threatening peak, did he begin to realize what had actually occurred. "What is it to be admitted to a museum," he exclaimed, "compared to being shown some star's surface, some hard matter in its home." Here Nature was worse than hostile, it was indifferent. And not even the loftiest imagery of myth and epic, which he had strenuously invoked, could master that awful fact. Indeed, the language he loved as a writer was working as much to conceal as to reveal the truth about nature. Language was no Jacob's ladder to the stars; it simply could not be trusted. In the account I could feel Thoreau's syntax breaking apart as he opts for direct encounter: "Talk of mysteries!—Think of our life in nature,—daily to be shown matter, to come in contact with it,—rocks, trees, wind on our cheeks! the *solid* earth! the *actual* world! the *common sense!* *Contact! Contact! Who* are we? *where* are we?"

A knife-edged ridge leads east from the summit of Mount Katahdin. Thoreau never got that far, but I often imagined him picking his way along it, teetering in the wind between the abyss of language with its dark, deconstructive horizon, and the abyss of nature, where the intensity of I-Thou encounter must end in a radiant silence. I knew that Thoreau could never have stayed in the underground library, yet I felt that his dilemma had arisen in part because he had come to the woods as a writer. Whatever the case, his Katahdin journey is not recorded in *Walden*.

Next came John Muir, who was much less well known at Yale. He had found nature first and Emerson second, a providential sequence as it proved. A hundred years before I entered graduate school, Muir had been building a cabin in Yosemite Valley, determined to live for as long as he could amid landscapes with which he had fallen in love. He was thirty-two years old, with immense talents for mechanics, business, and agriculture, yet he set all these aside for the life of a hobo naturalist. To his family it seemed a crazy decision. Muir had no wife, no job, and no prospects. His letters reveal periods of anguish. Yet he was sustained not only by the beauty of the Sierra and its community of life, but by Emerson's essays, which praised the very life he was trying to lead. On his long, solitary excursions into the backcountry—these were the days before topographic maps and down sleeping bags—Muir would take only a tin cup, a handful of tea, a loaf of bread, and a copy of Emerson. At night he would build a fire and read, wrapped in his overcoat, under the enormous stars.

Over time Muir became a fixture in the valley, renowned for his skill as a guide, his knowledge of natural history, and his powerful stories. Scientists, artists, and celebrities visited him. He had lived in Yosemite for three years when Emerson himself arrived on a grand tour of the West, accompanied by a doting cluster of Boston intellectuals. Naturally shy, Muir hung back at first, yet when he finally made bold to introduce himself, the two men took to each other at once. Emerson was delighted to find at the end of his career the prophet-naturalist he had called for so long ago. And for Muir, who was born a year after *Nature* appeared, Emerson's visit came like a laying on of hands. In vain he tried to persuade the old philosopher to camp with him in the high country, and when he waved farewell at the edge of a sequoia grove, he recalled feeling lonely for the first time since he had come to Yosemite. Later he wrote to Emerson in Boston, enclosing pine cones and sprays of incense cedar, urging him to return for a High Sierra baptism. "Your first visit was only a sprinkle," Muir pleaded, "come be immersed." Emerson responded with copies of his books and an invitation to teach at Harvard. Muir demurred, saying he had more fieldwork to do, but later he confided to a friend, "I never for a moment thought of giving up God's big show for a mere profship!"

Muir's decision caused me a great deal of anguish. At that time I would have loved to teach at Harvard, but I also wanted to live authentically with books and mountains. Although Muir was not on the reading list for American Romanticism, I began to study him on my own. I wanted to find the white thread that had led him through Emerson's garden of forking paths, up to Thoreau's great divide, and beyond to the light-filled place from which his own books had been written. It was not hard to detect a transcendentalist strain in Muir. Like Emerson he had seized on the metaphor of the Book of Nature; like Thoreau he had used nature as a standard of value for measuring people and institutions. But in each case he had made the concept his own. Whereas Emerson had approached nature with theology and exegesis, Muir had come to it as a botanist and geologist. You could tell that he was not interested in reading the land as a catechism, but rather as sacred history. To him the landscape was made up of stories, written and rewritten one upon the other. Glacial striations, the branching of trees, even the placement of lakes, meadows, and waterfalls bore witness to divine creativity and love. For Muir's god was an artist, deeply engaged even now in making the world, and reading the Book of Nature meant telling the story of this creation in words any reader could understand. It was science but also prophecy, for it sought to change our angle of vision.

Though he lived alone, like Thoreau, Muir was also never far from community. Even on his most remote journeys, the human world was constantly on his mind. I could see it in his abundant personifications and his praise of wild creatures for virtues like energy, thrift, grace, cleanness, and self-reliance. Yet such associations were not gratuitous. Muir's exhaustive field studies had given him an intimate, ecological sense of the landscape. The natural communities he observed in the Sierra seemed to be functioning so much more efficiently, sustainably, and joyfully than the human world he had left behind—a world of slavery and civil war, overgrazing and sluice mining—that he began to see wilderness as more humane and desirable than civilization itself. I saw that his imagery collapsed the biblical distinction between wilderness and paradise. For Muir, the Sierra *was* paradise; it was civilization that was fallen and depraved. So Muir came implicitly to reject the Edenic dreams of the Puritans, who had founded places like Yale, and the pioneers, who had sought to domesticate "virgin" lands in the name of God. Muir felt that if people simply came to the mountains and experienced wilderness directly, their eyes would be opened. They would realize that paradise lay all around them, that as far as nature was concerned, there had never been a Fall, that the world they lived in was full of original grace, as fresh and beautiful as the dawn of creation.

In the midst of these researches I found, buried in a footnote, a reference to Muir's copy of Emerson, which had somehow found its way to the Beinecke Rare Book Library at Yale. I had passed the Beinecke often but had never been inside. It was a windowless, white cube set on a granite plaza like some kind of Bauhaus confection, not a John Muir sort of place. Yet inside the effect was completely different. The walls were paneled with thin, translucent marble that admitted light in fantastic designs. They enclosed a vast open space at the center of which the books rose, stack upon stack, inside a plate glass column. Temperature and humidity were carefully controlled. In case of fire, the column could be sealed off and flooded with nitrogen. Only librarians were allowed inside. I filled out a requisition and waited for them to bring the book. No pens, metal objects, or briefcases were allowed in the reading room. Each table had easels of polished wood with thin, sand-filled tubes of green velvet to hold down the pages while you read.

I had no intention of using one of these things, yet when the librarian finally brought me the book, I stared at it, momentarily afraid to touch. The cover was scuffed and scratched, with a smear of pitch on one corner. The edges and spine were rough with small dents and punctures. Inside I found the pages supple and felted from much handling. Many passages were neatly underlined, with notes in Muir's slender, flowing hand. On one page I found a colored sketch of a red fir only two inches high. As I leafed through it, the book felt warm in my hand. Grandfather, I thought, was this your companion on so many journeys? Was this your map of solitude? Certainly the book had a history. I could see that dozens of campsites had left their marks upon it. No wonder Emerson had cleaved to Muir in his old age; Muir had loved his ideas and made them real with his life. Out of Emerson's exhortations and prophecies Muir had enacted stories.

Yet as I tracked Muir's markings, I found places where he had departed from Emerson's path. He consistently noted passages dealing with the beauty and joy to be found in nature, as well as the immanence of spirit and the sense of landscape as divine writing. But he left unmarked those passages where Emerson argued that nature must be surpassed on the way to spirit. Muir, it seems, had been unwilling to climb the transcendentalist ladder. This world, full of "divine hieroglyphics written with sunbeams," was more than enough for him.

As I left the Beinecke that afternoon, I felt a wonderful lightness, as if many things had fallen at last into place. I knew that I would be studying Muir for a long time, along with others who, like him, had followed the path of story. This was the path that led out of the Emersonian maze, up through the roof of the underground library and into the open air. But it was also the only path by which one could return, with sanity, from the prophetic clarity of a wilderness journey to the complex human world with its fortresses, monasteries, and bitter streets. By telling stories and writing books, Muir had made the Sierra real to his contemporaries and so returned some of the blessings he had received. Yet he understood that stories would not be enough. "No amount of word-making," he wrote, "will ever make a single soul to know these mountains." He wanted people to be immersed, so that their bodies, souls, and communities could be healed. So he had conceived the Sierra Club, with its outings program.

But I thought, why not combine the two, create a course that would put students in contact with story and wilderness both? Suppose we read books and then went to the mountains ourselves? Let the land speak directly. That would blast a hole in the monastery wall.

CHAPTER FOUR

The Dark Side of Katahdin

At the top of the slide the wind slams into us. Star tries to stand up, but his pack offers too large a target. He staggers backward, toppling into a clump of small fir trees. The rest of us crawl toward him, sweaty from climbing, shivering in our thin shirts. He tears open the pack, pulling out sweaters, parkas, ski hats. Someone's pink scarf goes sailing off, twisting like a snake as it disappears. We huddle around with weeping eyes, pulling on clothes and keeping our backs to the wind.

All we can see at first are rocks, acres and acres of rocks. They are covered with blue-green lichen and clustered in odd, polygonal patterns, the result of centuries of freezing and thawing. To all appearances, we ought to be somewhere in the Arctic, but this is the Tableland of Mount Katahdin, where the Maine woods are reduced to their elemental expression. Dwarf firs cluster in every hollow, their tops pruned to an aerodynamic curve—"as if," Thoreau observed, "they had for centuries ceased growing upward against the bleak sky, the solid cold." At the moment we are sitting on some of these trees, and the effect is not altogether pleasant, but at least we know what Thoreau had in mind. We have come here to see what he saw and so learn the secrets of his life and art.

A month ago we met for the first time in a Yale College seminar on wilderness literature, sixteen strangers plucked from every part of the country. Star, a blond giant with a sunny temperament, grew up on a forest preserve in Connecticut and has hiked all over the mountains of New England. Shelley, who grew up in Kansas, is used to treeless horizons and has never stood on a mountain; neither has her tent mate, Kathy, who grew up in Beverly Hills and is now on her first camping trip. Jennifer, who comes from northern California, started the class with patronizing ideas about eastern mountains, and Star has been teasing her ever since we left New Haven, much to the amusement of Paul, a quiet premed with lots of experience taking high-schoolers on backpacking trips.

I'm relying heavily on the skills of people like Paul and Star. The class is divided into groups of four, each responsible for their own equipment and meals. We had planned to hike separately during the day and camp together at night, in order to share impressions of Thoreau and the Maine woods. But things have not worked out so neatly. Rangers have closed all campsites along Thoreau's ascent route because of fire danger, and the trails on the other side of the mountain have proven more strenuous than expected. We have been forced to change our itinerary twice. Several people have had to abandon the climb because of injuries. And one group, eager to prove itself, left early this morning to follow Thoreau's descent route back to the van we had left at the base according to our original plan. They set off at dawn, led by Chase, a taciturn Yankee who has climbed Katahdin before and has been chafing all trip at the slowness of the beginners and my attempts to maintain an intellectual focus. I hate his attitude, but I can see his point. I've had to goad people into keeping journals, which was no problem for the sedulous Thoreau; and as for his life and art, we haven't discussed them at all. We've been too busy trying to stay warm and figure out where to go next.

This morning has been no exception. The blasting October wind numbs bare flesh instantly. Hunched against it, we can look back down along the white scar of the slide as it disappears into the floor of the Great Basin, where Chimney Pond, our last night's camp, glints like a dime dropped on a green shag rug. Over the pond rise pillared cliffs, and beyond them a great, dark spur juts out from the mountain. That will be our descent route, via the Knife-Edge, which we cannot yet see. Katahdin's entire north-western side is dark, but beyond the spur a cloud bank glows brilliantly in the morning sun. At its edge, torn streamers dance like hungry ghosts. Apparently, only the wind is keeping them off.

Paul mutters, "Those clouds are going to eat us alive."

"Nah," Star laughs, "our buns will freeze first!"

Kathy asks, "Did Thoreau have a down coat?"

"No," I say, "nor a sleeping bag, nor a topo map. Only a few people had ever been here before."

Her eyes widen. "He must have been crazy."

Paul laughs, "Come on, he was a writer. He was looking for a break-through."

"And for adventure," Star says.

"He was a rebel," says Jennifer.

"Like us," Shelley adds with an innocent smile. She's wearing a down vest lent by one of the injured, having resisted my plea to bring winter clothes.

Perhaps Thoreau was a little crazy, cooped up in a cabin no bigger than a dorm room, writing all day and hoeing beans for relief. No doubt he was motivated by a thirst for adventure, but adventure, like everything else, had layers of meaning for him. It was a way of asserting his independence from family, community, and utilitarian culture. It was a source of material for his art. And it was as much a spiritual as a physical undertaking. As he thrust out from Concord toward the purest and wildest nature he could find, he was really seeking the state of higher consciousness promised by Emerson, where his axis of vision would coincide with the axis of things.

As for the students, adventure seems motivation enough. For the beginners there's an initiatory challenge: will they survive with enhanced self-esteem? Some, like Kathy, are also interested in religious and moral questions, while others, including myself, are drawn to Thoreau as a social critic and storyteller. We admire his insight, eloquence, and integrity. In following his story and his path, we hope to connect with the power that spoke through him. For us, therefore, the trip has an aspect of pilgrimage.

In addition I have a few private motives. Katahdin has fascinated me ever since I first heard the name: a click, like a struck flint, widening into a long moan that evoked shaggy forests and desolate, arctic skies. Katahdin! There was ice at its core. I thought of lichened rocks and patterned ground, of ancient beasts like the mammoth and musk ox, or the caribou that once roamed the Maine woods. Katahdin always seemed like a beckoning place, austere and tantalizingly remote.

I've also justified this trip as a form of research applying Thoreau's empirical method to his own art. By enacting a parallel experience, I hope to learn more than I could from studying his text alone. You might say I am looking for "hard matter" to break the linguistic paradigm. And finally, I'm trying a method of teaching that seems out of place at Yale, where "adventure education" means something you do out West in the summer, using your body but not your brain. I'm seeking a more authentic mode of teaching, where both are engaged, where the instructor participates as a learner, and where the students will leave enriched, rather than merely dazzled, by greatness. This is my first professional course, and I desperately want it to succeed. I want to feel justified in my sense of a teaching vocation, my faith in a new kind of scholarship, my contempt for the spiritual dryness of theory and exegesis.

None of these motives were fully apparent three days ago, when our trip began as a pile of backpacks on the sidewalk at six o'clock in the morning. Whereas Thoreau had taken the packet boat from Boston to Bangor in 1846, we took the interstate from New Haven, skirting Walden and stopping at the New Hampshire line for gas and a six-pack, after Star reminded us that even Thoreau had drunk spruce beer at Tom Fowler's homestead, "the sap of all Millinocket botany commingled." We saw the remnants of Maine's last logging drive cast up along the banks of the Kennebec River, and "Moose Crossing" signs showed we were close to the north woods. But the land seemed comfortably settled till north of Bangor, where the trees closed in and the highway shrank to a single lane. Up here they were still cutting the interstate. The pavement beside us ran out to gravel, then dirt, then finally to piles of bulldozed trees before it ended in uncut forest. To our urban eyes this seemed like a real frontier. We turned off toward Millinocket, where a huge pulp mill had replaced the pioneer farm Thoreau had described. So far did our industrial world now extend, though even in his day, the old growth pines had been logged. The woods beyond Millinocket were all second or third growth, dark and dense. The road bored through them monotonously until, cresting a rise at the edge of Baxter State Park, it gave us our first view of Katahdin, a gaunt, solitary massif like Kilimanjaro that seemed to suck the landscape toward it. A storm was just clearing off, and the wind splattered pine needles and leaves against the windshield as we drove. That night we camped at a place called Avalanche Field, near a torrent whose roar combined with our highway fatigue and the rush of wind to create a sense that we were still speeding into the dark, joined now by the mountain itself.

After three days in the woods, people are stronger but the wind is still bitterly cold. We are half a vertical mile above where we camped that first night, but the summit is a thousand feet higher still. Star sets off, lurching against the gusts. We have to walk sideways to go straight. The trail is a pale streak on the green rocks. Cairns have been built every twenty or thirty feet, but if a cloud blew in it would be easy enough to lose them. One could wander for hours across these rocky slopes, disoriented by hypothermia. You could die on Katahdin any day. For the first time I sense the depth of Thoreau's courage—or madness—in climbing into the clouds alone.

As we ascend, the whole Tableland spreads into view. It's what the Swiss call a *Felsenmeer*, a sea of rocks, though the Alps never seemed this wild. The trail stitches across like a white thread, heading north past the top of our slide and over the edge of a secondary peak before plunging into a cirque called the Northwest Basin. That was to have been our ascent route, but the ranger at Russell Pond, where we camped on our second night, warned us against it. The cirque is so deep I can't even see the lakes at the bottom; we would have had to climb eighteen hundred feet to the Tableland at the end of the day. No doubt we would have come down to Chimney Pond well after dark, tired and hungry and weak in the knees. We would have been in no condition to try for the peak, even if the weather held. Still, the Northwest Basin looks like a wonderful place. I can see domed rocks breaking through its forested floor, like the *roches moutonnées* of Yosemite. Perhaps at their base we might have found glacial gardens of the sort praised by John Muir. That would have been a relief to Jennifer, who had expected a gentler wilderness, more like the Sierra Nevada.

In fact our first day was full of surprises for everyone. The seven-mile trail to Russell Pond had looked easy on the map, but under its carpet of leaves the trail was a cobble of roots and rocks that forced us to pick our way carefully, eyes on the ground. Here were no moist and cavernous groves such as Thoreau had described, but dense, second-growth stands of beech and maple, interspersed with thickets of spruce and fir. As Jennifer pointed out, it would have been very hard bushwhacking here, not like the High Sierra, where one can strike off in any direction. Here we needed the trail, which seemed just an extension of the road. The blue painted blazes on trees and rocks reminded her too much of highway markers. What kind of a wilderness was this, she wanted to know, where you had to stay on the trail and reserve campsites thirty days in advance?

Between wrangling over such questions and watching our steps, we forgot all about the mountain. But then, about an hour into our hike, the woods suddenly opened. The trail ran along the edge of Whidden Pond, a shallow lake dotted with rocks and fringed with brush. Beyond the west shore rose a distant ridge, steel-blue and dented with steep ravines. Over the top we could see clouds racing across, though where we stood the air was utterly calm. The pond spread toward the mountain like a reflecting pool. Each protruding rock seemed to match part of the skyline, as if the mountain had strewn small replicas at our feet. The effect was to magnify its power while increasing the sense of intimacy. This was not a place where human beings could live without conflict with nature. Even the trail itself seemed like a defiant gesture to which the mountain had responded, whimsically, with roots and rocks. I sensed the mountain as adversary, a brooding presence that had chosen to conceal its power. No animals had appeared to us in the woods; the contrast between the violence on the ridge and the still pond was unnerving. This was no landscape "beaming with consciousness like the face of a god." Katahdin looked as if it had weathered too many storms. It was a presence older and darker by far than anything John Muir had seen in the Range of Light.

It took us all day to reach Russell Pond. The trail switched back and forth across the stream, which, in this dry season, looked more like a chute of boulders. Some were bigger than barrels, and the thought of leaping from one to another completely unnerved the beginners. Paul and I spent many tense moments coaxing people across. By the time we got to the campground we were tired, discouraged, and hungry. At this rate, I did not see how we would ever get up the mountain. Then Chase, whose group had arrived two hours before, said the ranger wanted to see me about our plans.

We found the ranger in his cabin down by the shore, listening to the World Series on a transistor radio. On the shelves were all kinds of packaged food;

none of Thoreau's pork, beans, and flour, but pancake mix, beef stew, and instant pudding. The ranger himself cut a more authentic figure. He was a lean old-timer dressed in the green wool pants and checked shirt used in the Maine Woods for over a century. He mashed his "a's" like a good Down-Easter, an accent dry enough to salt cod.

"That Northwest Basin's a pretty trail," he said, "but it's hard. You'd get in after dark. If it were me, I'd go back to Roarin' Brook and up Chimney from there. Then you ask Loren Goode; tell him you talked to old Roger Chase—he's a heck of a nice guy—he'll tell you if the peak's open. Been closed prett' near all week," he added.

"We could hike out around the north side of the mountain," Chase offered. "I could take us to Walden on the way back."

"Whoa!" said Star, "You mean give up the climb? After I drove four hundred and fifty miles?"

Chase shrugged. "We're moving too slow. We should have gone up today."

"You mean," Jennifer said, "we should quit now and settle for Walden or climb two thousand feet and hope for a clear day?"

We turned to the ranger. "If you ask me," he said, "it's like bettin' on two crippled horses."

Back at camp we cooked dinner and held a council. Star and Jennifer wanted to forge on into the Northwest Basin despite the ranger's advice. Chase scorned the idea of retracing our steps, though Paul reminded him that everything would look different when seen from the other side. Several liked the idea of visiting Walden, even though it was not part of our course. Others held out for the peak, the Knife-Edge, and the chance to set foot on Thoreau's trail. Some even thought we should split the class. There was no consensus. Finally, I made a decision.

"We'll go back the way we came," I said. "We'll camp at Chimney Pond tomorrow night, as we'd planned, and those who want to can try for the peak in the morning. If it's closed, we can hike out and stop at Walden just the same. If it's open, at least some of us will make it." No one spoke. In the firelight I read mild shock on their faces. I suddenly realized that by exerting authority I had ceased to be part of the group. I had become the Instructor, arm of the institution. I had become Yale! Across the fire Chase scowled but said nothing. Then, mercifully, someone produced a bottle of rum.

Hours later, I went to sleep half-drunk, worrying that I might have lost the class. I wanted us all to be in this adventure together, sharing a lofty purpose. But things were not working out. I was too young to stop being a student. I still *was* a student, just at a more advanced stage. I was not much older than they were, about the same age as Thoreau when he had come. But Thoreau had had no one else to worry about. He could afford to climb into the clouds alone, seeking immaculate consciousness. There was so much more to learn! How could I presume to be teaching?

Halfway up the slope, Star halts for gorp and we huddle around. Sharing food has become a ritual, and today we eat constantly to stay warm. Below us the Abol Trail stitches across the Tableland before dropping off its western edge onto Abol Slide. That's where Thoreau came up; Chase's group must be on his track by now. Past the rim the Maine woods spread out in all directions, lakes glinting like shards of mirror just as Thoreau had described.

These are the woods in which we awoke yesterday morning after a night of bitter cold. I remember tugging at the frozen zipper of my tent and peeking out into a world of glittering hoarfrost, beyond which the pond was steaming like a hot spring. I had walked around knocking on stiff, creaky tents, provoking moans and growls from inside.

Kathy had poked out her head. "Wow!" she exclaimed. "How cold was it last night?"

"Look at this!" Paul laughed, picking up a bowl and spoon he had left by the fire. When he lifted the spoon, a disc of ice had come with it.

Kathy said, "I don't believe people actually live in Maine!"

An hour later the sun had risen, dispelling the mists and melting the magic frost. Roger Chase waved as we passed his cabin. "Have a good 'un," he called. "What you need is common sense, and I think you have it."

The sun had climbed rapidly, filling the woods with golden light. Shelley and Kathy took turns helping each other across the stream. Despite going uphill, the trail had seemed easier than before, as if we were gaining a new sense of balance—not just the beginners, whom Paul teased about getting their mountain legs, but also the more experienced hikers like Jennifer and me, who had felt so attached to other landscapes. As Paul had said, everything did look different when seen from the other side. I thought of the wakefulness preached by Thoreau, of his dedication to "morning work" and his desire to live in "infinite expectation of the dawn." Such pronouncements could only have come from one habitually beset by memories and desires, as we had been during our first day in the woods.

The past has a way of dulling the edges of things, but yesterday the land had presented itself with a bracing clarity. We had noticed all sorts of things we had missed before: a pure stand of white canoe birch, the copper of beech leaves, a boulder peaked like a house and draped with bright green moss. Animals had appeared. A party of ruffed grouse had crossed the trail, their speckled coloration of black, brown, and white blending perfectly with the forest litter. Though we stomped after them into the woods, they had refused to fly; they just waddled faster and gave us the slip. We had seen many other birds as well: hawks, sapsuckers, Canada jays. And at Whidden Pond we had spotted a cow moose feeding in the shallows, as shaggy and humped as the ridge of Katahdin itself. Thoreau had searched in vain for a moose throughout his trip, and for us to encounter one here, just as the mountain came into view, had seemed like a favorable sign. It climaxed a morning of small epiphanies during which we had felt rather than seen the mountain, sensing it as an organizing principle above, behind, and within the landscape. There were hints of its presence in the gradients of streams with their varied tones, in the peaked rocks beside the trail, in the colors of lichen—slate blue, gray, or oxide green—and in the sharp-edged movements of birds or animals cutting across the corners of sight. The day before the woods had seemed empty, but now they were full of life. Was it simply that we had failed to notice these present things, burdened by memories and dreams carried from Yale? Or had they somehow been hidden from us, as the summit had been, by a finer species of mist? Whatever the case, Katahdin that morning had seemed to exert a power of revelation.

Now, three thousand feet below us, clouds have moved in over Whidden Pond and the Roaring Brook trailhead, where we stopped to stow our extra gear in the van. What were hints yesterday are clear today. We can see how the mountain radiates down and out into the surrounding country, organizing the waterflow, the placement of soils, the associations of plant life at various altitudes. Up here nothing grows but the hardy, ubiquitous lichen. We're on an island of rock in an ecological sea. Though glacial features abound on its slopes—we can see deep cirques, like the one holding Chimney Pond, and moraines twisting through the forests above Roaring Brook—Katahdin's summit remained ice-free during the Pleistocene. It must have looked pretty much as it does now, a dark nunatak in a desert of crystal white. I can feel its endurance through my boot soles, climbing on rocks that appear loosely scattered but don't shift underfoot. Up ahead Star is shouting something about pink granite rich in potassium, large crystals indicating that it cooled slowly, deep in the earth. It's millions of years old yet just now exposed to sun and frost, like the pink skin of the planet itself peeking through. The mountain endures yet casts off water and minerals into the living world below. As we climb, we feel ourselves moving toward some focus of elemental origins.

It was this way, too, on the ascent from Roaring Brook yesterday afternoon. Almost at once the forest had begun to change: the trees grew gnarly, and the brown soil gave way to sand and gravel mixed with rocks the size of basketballs. These were the tracks of the last ice to spill from the Great Basin; I could almost feel its chill exhalations flowing downhill through the stunted trees. Before long we had left the birches and entered a belt of spruce and fir growing thick as hedges along the trail, This was no graded Sierra path but a cascade of rocks, as if someone had just peeled off a strip of the mountain's skin. Flushed and puffing, Jennifer had exclaimed that Sierra trails made a lot more sense, but Star had just laughed and quickened the pace.

We found them fifteen minutes later, collapsed by the shore of a pond at the top of the moraine. The water was absolutely calm, reflecting blue cliffs now less than a mile away, and a pale, warm sunlight seemed to gather in pools among the white rocks lining the shore. Only the wind-pruned firs at the pond's edge, bare on the uphill side, suggested violence. We had stared at the pond, too tired to move until Kathy threw out her arms and exclaimed, "This is wilderness!"

For a quiet half hour we wrote, snacked, or dozed in the sun. I remember Shelley curled on a flat rock out on the water, writing, the yellow covers of her journal spread open like tropical petals, while Kathy stood looking up at the cliffs. It was a moment of peace and clarity such as we had seldom experienced here. I know more than one of us would have been happy to stay. But we had to camp at Chimney Pond, and, once back on the trail, we had felt the woods close in again. The map shows Chimney Pond enclosed by cliffs, like a coin in a cupped hand. As we climbed toward it, the cliffs had seemed to lean in. The afternoon light had turned them a smoky blue, and we had an odd sense, as we passed beneath them, of going down instead of up, of descending toward some hidden, portentous place. By the time we reached the campground, the sun had dropped behind the ridge. A bunkhouse, a ranger cabin, and a row of lean-tos sat neatly among the shadowy spruce. The scene suggested a pilgrim hostel or shrine, such as one might find in a rustic part of Japan, but the place had no air of Zen-like serenity. Instead we had felt a brooding force, as if the energies of weather, ice, and rock flowing down from the peak were focused here.

We checked in at the ranger cabin, where an American flag waved optimistically from a pole in the yard. Loren Goode turned out to be a nice guy, and voluble as well. He advised us against the Abol Trail, which was very rough; he himself would be hard put to do it in five hours, even without a pack. We should leave our packs here, go up the slide to the Tableland, cross the Knife-Edge, and loop back down by the Dudley Trail, which was rocky but well marked. The peak might be open tomorrow, but the Tableland and Knife-Edge were very dangerous in bad weather, even in summer. Hikers had died; he had rescued several this year already. I could tell that he liked his work. Though he was thirty years younger, at least, than Roger Chase, he wore the same green wool and spoke with the same Maine twang. He had a crew cut. His honorable discharge was framed and hanging on the wall.

We cooked dinner in the gathering dusk. Chase had asked permission to take his group down the Abol Trail to retrieve our other van, and since they seemed strong and eager, I had agreed. I had no more stomach for conflict. Several of the other students were suffering knee and ankle problems, which meant they would probably have to stay behind. The class seemed to be breaking apart, but I realized that there was little I could do. Tomorrow those who could would climb, and later we could at least share stories.

After dinner Paul, Kathy, and I had walked down to the edge of the pond, which lay like a black mirror at the base of the cliffs. We could see the pinpoints of stars reflected in its depths; it felt as if we were sitting at the bottom of a well. Here the mountain's power seemed like something drawn up from deep in the earth, chthonic, primeval—a "force not bound to be kind to man," as Thoreau had written, though at that moment we felt no hostility. Rather, it was as if we had entered a strong magnetic field or a zone of spells. The mountain possessed a power to shape our view of things, to cut us off from accustomed reality. It was the ancient power that worked through oracles, the power to stun with dreams. We stared at the cliffs, which rose to a crest as sharp as cut metal. Kathy asked what it was.

"It's the Knife-Edge," Paul said.

And Kathy said, "There's no way I'm going up there!"

That was last night. Now Kathy picks her way up the final rock pile. Two thousand feet below, Chimney Pond has vanished behind a spur. The wind seems less severe; we no longer have to step sideways to go straight, and we can open our eyes without weeping. We keep a slow, deliberate pace, one step at a time, pushing the mountain down. Then Star hollers up ahead. He's silhouetted against the sky, pack off and arms flung out. A few moments more, and we're with him, hugging and laughing. A sign tells us that this is the summit, 5,267 feet above sea level, the northern end of the Appalachian Trail.

"Enjoy the land," said Thoreau, "but own it not." No doubt he would have found some irony in this sign, but for us it's something to lean against while snapping pictures and gazing out over the Maine woods. We are far beyond Thoreau in space and time, standing on the summit he was denied and enjoying the godlike view to which he aspired. From here we can look down and see almost all the country through which we have come since our first glimpse of Katahdin three days ago: the dirt road winding into the park through a necklace of lakes, the glacial valley through which we hiked to Russell Pond and back, the Roaring Brook trail threading up through gaunt, fairy-tale woods toward the Great Basin and Chimney Pond. Each of these had seemed a real challenge, but each made us stronger, and that strength has finally lifted us into the sky. The summit is a gathering place, not only for our bodies, but for our memories, hopes, and fears. It is the high point but not the end. We still have to cross the Knife-Edge to get down.

I can see it from here, a glacial arête twisting off toward the secondary peak of Pomola, named for the Indian god who Thoreau said was always angry with those who climb to the summit of Katahdin. Today it does not look so difficult. I had expected a thin crest with granite blocks maybe four feet wide, dropping off sharply on either side, the sort of place where, if you slipped, you would really fall. But the ridge is peaked no more steeply than the roof of a house, and the rocky slopes end in cliffs a few dozen feet from the crest. If you slipped, you'd probably just turn an ankle or bruise a shin. The main challenges posed by the Knife-Edge seem to be its length—nearly a mile, though it looks shorter from here—and a notch at the base of Pomola, where the ridge ends abruptly in cliffs. I expect we will have to do some rock climbing there.

The wind has picked up again, but it has changed direction. It's now blowing up and out of the Great Basin. The cloud bank in the east has begun to break up, sending long misty arms over the moraine ponds. No doubt our last night's camp will soon be obscured. Everyone's restless, eager to go. All trip long people have been muttering about the Knife-Edge, as if it, not Baxter Peak, were the real test. But we never saw it till yesterday afternoon. Perhaps they were reacting to the name, with its connotations of sharpness and danger. "Edge" suggests some sort of boundary or divide, a place where you need to maintain balance and control, a place of risk, exposure, or separation where you cross from the known to the unknown. And a knife is a moving edge, wielded by some intending hand and capable of inflicting wounds, like the obsidian blades used by our Ice Age ancestors to mark young women or men for initiation. The knife cuts away the old self, for what does growing up mean if not learning to live with scars, accepting your wounds?

We share a last handful of gorp, then Star takes off, leaping from rock to rock with his blond hair flying. Jennifer and the others follow in single file. Paul and I come last, with Kathy and Shelley. The wind has risen to gale force, tearing our jackets and knocking us sideways at every step. The mists are boiling over Chimney Pond; though still far below, they could lift to the ridge at any time. It's only now, when we're actually on it, that I realize the true danger posed by the Knife-Edge. In this brutal wind, every instinct tells me to get off the crest. The slopes seem safer and more protected. But they are incised by the headwalls of ravines, some of which cut nearly up to the ridge. In a cloud as thick as the one Thoreau described, you might suddenly come to the brink, where a stray thought or footstep could pitch you over the edge. Avoiding that, you might wander for some time before finding the headwall, or even the crest itself—for deceptive spurs do jut out from the ridge—and all the while insidious hypothermia would be sapping your judgment and resolve, until finally you might be tempted to hunker down and wait out the weather. But that would be the worst thing to do. I realize that survival means acting against all instincts: I have to keep moving along the crest. It's the most violent, frightening, and exposed place, yet paradoxically, it's also the safest. With this insight comes a rush of exhilaration. Up ahead I hear students shouting, "Contact!"

By the time we reach the cleft below Pomola, the Great Basin is full of clouds. Every ravine is boiling with mist, and long fingers search up the headwalls, sucked by the wind. The notch is deeper than it appeared, with steep, green walls on the far side. As we bunch at the rim, squinting to make out the trail, a thin stream of fog begins sluicing across. Soon the floor of the notch disappears. Star begins clambering down, and his blond head vanishes. Jennifer follows, then the others disappear one at a time. The mist rises by degrees, streaming and ectoplasmic. When it reaches our feet, Kathy, Shelley, and I go down. Inside it's damp and cold, with a shadowless, frosted-glass light. The blue painted blazes are hard to see. I can hear people shouting encouragement but have no idea where they are. We pick our way over the grassy floor of the notch, distracted momentarily by the wonder of finding plant life in such a place. And then we run smack into the far wall, with a blue blaze at eye level. Boot-wide cracks lead up from the grass. We start climbing, our fingers grasping like roots. The rock is cold; the lichen grates like sandpaper; the grass disappears, and once more we lose all sense of depth or height. All we have is the obdurate hardness of the mountain, and we cling to it, feeling it press against our bones. Our hands numb rapidly; our skin feels as thin as cellophane. The cold mist seeks out every loose seam in our clothes, hunting our body heat. And then, suddenly, the air grows brighter, the wall slopes back, and we burst up into clear air on Pomola's bouldered summit, where the others welcome us with cheers. Kathy and Shelley look around, blinking, then hug each other. The others are beaming, giggling, making faces. Star pulls our lunches from his pack. And soon we are sharing bread, cheese, and oranges, creating a circle within a circle of blessed but temporary light.

As I savor this meal that never felt better earned, I realize that something wonderful has happened to us. I feel tired but exhilarated, almost weightless. No one seems worried about the descent, which Loren Goode said would be very rough, nor about the weather still gathering ominously below. People are already telling stories about climbing the slide and crossing the Knife-Edge, expressing regret that the others couldn't be here, wondering if they had as good a journey as ours. It's as if the trip had already begun to turn into stories, even before it's done. Will everything from here on out be a dénouement? When the clouds lift momentarily, we can still see our whole route, as we could from Baxter Peak, but now both the peak and the Knife-Edge are behind us. We have crossed the notch with its cloud of unknowing. We are "past the steep ways and the narrow part." What is there left for us now but to return?

Interestingly, no one mentions Thoreau. As I realize this, I'm tempted to start a discussion. But it seems wrong, somehow, to break this mood of communion. Besides, we have left Thoreau's story behind. It gave us our bearings and set us on our way, but we have seen things he never saw, gone far beyond his footsteps and visions. So we encounter the paradox of all pilgrimage, which is that one's own journey finally displaces that of the saint or poet one has elected to follow. This may mean we've failed as a class. But who knows what the students are really thinking? I'll be eager to see, in three weeks, what their journals reveal.

When the sun dims, we pack up and go, striding over the boulder fields toward the steeper slopes below. We descend along the spur we saw from the slide this morning, the dark side of Katahdin. Soon we are clambering down small cliffs, picking our way around and under rocks as big as trucks. Without the blue blazes we'd soon be lost in this labyrinth. The descent is so steep that my legs and knees begin shaking. At one point Kathy turns back with a serious look and asks, "John, do women ever come on this trail?"

"You're here, aren't you?"

"Yeah," she says, "but I'm crazy!"

By the time we reach Chimney Pond, we've fallen far behind, and the others are waiting with Loren Goode, who says he closed the peak more than two hours ago. We look up to see the summit and Knife-Edge engulfed in cloud. Soon a light rain begins to fall. We pack up and head down.

Despite bad knees, the trail feels easy after so many miles of rock. We hike in a state of trance. When we reach the cars at four o'clock, we find the Abol group has been waiting for over two hours.

"Where have you guys been?" Chase growls.

Star grins, "Up where the spirits dance and the clouds caress the earth, long, lovely and lush. I've had a vision most rare!"

Chase grunts, shaking his head. Then he smiles. He takes Star's pack and heaves it into the van. Star reaches under the seat and hands him a beer. We all pile in. The woods flash by in a yellow blur. At the park entrance we stop for one last look at the mountain, but the summit is veiled in cloud. As we turn toward Millinocket, the rain increases to a downpour. The road bends south. We seem to be falling away from the mountain, carried downstream like discarded leaves. At two in the morning we wash up again on an empty street beneath the towers of Yale.

Three weeks later I sit in my study reading the students' journals, which have been typed and xeroxed for everyone in the class. The mood of our seminar has changed completely. No one is furtive or reticent anymore, and the air of pretense so common in elite, competitive schools has vanished. People kid one another, listen intently, and take a personal interest in the material, even though we've moved past Thoreau and John Muir into the twentieth century.

I'm struck by how good the writing is, even though much of it was composed on the spot, in "forlorn and savage places." It's candid writing, succinct and unadorned. The voices may not be mature, in a literary sense, but the students have written from what they know, setting a tone of candor and authenticity. I can feel the wind behind the words, the hearts pounding, the aching knees, the rush of insight.

But I'm also struck by how different each story is, though each is told within the frame of our common journey. I had no idea—to echo Thoreau —that so much was going on, nor that the trip could have meant so many different things. I see how skewed some of my own impressions were. Star, the laughing mountain troll, had turned a cool naturalist's eye on the Tableland: "On the ground, armored clumps of *Diapensia lapponica* cling tenaciously in the lee of rocks . . . *Rhizocarpa geographica*, a familiar lichen for dating deglaciated surfaces, has covered every square inch of bare rock."

Chase, the rebel, had also devoted pages to natural history but, more surprisingly, had praised the trip's organization, process, and "strong feeling
of camaraderie."

Kathy, who had faced so many challenges, revealed the strength of a
deep humility. The climb to Chimney Pond had nearly done her in. "I
mutinied," she wrote, "but just when I'd be giving up, Nature would offer
a comforting pond or view. When we reached the camp, I wrestled with
tears. I was lonely, deserted by my mind, confused. I felt like a wilderness.
Nature had done as much as possible for me. I had failed Nature." Yet
the next day she was crossing the Knife-Edge, where even Jennifer had
needed help. "I think most of us had moments when we wondered if we
would make it," Jennifer wrote, describing her fear at the notch below
Pomola and the encouragement she had received. Paul, I remembered, had
been present at every such place, yet his journal shows that he had wrestled with the urge for solo adventure before opting, finally, to go with the
group. "There is no ecstasy à la Thoreau on top of the mountain for me,"
he wrote. "I like it here. I feel free, and I feel a sense of completion about
all these days. It is enough to enjoy this time as it is. It's great being here
all together."

I know he means everyone, experienced and beginner, student and
instructor, for on the summit's initiatory threshold we felt all such differences finally converge. "The wind blows up here just like it does in Kansas,"
Shelley wrote, "strong and steady, clear and clean. If I take away all the
gray-green rocks, only the sandy colored grass is left. Then, it's home."
How poignant her loyalty appears at this moment of transformation. "A
friend had told me that I would see the whole world from up here," she
went on. "He was right. There are mountains and strong sun. There are
clouds below that stretch past the sea.

"Boiling, boiling, boiling up fast, they cover everything.

"That horizon a mile away could be the edge of the world for all I know.

"I have climbed a mountain now.

"I never did that before."

Moved, I read on and on into the sixteen journals before me. When I
finish, near midnight, my eyes are sore and blinking. They feel like they
did on the Tableland, though now it's not orographic winds but a wind
of words that they feel. I search the voices rushing behind my eyes, feel-

ing in vain for the most authentic one, the one that approximates the voice of the mountain itself. But all I hear is a chaos of individual voices, turbulent, unpredictable, yet manifesting a strange coherence, like dancing flames. And then I realize my error: the mountain speaks with multiple voices, addressing each of us in the dark of our minds according to our own needs, issues, and aspirations. In an absolute sense it remains elusive, while appearing with vivid particularity to each. So it withholds authority from those who, like Thoreau, come seeking to prophesy and confers it instead upon pilgrims through strenuous rites of passage. I realize at last that the mountain's greatest power is transformation, like the power of pagan gods who turned people into beasts or immortals, or even the Christian god who could heal with a touch or convert with a whispered word. And the mountain's gift is not some slate of divine commands by which we could all live perfectly, but the power to tell our stories and so, speaking and listening to one another, enter into community.

I think of Thoreau, who appears only fleetingly in these journals. It's clear now that he, too, experienced the mountain as a place of unlooked-for transformation. It came to him most vividly while crossing the "burnt lands," where he began to sense that his body, like the mountain itself, was made of raw matter indifferent to human concerns. He had come to the wilderness hoping to meet nature unveiled, but he found that Katahdin had no human face, nor any face at all, save that which stared up at him from the mirror of language itself. How could he love or write about nature in the same way as before? It was as if he had come seeking visions and received an injection of darkness. I could see the darkness emerge in his later work, first in *Walden*, which celebrated a dream of balance and purity that he could no longer fulfill in his life. In telling that story of an idealized year, he had created a language that calls attention to what it does not say, a language of paradox like the Zen koan where the shadow speaks from an eloquent silence. And later, in *Cape Cod* and *The Maine Woods*, he had turned more and more from philosophy to storytelling, for narrative alone can overcome contradictions of thought and character by creating a space that contains both, as ecosystems provide niches for mortal enemies.

I imagine Thoreau after his return from the mountain, writing by lamplight in the cabin he had built on Emerson's land. He sits alone in a small circle of light. Outside a loon calls. The pond's surface twinkles with constellations. From time to time he makes a mark. The sentences uncurl slowly, like ferns, like melting streams, like time itself. He writes of his brother, using the names of New England's mountains and rivers. He writes of hope. Outside the enormous darkness cups him like a hand. I imagine him wondering, in the spaces between words, whether he will ever return to Katahdin.

CHAPTER FIVE

Among Shining Mountains

IN WANT OF A POSITION

Two years later I left New Haven, heading west again. This time the Volkswagen belonged to me and, as I stepped into it on a steamy August morning, I felt it sink noticeably onto its springs. This car held everything I owned except for fifteen cartons of books that, like museum specimens, had been shipped on ahead. As I started the engine, I thought of sheepherders, who still live in tin-roofed wagons on Wyoming's high plateaus, or the pioneers who had crossed the Great Plains in covered wagons while John Muir was exploring the High Sierra. They had had oxen; I had a gasoline engine, nomadism in a late industrial model.

It is a truth universally acknowledged that a single man in possession of a degree must be in want of a position—a teaching position, specifically, and as close to the mountains as possible. After Katahdin I realized that the paradoxes of pilgrimage would inhere in any course where the land spoke directly to students. And the paradox of teaching itself—the conflict between one's desire for adventure and one's responsibility as shepherd and guide—would always tempt me to seek control, leading to anxiety, rationalizing, or even self-deception. Perhaps true teaching would require an ongoing relation with someplace beautiful and wild. Both teaching and living would then become aspects of a single practice enacted through periodic returns to the wilderness.

In this frame of mind I went looking for work, but the prospects were not encouraging. Two years after Katahdin I was writing a dissertation on narrative artifice in the literature of exploration, hoping to finish by June so that I could move west over the summer. I had joined the Modern Language Association and subscribed to their job list with great expectation. But the fall issue showed only forty openings in American or comparative literature, and most of these lay east of the Mississippi. My friends and I had heard that each job would draw between fifty and one hundred applicants. These numbers were no more encouraging than the geography. Nevertheless I typed thirty letters, received ten dossier requests, and eventually secured two interviews at the big New York convention just after Christmas. Opinions were mixed on the MLA. Most professors considered it a necessary evil, but to graduate students it was known as "the meat market."

I remember standing on a Manhattan sidewalk, looking up at the soaring glass facade of the Americana Hotel, and wondering how it would feel to have five thousand English professors stuffed into one building. Dante had imagined Hell by subjecting the human world to a kind of fractional distillation: people of like temperament and behavior wound up together, violence and agony ensued, and the ultimate horror was that nobody wanted out.

Those entering Dante's Hell had been warned to abandon hope. Yet inside the Americana I found hope seething and bubbling everywhere. Crowds pressed toward the elevators, clutching programs and briefcases. People would jostle each other, exchange a few words, and then spin off like colliding particles. Perhaps this sort of Brownian movement kept professional life in a fluid state. I soon learned to pick out the graduate students: they were the ones in new suits with darting eyes and famished looks. Senior professors often wore faded trench coats or shapeless tweed; they sailed through the crowds like yachts, fending off envious looks with ease. And all the while, in hundreds of seminars, lecture rooms, and suites that made up this vertical hell, ideas and careers were being sifted like wheat.

I considered myself fortunate to have gained interviews at two schools close to the Sierra. The first was a large public university. When I presented myself, the chairman showed me to a seat facing a ring of tenured professors. It felt like the focal point of a solar cooker, but the army had trained me as an interrogator, and I was curious to observe civilian techniques. One professor in blue blazer and khakis used his pipe stem for emphasis, thrusting it forward like a dirk. Another, recently tenured, wrung her hands as she asked what wilderness had to do with intellectual history. I detected a note of empathy there. The chairman, a glistening hairless man, presided silently in a sharkskin suit and a hot pink raw silk tie. When he finally broke in to conclude the interview, he spoke without parting his teeth. As I shook his hand, I saw that he had no eyebrows. His face was smooth and rosy, as if it had just been boiled.

The next school was a small college known for excellent teaching. My host showed me into a room with drawn blinds and offered a drink, though it was only one in the afternoon. We sat on the couch and chatted about Yale. Finally he asked how I would teach Henry James. When I hesitated, alarm crept over his face. He asked me to remind him again of my dissertation topic. The literature of exploration? Was that "inner" or "outer"? Muir? Oh yes, the Sierra Club man. He had not known Muir was a writer. Yosemite? He had once driven up there with friends from the East. It was beautiful, to be sure.

I left the convention feeling as ripe and bruised as a supermarket melon. Back home, New Haven had sunk into a wintry slime. I waited by the phone and worked on my dissertation, but neither school called for a campus interview. By March I had despaired of finding a job and was beginning to brood anxiously on what Muir had called "the bread problem," when my department called with news that the University of Utah wanted someone to teach humanities survey courses. The secretary sounded apologetic; it was only a three-year position, she explained, and Utah was rather far from the center of things. But she thought I might be interested, given my unusual area of research. I applied that afternoon. And three weeks later I found myself on a plane bound for Salt Lake City.

Such reversals of fortune are always exhilarating. I remember soaring over the Great Plains in dazzling sunlight, marveling at the Mondrian patchwork of plowed fields and open range. West of Denver snow clouds loomed over the mountains, great porcelain-white cumuli through which I occasionally caught a glimpse of white slopes or dark, pointed evergreens. Over Utah we disappeared into a gray unknowing and then, suddenly, broke into clear air over a welter of peaks with avalanche scars sweeping into the canyons and yellow cliffs reflecting the light of noon. These were the westernmost range of the Rockies, which the earliest trappers had called the Shining Mountains. I could see dozens of summits linked by knife-edge ridges, a vast labyrinth of initiation. When I stepped out of the plane onto the floor of the valley, I thought Salt Lake must be the most beautiful city on earth.

Perhaps it was really enthusiasm that got me the job. Three years seemed like a wonderfully long time, as long as I had spent in the army, and with much more room for adventure. Back home I worked hard to finish my dissertation. In August I mulched the asparagus beds I would never harvest, pruned my fruit trees one last time, and said good-bye to the hills of Lake Waramaug, thinking only of delectable mountains. As I turned onto the interstate highway again, I remembered leaving Philadelphia four years before. But now I was seeking more than just adventure or purification. Utah promised a home, a career, and a place to enact my vocation. Crossing the Hudson, I watched my childhood landscape flash by and disappear. Speeding west with all I owned in the car, I felt as buoyant and free as a winged seed.

MORMONS AND MOUNTAIN MEN

Travel has sometimes been thought of as writing, and not just because travelers like to tell stories. The act of travel inscribes itself in your personal history, and a journey marked on a map makes a kind of cipher. So when you retrace a journey, it's almost like reading an old letter or journal entry. Following in your own footsteps, you meet a part of yourself and fall in with him or her as a new companion. This lends a holographic depth to your enterprise, and the feeling is enhanced if you travel, as I did, over routes used by generations of voyagers. Especially west of Kansas City, with the road lifting onto the Great Plains, I sensed the richly layered texture of journeys. I had crossed here before, with millions of other motorists, and before us had come the interstate highway builders, moved by the Cold War to lay a thin ribbon of concrete over a path inscribed by wave after wave of traders, emigrants, and explorers: the Dust Bowl refugees seeking new life in California, the vanguard of motorized tourists created by Henry Ford, the Wells Fargo stage and Pony Express, the army, the settlers heading for Oregon, the Forty-Niners, the Mormons fleeing persecution, the trappers and traders who had come to cash in on the wild wealth they had tasted with Lewis and Clark. These Euro-American travelers had followed paths dictated by the lay of the land, as had their predecessors, the Plains Indians, who stampeded buffalo, and the Paleo-Indians, who hunted mammoths in the shadow of ancient ice. As I raced across Kansas and Colorado, I sensed the richness of these layered texts. I was adding my own layer, thin as it was, to the history of westward passage.

On the Plains with their gridwork of farms, I thought most of the Mormons who had crossed in 1847, fleeing from persecution. They had started two decades before in the "burnt-over district" of upstate New York, where the fires of religious revival had swept through frontier communities. Living next door to wilderness in a land once ruled by the warrior nation of Iroquois, these settlers were ripe for prophets like Joseph Smith, who claimed that angels had delivered into his hands a book proving that America had been settled originally by the lost tribe of Israel and that Jesus, after his resurrection, had come here to preach the gospel.

The Book of Mormon explained the origin of the Indians, legitimized a Christian presence in America, and sanctified the pioneer impulse to transform the wilderness into a garden. It spoke, at a latter day, to the same Edenic aspirations that had brought the Puritans to New England and led to the founding of places like Yale. The Mormons were disciplined, idealistic, clannish, and highly successful. Their utopian farm communities prospered while their people increased and multiplied. Naturally this kind of success aroused both envy and fear. But not until Mormons began voting in blocks to capture local elections did these feelings actually ignite. All over upstate New York, Mormon homesteads were vandalized and burned. And the Mormons reacted in classic American fashion: they packed up and headed west, first to Ohio, then Illinois, where Joseph Smith was killed by vigilantes, then across the Mississippi to Iowa. It was then that Brigham Young, a Vermont Yankee and visionary entrepreneur, took over the leadership of the church. Inspired by Smith's dream of a western utopia and impressed by John Charles Frémont's vivid accounts of the Great Basin, Young decided to move out of the United States altogether. At that time the intermountain West was technically part of Mexico, but there was no government presence to question the Mormon enterprise. In 1847 Young led an advance party across the Plains. By July they had reached South

Pass, at the lower end of Wyoming's Wind River Range, and soon after they encountered the legendary mountain man Jim Bridger, who confirmed Frémont's report of a desert valley beneath snowy peaks, where a north-flowing river connected a freshwater lake to a much bigger, saline lake. Bridger did not think the valley could ever be farmed, but to Young its geography proved irresistible: here in the New World was a landscape that mirrored the Holy Land, as if nature itself were confirming Mormon mythology. When Young's party looked out on the Salt Lake Valley three weeks later, he murmured, "It is enough. This is the right place. Drive on."

The Mormons camped on City Creek, the northernmost stream in the valley, and immediately set about planting corn, peas, and potatoes. They dammed the creek for irrigation, and Young drew up plans for the new city; it was to be centered upon a temple erected over their campsite, with one-and-a-quarter-acre lots and streets wide enough for a wagon team to make a full turn. The Mormons built houses of logs and adobe; later they used bricks fired from the desert clay. Some of these early homes are still standing; they have a compact, fortified look, as if their owners were taking no chances.

Young established survival routines for the people: each household was ordered to store a year's supply of food; each neighborhood congregation was organized for a quick response to fire, flood, or other disaster. When colonists set off for outlying parts of Utah, they traveled as whole communities, with every essential skill represented. Wherever the Mormons went, they built dams, watered the desert, and planted gardens and fruit trees. They put down roots and prospered in strange lands.

As I followed the Mormon trail over the high plains, I realized how much their story attracted me. The Mormons I had known in the army were all upstanding, earnest young men devoted to family and place. Their myths seemed odd, but no more so than those of other faiths. I was more interested in their culture's Edenic dreams, their sense of husbandry and community, and their choice of a promised land. Thoreau had written that a village should be spiritually and culturally nourished by the woods around it: "We need to see our limits transgressed, and some life pasturing where we never wander." A clean city surrounded by shining mountains seemed the perfect place to build his kind of society. People living there would be exposed daily to the invigorating spiritual influences of which he and Muir had written. In such a place professional life might well be redeemed by contact with nature.

Meanwhile the interstate had carried me through Denver and into the Rockies. Climbing toward Berthoud Pass on the Continental Divide, my car began laboring with the altitude, and I finally had to pull over to adjust the carburetor. Even then I had to shift down into second gear, but this was better than cutting roads and hauling wagons in pieces, as the Mormons had done. I stopped on the pass to gaze into the land of the mountain men. From here all streams ran west and south toward the Pacific.

A famous photograph taken by William Henry Jackson shows a mountain man standing on Berthoud Pass dressed in skins and cradling a flintlock rifle. In the foreground scattered rocks and stunted firs suggest a climate as harsh as the Tableland of Katahdin. In the background successive ranges advance from a bright, indistinct horizon, their crests converging upon the silhouette of the hunter. There is no sign of any trail. You get the sense that this man has just reached the top of the pass after crossing hundreds of miles of wilderness. His rifle follows the crest of the nearest range. He looks eastward past the edge of the frame. What does he see? Not game, certainly, but his stare is fierce and intent. Perhaps he sees people coming. Are they Indians, explorers, or pioneers?

The man in the picture is Harry Yount, a hunter for the Hayden Survey of 1873, who would later become the first ranger in Yellowstone National Park. The picture was taken more than thirty years after the last rendezvous of the mountain men. So Yount is posing to model an image out of the past. The figure he represents is already becoming a myth as the wilderness perishes, transformed by war, exploration, settlement, and technologies like the railroad and the camera. What we do not see in this picture, of course, is the photographer behind the lens, and behind him the expedition itself. Nor do we see the lens, whose very transparency is also a fiction, asserting that the image it presents is not art but reality—and more, that the world outside the frame is simply an extension of the image within it, a world of "mountains and rivers without end."

Perhaps it was only after the mountain men had passed into history that such an image could have been composed, for by then their way of life posed no threat to the culture advancing from the East. They could be contemplated in safety and safely romanticized. In the photograph, Harry

Yount appears to be striding forth out of the landscape that has produced him. He meets the viewer on the pass. To the viewer it feels like meeting a grizzly bear: you stop dead in your tracks, aware that you have stumbled into the realm of a powerful, alien being. So the photograph depicts a meeting of two worlds: you and civilization stand on one side of the lens, the mountain man and the wilderness stand on the other. And the lens coincides with the pass itself: it stands on a great divide.

As I looked north from Berthoud Pass, I realized that what fascinated me about this image was its call to adventure. For unlike the Mormon pioneers who carried the line of civilization forward, the mountain men had crossed the line to live on the other side. The pioneers had reshaped the land to suit their needs, but the mountain men had entered into the land, eschewing homesteads, adopting Indian dress and woodcraft, even taking Indian wives. They had become border people, living between worlds. As such they represented a path that America, bent on conquest, had chosen not to follow. They emerged as a kind of shadow for us, antibourgeois, empowered by savage secrets, men not of reason but of the earth. They had jumped off into remoteness and anarchy, becoming explorers and renegades, embracing the Other. So to me they stood forth as icons of transformation.

As I headed north and west from the pass, I realized I was trying to follow a twofold path. The pioneer and the mountain man were natural enemies. Yet I felt attracted to both. I wanted to settle and practice my trade, pursuing a Jeffersonian ideal of professional husbandry and citizenship. But I also thirsted after experience and extremes. I was eager to taste the land's intricacies and perfections. And above all, I wanted the freedom to move back and forth between worlds.

All day I drove down the western slope of the Rockies, through canyons and desert valleys, past the feet of the Uinta Mountains, up the Strawberry River, where rain and darkness began to fall, and into the Heber Valley above Salt Lake, where I ran into thunder and hail. The road turned west into a canyon that seemed, in the dark, like a tunnel boring through solid rock. Then it swung down and down until all at once the walls flew back and there was the city, spread out like a carpet of fire with lightning dancing above dark peaks on the other side. Could this be nature? It looked more like a scene from *The Ten Commandments*. But I was too tired from driving to stop and think. For better or worse, this was the place.

I drove to an address the department secretary had given me, where another new assistant professor had offered to put me up. As I turned off the engine, rain began falling in sheets. I ran up the walk toward a sound of loud rock music. A man with a black ponytail and a gunfighter's mustache answered the door. "You must be John," he grinned. "Come in. Have a beer."

I stepped into a throbbing envelope of sound. Two magnificent Persian cats lay curled on the couch. The coffee table was strewn with papers and books: Nietzsche, Husserl, Gayatri Spivak. A folder said "Longhorns" in big orange letters.

My host handed me a beer. "Sorry it's only three-two," he shouted over the stereo. "This is Utah."

"Where did you come from?" I asked.

"UT Austin. How about you?"

"New Haven. Yale."

"Wow!" he exclaimed. "Do you know Jacques Derrida?"

THE NEW WEST

Those first two weeks I traveled a good deal in Salt Lake, seeking a place of my own before school began. It was a time of disorientation. On the one hand, I found the city more clean and beautiful than any town of comparable size I had known in the East. It was full of bright gardens and well-kept homes. The people were handsome in a Nordic sort of way, for the Mormons had proselytized heavily in Scandinavia, and they smiled easily on the street or in stores. To a displaced person like me, such western openness felt like a touch of grace. I was used to feeling at risk in cities and to cultivating a tense, guarded look as a means of defense. But here the people all seemed relaxed and secure. The town glowed with prosperity and a civic pride I could easily understand.

But on the other hand, I was bewildered by the dissonance between the urban culture and the surrounding landscape. I suppose I had come with the idea, borrowed from Muir and Thoreau, that magnificent country would produce a magnificent culture. Yet here were tract housing, fast food restaurants, motels and gas stations, high-pole signs, shopping centers, and skyscrapers—all the insignia of life in the age of the automobile. Some days I felt I might be anywhere in America—Illinois, Pennsylvania, or California—instead of *here* at the feet of the Wasatch Range. I could see the mountains from anywhere in town, yet at times they looked almost fantastic, like cardboard cutouts or painted scenery, a mere backdrop to the dramas of commerce, religion, and entertainment going on at their feet.

Brigham Young had platted his city on a grid oriented to the four points of the compass, and even his side streets were as wide as major arteries back East. One had the sense of space to spare: the city seemed to project itself out across the valley as if trying to capture it in a net. I could imagine the lattice of streets expanding indefinitely across any flat surface, and I thought more than once of the grid of fields and roads that now covered the Midwest. That was the square dance of the pioneer dream. But here, where the fractal skyline of the Wasatch stood in such bold contrast, I experienced the grid as an effort to subdue an alien landscape by imposing an artificial concept of space. In much the same way, medieval philosophers had used geocentric cosmology to marry the physical world with Christian morality. But although the Mormons had built their temple at the center of the grid, it did not stand at the focal point of the landscape in the manner of, say, Greek temples or Himalayan monasteries. Whatever spiritual power it possessed seemed to derive from a source outside the land.

These contradictions were sharpened for me by the fashions of landscaping and architecture I observed. In eastern cities I had generally found more greenery the farther I got from town, yet here that pattern was reversed. The streets were lined with shade trees and irrigated lawns that contrasted handsomely with the dust-gray sage and scrub oak of the foothills. Even in town, any plot of ground that was not watered daily soon looked as if it had been baked in an oven. A vacant lot near my house bristled with rattling weeds, yet across the street lay a park where the grass actually squished underfoot.

I was accustomed to plants being watered from the sky, not from a buried pipe, but soon I began to give thanks for water of any kind. From the time I arrived until mid-October, the sun beat down on the valley like a hammer. By nine in the morning the streets would be shimmering like hot iron, while a smell of dust and alkali rose in the air. The intense, unvarying light felt almost corrosive; I began to believe that over time it could even flake stone. People escaped into houses defended by broad eaves, air conditioning, and irrigated trees that were native to other parts of the world.

But there was nothing particularly indigenous about these houses, nor about the larger public or commercial buildings. The settlers had built snug, compact homes, but later generations had turned to ranches or bungalows. There were plenty of high-rise apartments and office buildings, too, and the state capitol had been built from a neoclassical design, complete with gilt dome and columns. What made it distinctive was its location on a spur overlooking the city, and the contrast between its viridian lawn in front and the parched chaparral spreading up from the parking lot out back. Like every other building except the temple, the capitol seemed to have been brought in and plunked down. I had expected, perhaps, more stone, since that was the local material, and designs more in tune with the land, like the adobes of New Mexico, the Gothic of Alpine Europe, or the wind towers of Iran. But this was imported architecture, a way of costuming space.

As for the university, it reflected both civic pride and the optimism of Cold War America. Set up to overlook the city, as scripture advised, it consisted of crisp, rectilinear buildings set out on felt-green lawns. Between them ran concrete esplanades accentuated by huge beds of marigolds, petunias, and snapdragons that looked like flags spread out to dry in the sun. From any point on campus inside or out, you could see both city and mountains. This was no monastery, I thought, but a true "university without walls." And indeed, as fall quarter began, I realized how intimately it was linked to the culture of this city, where most of its twenty-five thousand students lived. A majority of them were Mormons, infused with a strong work ethic and encouraged to marry young. Since most held full-time jobs while attending school, early classes were most in demand. I found the students earnest, pragmatic, careerist, respectful, and somewhat in awe of the East—like Jay Gatsby, though too pure in heart for his kind of dealings. Most were not interested in wilderness, and besides, their work lives precluded backpacking trips. So that fall I gave up the idea of replicating Katahdin.

The first year in a new place is always pathological to some degree. Your inner rhythms have to adjust; you have to extend your roots into new psychic soil. In the nineteenth century "nostalgia" was considered a bonafide medical problem, though in our rootless age it's more often viewed as a weakness in character. That fall I was not homesick exactly, but rather perplexed and disoriented, for I had come west seeking a new place and found instead a place that seemed in some ways very much like the old. Just as Emerson's friends had longed for the high culture of Europe, so the people of Salt Lake seemed to be fascinated by eastern cities and colleges. Travel agencies advertised shopping and theater trips to New York. There was even a fancy dining club called "The New Yorker," whose walls were adorned with framed covers from the eponymous magazine. High arts like the symphony and the ballet were promoted aggressively. And the university, too, was seeking to emulate research institutions like Harvard and Yale, to the despair of some older faculty who, like myself, felt that its true business ought to be teaching. In the English Department the most influential professors were in their forties and eager for all the latest news from New Haven. They wanted to build up the department by recruiting hot, young publishing scholars. But I found myself more drawn to the senior professors who had come when Utah was still on the academic frontier and learned here the delicate art and craft of teaching. They were not above taking a class to the mountains or dressing up like Emerson and Thoreau to make the Concord Renaissance come alive for their students. But now they, too, were leading a border life.

The New West I encountered was full of such contradictions. At times it seemed fresh and exciting, at times depressingly familiar. As fall term progressed, the contrast between landscape and culture impressed itself ever more deeply upon me. Everywhere I looked were dramatic views, but the mountains' energy had been pushed to the edges of the frame. At the center lay the Euclidean certainties of the grid, the formal prosperity of church and garden, where eastern roots were maintained by a kind of psychic irrigation. I sympathized with the pioneers, for the Great Basin desert could be a fearsome place. But I could never quite shake the sense that I now lived in an artificial paradise, where the goal was not baptism or grace, but protection from nature.

LIVING WITH GEOLOGIC TIME

Fortunately, beyond every street and rooftop the mountains beckoned. Between classes I found myself gazing across campus toward the slopes of parched grass and scrub oak that marked the limits of civilization. I could drive half a mile to the topmost street, then step off into de facto wilderness. Once I got out of town, the mountains looked even larger. They rose eight thousand feet from the valley floor, a great wall cleft by the dark mouths of canyons. Some canyons had roads and ski areas; others had footpaths and cougars. The Wasatch Range gave Salt Lake the most spectacular backdrop of any city I had ever seen.

The term "Rocky Mountains" had always seemed trivial to me: what else would mountains be made of? Yet living here I encountered rock as a constant, overwhelming fact. The mountains I knew back East had been clothed with vegetation, yet here the biological world was suppressed for months at a time by dryness and heat. Moreover, the slopes were often too steep or unstable for plants. I learned that an active fault ran along the base of the range, which was rising faster than erosion could wear it down. Looking along the scarp, I could read the bedrock geology in the fracture patterns of the cliffs, which were often highlighted by dark lines of trees. When I entered one of the canyons, it felt at first like driving into a railroad cut. The cliffs looked as jagged and raw as if they had just been dynamited. Farther up the walls sloped back, scored by rock slides and ravines that poured great fans of talus and scree toward the road. Boulders would occasionally break off the high walls and come bounding out of the ravines to crash into the aspen groves on the other side. Luckily I never saw one of these events, but I noticed the dents that several had left in the pavement.

Never having lived in such dramatic country, I soon developed a visceral sense of geologic change. Of course I seldom saw the earth actually move, but its surface preserved a trace of each past event. Looking along the Wasatch Front I could see the beaches of glacial Lake Bonneville, which had filled the valley ten thousand years ago. The campus had been built on one of these "benches." I could see the marks of recent earthquakes along the fault zone and evidence of more ancient upheavals in the twisted strata exposed by eroding streams. Everything seemed huge, sharp-edged, and abrupt. The landscape's history stood forth in gigantic characters, and marks of violence seemed to be everywhere. It was hard to escape a sense of tragedy. In the Greek *agon*, character and fate coalesce in a moment of visionary destruction. Why shouldn't the metaphor apply here, where landforms arose from the joint structure and mineral composition of rock exposed to relentless mechanical force? Like tragedy, geologic time moved forward linearly from one heroic gesture to the next.

Given the grandeur and extremities of this landscape, I could see why people might want to live indoors. But I found myself going out even farther and higher. During the Ice Age the Wasatch had formed alpine glaciers that had gouged the upper canyons into deep U-shaped valleys. Soil had accumulated there, supporting groves of aspen, spruce, and Douglas fir. It was lovely to drive a half hour up the steep, crooked roads to emerge, all at once, in a landscape refreshed by wild flowers and evergreens. Side canyons and hanging valleys, each with its own snow-fed stream, led back toward the high peaks and connecting ridges I had seen from the air. Here were gardens wild enough to delight John Muir. But they were tucked back up in the labyrinth, invisible from the valley.

I learned that the Wasatch were very young mountains, still being twisted and shoved by the forces of planetary growth. Rocks of all ages and types appeared to have been thrust together, and each canyon bore a distinctive character, depending upon the formations it cut. Parley's Canyon, through which I had entered the city, sliced through Jurassic sandstones and limestones. Driving down Parley's was like entering a wound in the earth. A few miles farther south, Big Cottonwood Creek had exposed Precambrian quartzites more than a billion years old. This rock splintered into palm-sized fragments sharp enough to cut shoes. But I was most attracted to Little Cottonwood Canyon, where the glaciers had reached down almost as far as the valley. Here the mountains were made of a young, gray granite as fine-grained as that of Yosemite. It was here that the Mormons had quarried for their temple and, more recently, excavated their own sort of underground library, a vast genealogical archive that was now deemed safe from nuclear war.

I remembered how Darwin, admiring the coastal ranges of Chile, had once exclaimed, "To the geologist, granite is classic ground." That made sense to me. I had always loved granite and felt its strange attraction, on Half Dome, for instance, whose Cretaceous granite had cooled while the muds of eastern Utah were burying brontosaurus bones, or on Katahdin, whose pink granites had crystallized 250 million years earlier, in a time of coal swamps and giant dragonflies. Such were the deep, unforeseeable turnings of earth's mind. By comparison this Wasatch granite seemed positively youthful. It had pushed into the bedrock a mere 26 million years ago, while rhinos, camels, and tiny horses were roaming the grassy plains of Utah.

Elsewhere this rock had erupted as lava or volcanic ash, burying whole herds of these early mammals, but here the small crystals of quartz, feldspar, and black mica showed it had cooled underground. I sometimes thought of granite as frozen fire. Perhaps that sense of fierce energy contained made its cleanness and impenetrability even more precious to me. A piece of granite rounded by years of tumbling in a stream seemed like some original word of the earth. And whenever I stood on a granite summit like Half Dome or one of these Wasatch peaks, I felt the roots of my awareness probing downward, unmediated, toward the ancient energies that still moved mountains.

The Wasatch looked out across the valley like a file of watchtowers. Going up into them was an exercise in emptying. For a day or two before I would always be restless, then I would finally get up, walk out, and drive south along the fault zone through pastel suburbs until I reached the alluvial fan at some canyon's mouth. I would then turn upstream through towering gates of rock, following a crooked path through that needle's eye, until I reached the sunny openness of the glaciated zone. If I looked back then, I might still glimpse a sliver of valley obscured by the light brown smog that grew thicker every year. The higher I went, the more I cast off. I would leave the car, cross the creek with its white sand bed, and climb through spruce and aspen woods where mountain bluebells nodded beside the trail. A thousand feet higher lay pocket lakes with waters as green as beryl, and above them a talus staircase, whose boulders would rock and clink underfoot. Sometimes I might find snow here, even as late as July, and clusters of blue lupine on the ridges above. I would always stop for a snack, enjoying the first rush of space before climbing the last eight hundred feet to one of the summits—the Pfeifferhorn, say—from which all the mountain realms of Utah would spread into view.

Standing like this on a granite watchtower made me feel as I had on Berthoud Pass, except that the mountain man, the lens, and the eye behind it had fused into one. I saw both the physical and the spiritual geography of the New West, so different from what I had known as a child and yet curiously linked to those red sandstones and dusky cities. Salt Lake's grid of streets, parks, and housing developments spread out as crisp as an architect's drawing, yet in the immensity of the total landscape it seemed meticulous, delicate, almost trivial. The Jordan River wiggled through it like a piece of discarded string. Beyond rose the silver heaps of the Oquirrh Mountains, punctuated by two huge artifacts: the Kennecott smelter with its thousand-foot stack, and the terraced piles of tailings from the Bingham Canyon Mine, where a small mountain had been ground up and cooked into copper. The tailings ran for several miles and looked, up close, like the benches of Lake Bonneville, but from here they seemed no more significant than a sand castle on a beach. Such were the gestures of humans in this vast theater of geologic time.

I could also see how the New West's patterns of land use differed from those in the East. Here both culture and wilderness were concentrated and distinct. But in New England, wilderness, farmland, and urban areas all intermeshed, so that even Connecticut, the most densely populated state of all, supported abundant forests and large mammals like bear and deer. Back East, wilderness survived in thin corridors that swelled into nodes of several hundred acres, instead of in five-thousand-acre blocks as prescribed by the Wilderness Act for public lands. But in Utah, which was twenty times bigger with one-tenth of Connecticut's population, 80 percent of the people lived in cities along the Wasatch Front. Ironically that made Utah one of the most urbanized states in the nation. From any one of these mountain towers, I could look down on about half the population.

No doubt the idea of vast and untouched wilderness had largely attracted me to the West. I was a young man at the end of his formal education. I had a degree and even a good first job, but I also wanted to find a place I could live in forever. I wanted to realize the life of adventure, inspiration, and joy that Muir and Thoreau had celebrated. To do so, I thought, meant finding a landscape that would respond effortlessly to desire. I knew that such a paradise did not lie in the city, enmeshed in paradox at the end of its pioneer dream, but somewhere beyond, in the purity of unspoiled nature.

So I stood on the Wasatch towers like Melville's Ishmael looking out to sea, "tormented by an everlasting itch for things remote." I looked first one way and then the other, as I had on Baldy Peak so many years before. To the south I could follow the tops of the mountains off toward the Colorado Plateau and the visionary deserts of which Edward Abbey had written. To the west, beyond the Oquirrhs, lay the smoke-blue ranges and saline valleys of the Great Basin, last outback in the Lower Forty-Eight.

And to the north and east rose the snowy Uintas, with suggestions beyond of Wyoming, the Tetons, the Absarokas, and, bearing the Continental Divide, the Wind River Range. In those days I loved immensity and the clarity of distance and every sublime utterance of geologic time. Desire and imagination knew no limits for me. Three years seemed like a kind of eternity.

CHAPTER SIX

Delicate Arch

THE WORLD IN A BOOK

That fall I learned to teach for a living. It meant sixty-hour weeks closeted with the *Norton Anthology of English Literature* or *The Intellectual Tradition of the West,* amid whose labyrinths I rediscovered Chaucer and Dante, emerging dizzy and overprepared. The English Department was housed in a rectilinear brick and aluminum building, and after class I would retreat to my steel box of an office to gaze at the Oquirrh Mountains across the valley or pull out one of the topo maps I kept stashed in my desk. The chaos of contour lines always seemed cooling to a hot, post-lecture brain. For inspiration I might also read a page or two of *Desert Solitaire,* Edward Abbey's famous book on the canyon country, which I kept on a shelf next to the dictionary.

Abbey was known all over the West as the desert's foremost spokesman and fiercest defender. Unlike the biblical prophets, he had found some honor in his own country. Most bookstores in Salt Lake carried his writings, along with commemorative T-shirts and wall calendars. Radical groups had drawn inspiration from his tales of environmental sabotage. A rare public reading could bring out hundreds of people and raise thousands of dollars for the cause.

Abbey had inspired me, too, from the time near the end of my army tour when I had first read *Desert Solitaire.* In those days I was feeling lonely and oppressed, contemptuous of institutions. I hungered for wilderness with its lure of anarchic freedom, and Abbey's book had drawn me toward a vision of thoughtful, irreverent, and active life. I found I could read it over and over without getting bored. And later, teaching it in my courses at Yale, I had discovered affinities with the works of Thoreau and Muir that were actively shaping my career.

Like them, Abbey seemed to write from the center of the world. His canyon country was suited as perfectly to his temperament as Thoreau's Walden or Muir's Yosemite. He expressed his love in descriptions of stunning, lyric intensity edged with bitterness, for he knew the canyons were threatened. I loved the combination of yearning and despair that peeked out from under his male bravado. This Abbey appeared well educated, too, quoting poets and philosophers as he hunted fruitlessly for visions in the labyrinths of the Escalante or burned out his eyes trying to "look at and into" a gnarled, cryptic juniper that grew near his camp. He, too, had tried reading the book of nature, but he seemed to take pleasure even in his failures. He was robust and full of lively contradictions, invoking ascetic ideals while boasting, like Whitman, that he believed in the appetites. After praying and fasting in the desert, he had come out like a true son of man, eating and drinking. No elitist, he could move gracefully among all kinds of people, an intellectual who wintered in the slums of Hoboken, New Jersey, and summered with park rangers, cowboys, and river rats in the deserts of Utah. He had a hearty, macho quality, like Steinbeck heroes, and a Yankee wit tinged with self-deprecation. He liked to hang out in bars or around campfires with men who worked in the open air, sunburnt with great ideas. In this respect, he recalled the great poet-heroes of American literature, the Ishmaels, Whitmans, and Mark Twains for whom roughing it merely sharpened the imaginative eye. He was one of the "isolatoes," a pioneer of the spirit, and he had found, in wilderness experiences of piercing clarity, the power to speak out and challenge our habits of vision.

Abbey's brand of social criticism appeared more belligerent than Muir's or Thoreau's, but I felt that was because he had had to deal with a crueller, more dangerous world. This was the age of nuclear weapons, mass advertising, the military-industrial complex, and the internal combustion engine, yet Abbey had the guts to attack them all. Here was a man whom nature had empowered to live without institutions. I found his rhetoric of rebellion hugely appealing.

Moving to Utah only increased my fascination with *Desert Solitaire*. The book seemed to speak directly to so many of the issues I was currently facing: the sense of rootlessness and alienation, the hunger for freedom and self-reliance, the quest for a spirituality of direct encounter, and above all, the desire to pursue a prophetic teaching vocation. Abbey had come to the desert driven by many of these concerns, and the desert had answered to his desire. I was amazed that one landscape could bestow so much power. Granted I had seen much the same thing in Thoreau and Muir, but Thoreau was a pastoralist, living close to the village in cutover woods instead of real wilderness, glorious and remote. He had retreated from Katahdin, as if, so I thought, he had just not been tough enough. But Abbey relished the brutal otherness of the desert, the "bedrock and paradox" to which all his excursions led. He could even turn a lackluster eye on himself, which made him seem even more genuine than Thoreau. As for Muir, reading Abbey made his rapturous descriptions seem overblown and naive, even though I had been to Yosemite and felt its radiance myself. Now I began to think of what Muir had left out of his stories: the wild creatures' desperate struggle for food, the cruel economies of predation, the violence of storm and avalanche, and the real dangers of traveling alone in remote and unmapped places. The High Sierra was hardly a peaceable kingdom; Muir had engaged in some editing. But Abbey imagined paradise as "the actual, tangible, dogmatically real earth on which we stand," complete with spiders, scorpions, flash floods, and epidemics. He would excise only minor blemishes, like Glen Canyon Dam or the federal government. Apart from such frankly quixotic hopes, he seemed more down to earth than Muir or Thoreau.

A generation brings all things to the test of itself, and Abbey spoke directly to mine. I found his romantic principles and feisty rhetoric as comfortable as old blue jeans. So it was to the south that I looked most searchingly when I first stood on the Wasatch towers. And in early October, less than six weeks after arriving in Utah, I set off with a friend toward Arches National Park to see for myself the world I had found—or thought I had found—in Abbey's book.

CITY OF ROCK

To get out of Salt Lake you must sooner or later go up. It's a reminder that the city lies on the floor of the Great Basin, in a place once covered by nearly a thousand feet of water. The road to Moab climbs up a canyon onto the Wasatch Plateau: you enter a slot in the great wall and emerge into rolling, hilly uplands reminiscent of parts of New England. Thick meadows sweep back from the road toward hillsides clustered with aspen and evergreens. Streams meandering through willow thickets still shelter the beaver that once attracted the mountain men. To the northeast the plateau rises into the glacial fold of the High Uintas, dimpled with hundreds of trout-filled lakes. To the south it breaks off in naked escarpments toward the Colorado and its canyons. In between lie places with wonderful names: Castle Valley, Slaughter Slopes, Sinbad Country, the San Rafael Swell. The first time I drove this road I felt as if I were journeying up from the coast toward some fabulous interior, like one of the Spanish explorers. It helped to have a map and a destination, to see the rectangular boundaries of Arches National Park tinted purple and studded with scenic markers. The Spaniards had dreamt of finding cities of gold, but I was following a different kind of story.

The road crested at seventy-five hundred feet on Soldier Summit before beginning a long, crooked descent from the plateau. There would be no major city for five hundred miles: between us and Denver lay only the Rockies and the canyonlands, delicious terra incognita. I felt as if we were nearing the wilderness by degrees, and I began watching eagerly for arches, monuments, or any other signs of approaching paradise. But instead coal seams appeared in the road cuts, followed by an incongruous, billowing power plant that seemed to have been thrust like a concrete wedge into the canyon's throat. The road swung down through Helper and Price, old mining and railroad towns, then turned east through a scattering of shacks and trailers. This, too, was the New West, and a far cry from Abbey's country. The bleakness of human life seemed reflected in the terrain. Past the towns lay a sagebrush valley broken by low clay hills that were rutted with cycle tracks. To the east rose the Book Cliffs, a wall of gullied blue shale capped by thick bands of sandstone. The cliffs looked morbid and inaccessible—hardly book-like, unless you imagined books splayed open and turned up on end. Certainly they suggested no book of nature or prophecy, like Abbey's.

The road turned east through the dusty town of Green River, then crossed the Green itself as it flowed from the Book Cliffs in a muddy trough. I thought of how some of this water must have started as pure snowmelt high in the Wind River Range, four hundred miles to the north. We passed the Green River Missile Base, another sign of the New West. Thousands of Utahns had been dusted with carcinogenic fallout during the atomic tests of the 1950s, yet uranium was still being mined and processed near Moab. I felt a prickle of anger. Thank God for Abbey and his words.

The road turned south into featureless scrubland. There was still no sign of the place that Abbey had described, just red dirt, dry washes, and endless sage. We drove in silence for twenty miles, until the road entered a fold in the terrain and a red cliff rose abruptly on our right. The road sliced into the land, curving down toward the Colorado, and there, suddenly, we found the park entrance, a pink stone visitor center and parking lot tucked in at the base of the cliffs. The rangers said we could camp anyplace that was three hundred feet or more from a trail. We bought maps and filled our water bottles, tingling with expectation, and then headed off into Abbey's country.

The road had been chiseled into the cliffs behind the visitor center, climbing in alpine switchbacks toward the park's interior plateaus. The blacktop looked fresh. No doubt this was the road Abbey had tried to sabotage when, as he tells it, his desert reveries were interrupted one afternoon by the growl of a jeep coming from an unexpected direction. A party of civil engineers had pulled up, obviously dehydrated. Abbey had given them the last of his ice water along with careful directions back to the highway. Then, knowing their mission, he had hiked down their tracks and pulled up their survey markers. I admired the gesture but was also enjoying the road, which had been designed for dramatic effect. It topped out in a cluster of towers and promontories that glowed in the late afternoon sun like Egyptian ruins.

We drove north across rolling valleys and ridges studded with huge formations, some of which were marked with signs and turnouts. With darkness less than two hours away, we could not afford to stop, but we spotted occasional arches, small in the distance, with patches of sky or shadow peeking through. Whenever the road topped a ridge, we could see the La Sal Mountains, a cluster of gray pyramids rising beyond the trench of the

Colorado. The peaks contrasted violently with the curves, cylinders, arcs, and rounded columns of sandstone in the foreground. Conventional mountain forms, angular and chaotic, seemed out of place in this curvilinear geometry more suggestive of Frank Lloyd Wright or Le Corbusier.

The road ended, eighteen miles later, at Devil's Garden, so named for its abundance of arches, though it seemed to us a serene, even blessed place. There were only a few people camped there, but we wanted to sleep in the back country, so we set off down the trail. Here the brick-red Entrada sandstone had been cracked in long parallel joints, which erosion had widened and deepened to leave great standing fins, domed at the top and sapped at their bases by frost. We could see cavities forming in some of the fins, and it was thus, through a humble mechanical process, that the arches had been created.

A mile of walking brought us to Landscape Arch, which, at 291 feet, was said to be the "longest natural span in the world." These were engineering terms. From the trail it looked like a frozen leap of stone, curved upward just enough to enclose a bright sliver of sky. It appeared improbably thin, brittle as a breadstick, though I calculated it must have been at least as big around as a house. Beneath lay a heap of rubble in which sagebrush and juniper had randomly taken root, the remains of the landscape from which the arch had emerged. It was as if some portion of the earth had shrugged off its grosser elements as it struggled into the light. I remember thinking how much more beautiful the arch would have looked if someone had only cleared away the debris.

That night we camped on a slab beyond sight of the trail. Twilight filled the sky with the colors of stained-glass windows. Overhead, the stars glittered like frost. So far I had felt none of the fierceness Abbey had described. Perhaps it was just lack of imagination.

Next morning we woke to bird calls and a depthless, turquoise sky. The rising sun caught a jumble of sandstone blocks nearby, making them glow like huge flakes of gold. It was easy to see how the Spaniards could have been deceived. But I was seeking another kind of wealth.

We hiked back to the car on a primitive trail marked by cairns, immersed in the country instead of cruising over it on a road, and so exposed more intimately to its variety, intricacy, and form. The trail led alternately along the tops of fins, where the domed rock was spotted with lichens, or down into sandy troughs, where juniper, pinyon, and sage grew thick and bristly. I had not expected such profuse vegetation in Abbey's desert; it was richer, even, than the foothill chaparral above the university. We found water, too, when the trail crossed a draw cutting between the fins in a series of small, dry waterfalls whose plunge pools still held fifty gallons or more. In the haloes of mud, slick as fresh paint, we found tracks of insects, birds, small mammals, and even deer. A few late wildflowers bloomed in shady nooks at the bases of fins.

Along with this vivid, abundant life we discovered an intimate, architectural quality in the land. The bare sandstone was known locally as "slickrock," though it hardly felt slippery, but more like a clean, swept pavement. Walking along or up fins felt like climbing stairs or strolling down a sidewalk. The path led along the bases of walls, cool and clean to the touch, with shelves, nooks, or alcoves where one could sit down or rest a pack. We walked along alleys, touching the walls on either side before emerging through porticos into hidden, light-filled gardens. It felt very much like exploring some Mediterranean village with intricate passageways and thousand-year-old masonry. Every spot seemed possessed of immense character, inviting us to pause and savor. Oddly it was not wildness I felt here, but antiquity, comfort, even domesticity.

I found myself taking a lot of pictures that morning, snapping like a tourist at every secretive archway, potted flower, or abstract-expressionist wall. Emerging into open country beyond the fins, we could see the La Sal Mountains rising blue in the morning light like Greek ranges beyond the Acropolis. I snapped them. Behind us the Devil's Garden looked more like Bethlehem, or any hilltop city out of the Holy Land. I snapped that view as well. Back on the road, I found myself wanting to stop at every turnout. The country seemed to offer itself to the lens. Even an amateur photographer like me could hardly make a mistake.

At every scale the land seemed formed to the requirements of art. Each layered vista was framed by commanding verticals. The gauzy textures of distance accentuated the thrusting sublimity of nearby rock. Clean, changeless forms seemed to grow out of shifting sand, which the wind had raked into small and elegant waves. Everything seemed open to space, accepting light, offering itself to the eye as if posed. We visited several other groups of arches and were struck by their quality of display. They stood ranged against the sky like flying buttresses or the mounted skeletons of dinosaurs. I began to realize how the land's stunning beauty arose from its marriage of monumental architecture with the fluid geometries of bone. It suggested, oddly, the beauty of fashion models with their high cheekbones and translucent skin and the lure of ascetic ideals that promise, through mortification of the flesh, to reveal the elegant and essential truths that Abbey had called "the bare bones of existence." He had come here as a philosopher, a solitary man in search of the absolute. I began to sense why, in his narratives, he had been led to feminize this landscape, imagining it as some kind of unattainable woman. He was fascinated by the skull beneath the skin, the links between beauty and cruelty. There was in his philosopher's eye something contemplative and photographic, detached even from the fear of his own death. It contrasted with his vulnerable, sweaty manhood. I found it attractive, and slightly chilling.

That afternoon we hiked up a mile and a half of slickrock to Delicate Arch, the park's official emblem and most photographed formation. Even after seeing dozens of pictures, I was not prepared for the real thing. The trail led up the back of a tilted ridge, and for the last couple of hundred yards the path had been chiseled into the side of a cliff. We hugged the wall as we gazed across a hypnotizing gulf toward the Colorado and the blue La Sal Range. Then, quite abruptly, we came out on the rim of a sandstone bowl ten stories deep. On its far edge, thin as a wishbone, stood the arch.

I subsequently learned that Delicate Arch stands more than sixty feet high, yet on that day, with no human figure for scale, it looked frail, improbable, and pitifully exposed. A strong wind, I thought, might blow it away, and yet how wonderful to find something so perfect set out here in the wilderness, waiting to be discovered. I began to sense coherence in my varied impressions of the landscape. Unlike the others I had seen, this arch had no supporting fin. Its only contact with earth came from the two small points of its feet. Thus it suggested both grace and aspiration. There was, moreover, no sign of the debris that had been removed during its creation, a volume of stone that, to judge from the placement of strata, must have amounted to thousands of cubic yards. No fallen blocks were in evidence. Indeed, the curvature of the stone suggested erosion by frost and wind.

As I moved my fingers over the slickrock beside me, I could feel its surface granules loosen and abrade. I imagined the wind as a great hand scouring, rubbing, and polishing the rock with relentless intimacy. It had taken centuries to produce this graceful, Euclidean form, yet all traces of the creative act were gone. The process that had been only partially realized in other arches had reached its completion here. The result was a pure, geometric utterance, a naked parable of stone.

I understood now why people were drawn to photograph Delicate Arch. It could frame anything to stunning effect, particularly in the evening when the long, orange light made the rock seem to glow from within. Its splendid isolation and perfect form attracted the eye like sculpture. It seemed to radiate meaning, an omphalos or power place like the grotto at Delphi, though here there was no need for a temple architect. My scientific mind could see Delicate Arch as the result of natural forces acting over thousands of years. Indeed, from the perspective of geologic time, it was completely ephemeral, destined to vanish in the blink of an angel's eye. It was only the trace of a process that had no vestige of a beginning, no prospect of an end. But for this moment, captured in my eye or the eye of any human being who might come this way, it was a perfect creation, enduring and immortal. So part of its allure came from coincidence in time.

Just so, I realized, a photograph appeals because it claims to embody an actual trace of the world. It fixes the impression of a passing moment when everything seemed perfectly configured. Is this why we gaze at old portraits of ourselves, framed by a cunning hand to show off our "best features?" Great portraits are said to "capture" the character of a person or place, as if character were some sort of platonic essence peeking furtively through the chaos of history. Each photograph seems to affirm Blake's dictum that eternity is in love with the productions of time.

But Delicate Arch, as the trace of a natural process, offers the same kind of appeal: it suggests that nature possesses an underlying form that corresponds to the structures of the human mind. Here we see nature imitating art, geology approximating sculpture, the real coinciding at last with the ideal. So Delicate Arch offers, as Abbey said elsewhere, "a window into eternity." What greater lure could there be for a philosopher? Such a hope had drawn Emerson into nature, and Thoreau too, before his experience on Katahdin. Now I could see that it had also drawn Abbey, the romantic intellectual and writer of western novels. He, too, had come to the wilderness looking for affirmation.

We left Delicate Arch and drove to Courthouse Wash in search of a camping spot. The wash flowed out of the Courthouse Towers, which we had passed at the top of the entrance road. From a shallow draw it deepened rapidly to a canyon with high walls and inviting tributaries a mile downstream. There was water at this time of year, shimmering like a silk coverlet under the black, varnished walls. We crossed dry-looking sandbars that rippled underfoot like water beds, jumping off when water spurted around our shoes. Back toward the banks grew a silvery grass that was almost as fine as wool, young willows, and even cottonwoods where the soil had held firm for a decade or more. I recognized several wildflowers I had met in the mountains. Except for the vertical sandstone walls, this might have been any meandering mountain stream.

That night we camped in a side canyon thick with tamarisk. The stream trickled down over sandstone bedded as thin as the leaves of a book. The surrounding country was made up of petrified dunes, humped like pots in a kiln, but where we camped it was moist and intimate as a glade. I fell asleep gratefully to the clank of frogs.

I returned to the canyon country that spring and for several seasons thereafter, in search of other places that Abbey had mentioned. The land's beauty was a fact, incontrovertible yet somehow remote. Eventually I had to admit that the country did not speak to me as it had to him. I was enticed by curiosity to learn its intricacies, I lusted after its pure light and photogenic formations, but I never felt as much at home as I had in the mountains. And the spirituality that Abbey had sought seemed to elude me also. But whereas he had remained fascinated by the desert, for me it was his book that continued to beckon.

Part of the problem lay in the quality of the rock. Apart from its remarkable gift for creating vertical walls, sandstone held little appeal for me. It reminded me too much of the crumbling brownstone homes and Jurassic red beds of New Jersey. It was soft rock, even when glazed with the brown patina of oxides called "desert varnish." I remembered the way brownstone houses would disintegrate in the rainy, polluted East, spilling tiny piles of sand from salt-rimmed cavities just above the sidewalk. Given enough time, they might have formed small arches themselves. Likewise, wherever I went in the canyon country I found it hard to escape the impression of wastage. The edges of mesas were jagged as rusted iron, as if the country were being etched by acid. Everywhere I looked I saw corrosion, excavation, a tableau of flaking ruins and dissolving bones. I found myself longing once more for granite with its crystalline hardness polished to shining by glaciers. I wanted the sterile, distilled water of alpine lakes, not canyon water with its slight soapy taste, tainted with alkali and uranium.

Abbey had called the desert a "monstrous and inhuman spectacle of rock and sky and space," declaring that one of his principal aims was to suppress in himself the tendency to personify natural forms. Why, then, had he chosen a landscape that seemed to invite such analogies? If anything, the canyon country seemed all too human to me. Everywhere I looked were Euclidean, architectural forms, comforting in their familiarity. No doubt that was the reason Arches had been made a national park to begin with. Here one could well believe that nature was shaped like the human mind and so entertain Emerson's belief that in wilderness lay the hope for American culture. In this light Abbey's radical politics made sense. Yet there was a kind of narcissism, I thought, in worshipping places shaped to the features of intellect.

So I began to suspect Abbey's brand of spirituality. I recalled that his character did not change in the course of the book despite the intensity of his experiences. As far as I could tell, he had left Arches with the same ideas and attitudes he had brought in. One of these was his dream of "a hard and brutal mysticism in which the naked self merges with a non-human world and yet somehow survives still intact, individual, separate." Apparently he had succeeded, but to what end? Certainly he cut a heroic figure, emerging bloodied and baffled after wrestling the angels to a draw. His fascination with the desert compelled me. But his story revealed no initiatory transformation such as Thoreau had undergone on Katahdin.

To my mind Abbey resembled the young, adventurous Thoreau. Why, then, did his book share so many features with the mature and paradoxical *Walden*? I noted the cyclic plot structure of an idealized year, the pervasive learning, the Yankee humor, the mordant social critiques, the spirit of civil disobedience, the lyric descriptions and love of nature, the robust self-sufficiency, even the irony. But what *Desert Solitaire* lacked, I came to realize, was a paradoxical, self-questioning quality in the language itself. It was as if Abbey had missed Thoreau's injection of darkness. In his book the darkness and irony were all on the surface, in sarcasm, self-deprecation, and the worship of death and violence. In Abbey paradox was a pose; in Thoreau it was more like a wound. *Walden,* I realized, was a far more subversive book.

And yet in those days I still loved *Desert Solitaire* and envied its narrator, whose dreams and desires so closely matched my own. Though the desert did not speak so deeply to me, I still wanted to find what Abbey had found: a beautiful, wild, and sacred place that answered effortlessly to desire. It was just a matter of finding the proper landscape. Or so I thought until I met the man himself.

Prophecy and Debris

In the late 1970s Utah had vast tracts of roadless land but only one officially designated wilderness, a five-thousand-acre parcel on Lone Peak, just above Salt Lake City. Environmentalists joked that it was the only wilderness from which you could look down on a major metropolis. Politically Utah lay far to the right, more interested in using its land for defense industries, military bases, and power dams than for backpacking and vision quests. But a small, vocal group of activists had begun to advance the cause of preservation, and Abbey had lent them both moral and economic support. One day I got a call from Flo Krall, a professor of environmental education, who said that she was teaming up with Dick Carter of the Utah Wilderness Association to bring Edward Abbey to town. She had also invited a young nature writer named Barry Lopez. The two had agreed to meet with students during the day and give a benefit reading that night. Would I be willing to interview Abbey in her class and moderate the discussion?

At that time I had never heard of Lopez, but the chance to meet Abbey was irresistible. I began researching interview topics at once, settling at last on a set of open-ended questions I hoped would draw him out. Abbey was supposed to meet twice with students, over lunch for a session called "Books and Banter," and later that afternoon at an open meeting of Flo's environmental education class. The night before, Flo called me to say that Abbey had missed his plane and that Lopez would fill in at lunch.

It would take guts, I thought, to play to an audience of someone else's fans. But if Lopez felt challenged, he never showed it. He came in wearing blue jeans and a corduroy jacket, carrying an old satchel stuffed with papers and books. He was a small, intense man with a pale face, narrow beard, and clear, dark, penetrating eyes. For an hour he ranged over the landscape of western knowledge, taking our understanding of animals as an indication of how we comprehend both the world and ourselves. He used the Indian manner of calling animals by the generic, as if it were a proper name. Thus: "When Wolf hunts Caribou, he begins a conversation of death." It was a prophetic way of speaking. I felt woefully ignorant of wildlife—scenery, I realized, had always attracted me more—but Lopez respected the ignorance of his listeners. Whenever he answered a question, he seemed to be giving his full attention, as if there were no one else in the room. I felt doors opening in my mind, as if what I had thought all along were closets turned out to be windows.

Later that afternoon I went to Flo's classroom, where I found students crowding the chairs and windowsills. A few moments later Abbey arrived. He was a big man, over six feet tall, with a huge head and a grizzled patriarch's beard. He wore scuffed boots, green corduroy jeans, a leather vest, and a western shirt with ragged, shiny cuffs. His lined, somewhat flattened face was heavily tanned. It looked like a slab that had stood for years in the sun.

Abbey folded himself into one of those mass-produced chairs that torment students everywhere. He cast a bored, faintly hostile look around the room. I noticed that he had big, meaty hands with dirt ground into the creases, as if he were more used to handling leather than paper. He looked, in fact, as if he had just walked in from the corral. I tried a few leading questions. He had written extensively about the Southwest since *Desert Solitaire*. What were some of the themes that he still wanted to explore? Well, we should buy his books to find out. He was widely known as a desert writer; did he worry about becoming too closely identified with one landscape? Not much. Did he feel more comfortable writing fiction or nonfiction? The difference, if any, was academic to him; as we could see, most of his books were novels. His works were being studied in college courses; did that encourage him as a writer? Well, there was a difference between being studied and being appreciated.

After five minutes of this I was sweating hard. Fortunately the students began to ask about places he had described or defended. He warmed slightly to their questions, yet his manner remained laconic and aloof, irritable or diffident by turns. He grinned occasionally and spoke through the grin. Yet at the same time his voice quavered, his hands twitched, and he often blinked rapidly while speaking. All this suggested unease or dissipation, as if his powerful frame were being wasted from within. He gave an impression altogether different from that of the cocky, profound, and articulate speaker of *Desert Solitaire*, who seemed quite sincere in his effort to share a vision quest with the reader. In person Abbey kept fending his audience off. Clearly, I thought, he wants no disciples. I recalled the statement he had made to a *New York Times* reporter that "it would be a fate worse than death to become a cult figure, especially among undergraduates." Yet if Abbey felt that way, why was he here? What did he expect?

Afterwards Flo took us down to the Green Parrot, a watering hole for TV reporters, ski bums, and other young professionals. Dick Carter met us with a delegation of activists that included Doug Treadway of the BLM and the Sierra Club's June Viavant, whose life had been threatened by angry ranchers. The Parrot made the best margaritas in town, and Abbey soon grew relaxed and garrulous, inquiring about various desert places and trading war stories with Carter and Treadway. Obviously he felt more at ease with a small group of people he knew and respected for their love of a common place—people who had, so to speak, proven themselves in combat.

The reading was scheduled for seven-thirty. At seven fifteen we stumbled out of the Parrot and into Doug Treadway's camper. June and I rode in the back with three dogs, while Treadway and Lopez rode in front. Abbey drove with exuberance, heading up Fourth South in the wrong lane before screams from the others made him realize his error. He grinned, gunned the engine, and hauled the truck over the median, crunching the transaxle. Treadway groaned, but the axle held, and the lights were with us. Ten minutes later we walked into the university ballroom, where a crowd of two thousand people stood up and cheered.

Dick Carter began with a speech defending Kaiparowits, a plateau near the canyon lands where a power plant was scheduled to be built. He asked people to stuff whatever donation they could into a hiking boot that was being passed around. Then Abbey got up, to prolonged applause, and read, of all things, a book review. This was followed by a diary he had kept on a river trip in Alaska. Although he showed flashes of the irreverent entertainer—comparing glaciers, for instance, to "rivers of frozen blue snot"— neither piece struck me as learned, profound, nor especially beautiful. Abbey never once mentioned the canyon country. Could this be the author of *Desert Solitaire?* Apparently the question was not mine alone. Around me several people were nodding off, while others had started to leave.

By the time Lopez got up the hall was half empty, but it still held a good-sized crowd. Lopez rewarded us with three dazzling tales of humans and animals based on Indian legends. Each word seemed to whiz through the air, as if all his morning ideas had been gathered, fitted, and compressed by the potent economy of narrative. I realized there was something new for me in these stories that struck like arrows—not just the ideas, but a whole new way of thinking and speaking about our relationship to the land. It was something beyond what Emerson and his followers had conceived; an art that not only celebrated but required transformation.

Afterwards Flo held a reception at her house, and I screwed up my courage to speak to Abbey again. As he bent over the celery dip, momentarily free, I apologized for my dumb interview questions, the kind he must have had to endure on countless occasions. No doubt he considered *Desert Solitaire* old work, but I wanted him to know how much it had meant to me. I told him how I had used it in my courses and how much inspiration and insight my students had drawn from it. Whatever his present opinion of the book, it had moved and challenged them. I felt he was entitled to know. He nodded and thanked me graciously. He seemed to be looking down from a great height. He signed my book and I shook his hand, which felt warm and slightly limp. Perhaps it was just the lateness of the hour.

On my way out I exchanged addresses with Barry Lopez, who had been talking animatedly with some graduate students, off in a corner. In a few years he would be speaking to my classes about the writer's duty to respect his readers by keeping the private distinct from the personal. He would declare that "in North America, natural history is the preeminent metaphor for inquiry into the human condition." And on a warm spring night, he would pause in his reading to pick up a baby duck that had somehow wandered into the lecture hall, then carry it tenderly outside, whispering com fort. He would proclaim the need for a "conservation of darkness." But now he was still a young prophet, not yet at the middle of the journey.

I walked back to my house under the great dome of light that every city like Salt Lake projects toward the stars. I pondered my disillusion at meeting Edward Abbey the person instead of the living hero of *Desert Solitaire.* Better, I thought, if he had just stayed at home, out of respect for his readers. Why spoil their inspiration? Why spoil mine? And yet here was a man who was giving his time, his money—all the rewards of fame—and even his best words to the cause of wilderness preservation. He had not abandoned the land of his inspiration but was doing whatever he could to make return for its gifts. He was doing his duty. Yet what was so hard about that, with all your books in print and two thousand fans turning out for a reading?

Abbey had clearly felt ill at ease during both the interview and the reading. Flo had said he was suffering from a cold; others had said he was just being rude because, really, he didn't like people at all. But I felt there was something deeper involved. In choosing to view society through the lens of his wilderness experience, Abbey had placed himself in the Thoreauvian tradition of nature writing as jeremiad. Yet, unlike Thoreau, he had had to face the challenge of fame and literary success in his lifetime. What would it be like, I wondered, to be known and revered for a single work, even ten years after life and imagination had carried you far beyond its creation? And how much more challenging it would be if the subject of that work were yourself, captured, as if by a photograph, in some attitude of heroic perfection.

I realized then how much courage it must have taken for Abbey to come to readings like this. How exposed he must have felt, pursued, as it were, by a fictive double he himself had created. Most writers are shy by nature, preferring the quiet of desk and study to the hubbub of public life. As Keats once observed, "a poet is the most unpoetical of any thing in existence." Perhaps that is why, even after I had met him, I still thought of Abbey in terms of his book. His fictional self was more real to me than the man. And he must have known!

For a moment I sensed the loneliness all writers carry with them, knowing their words will live longer than they will and that the mask they present will be more loved than the living face. They must realize that readers come in search of perfection, and that their calling as writers is to minister to that need. The writer's work makes a kind of delicate arch; what's beautiful is the airy span, framing space and defying gravity. That's all the reader really cares about. But for each foot of arc there are tons of rubble to fall and be carried away. For beauty arises only out of our brokenness. At Landscape Arch the rubble lies in heaps; at Delicate Arch it has all been sifted away. But in either case the beholder's eye is drawn to the airy span. So always, seeking grace, we aspire to slough off the wreckage of human time.

But the nature writer cannot escape the past. Out of one's total experience of the landscape a thin band remains, like a sliver of rock enclosing a small piece of sky. One opens a window into eternity, but at a price, for one must then carry within oneself all the debris. The writer's real self, if it exists at all, must lie as much in the rubble beneath as in the parable overhead. The reader wants only some hero to admire—a life like a delicate span. How disturbing it is to be confronted with the debris of prophecy in the ravaged face of the actual writer. And with what feelings of relief do we turn again to the book and the infinite game of reading to which the writer becomes, for our sakes, a living sacrifice.

I never saw Edward Abbey again. Years later I heard that he had been buried, according to his wishes, beneath a heap of rocks somewhere in the desert.

CHAPTER SEVEN

Into the Deeps

Everyone harbors the dream of a mythic landscape, some distant, exotic region that feeds the imagination with visions of power and understanding denied by our normal life. For Melville's Ishmael it was the sea, which he sometimes took in masthead reveries for "the visible image of that deep, blue, bottomless soul pervading mankind and nature." For Darwin, voyaging on the *Beagle*, it was the arid plains of Patagonia, those "last boundaries to man's knowledge" that awakened "deep but ill-defined sensations" of the vastness of geologic time. For me that mythic land had beckoned variously from the High Sierra, the Maine woods, or the secretive canyons of Abbey's country. It was a protean thing, tantalizing but evanescent. Whenever my gaze would fasten upon some distant prospect, I would catch a flash out of the corner of my eye, like sunlight glancing on a pool. Then I would have to go out there. But when I arrived the light would already have diffused into the landscape or leapt to the horizon, leaving only the trace of a myth or a story.

From my urban base I explored all the more accessible parks and mountains, but after two years I still felt restless and unfulfilled. Ishmael had confessed to "an everlasting itch for things remote." I thought of these words every time I looked out the office window toward the barren slopes of the Oquirrh Mountains, the first of more than two dozen ranges advancing across the Great Basin like parallel waves toward the feet of the High

Sierra. I made inquiries, but people were not very helpful. The Great Basin was hot, barren, treeless, and ugly, they said, wild enough, certainly, but worthless for recreation: no lakes, no fishing, no good camping, just sagebrush valleys and drab, waterless mountains. They referred to it as the West Desert, a term of generic bleakness.

But the more people disparaged it, the more I was drawn to the Great Basin. It was the largest outback in the Lower Forty-Eight, yet in those days it had no national parks and only three designated wilderness areas. From the air it looked totally desolate, a corrugated landscape the color of rusty metal. At thirty thousand feet the mountains lost their relief; they looked like squashed centipedes, fringed by alluvial fans and dry gullies winding toward lake beds ringed with alkali. The valleys between looked smoky gray, as if dusted with ash. The maps showed few roads, mostly dirt, a scattering of towns with odd names like Winnemucca, and geographical features with darker, more romantic names like Skull Valley, Confusion Range, Ruby Mountains, and Black Rock Desert. The white space on these maps was surely deceptive, I thought. The Great Basin must have its secrets.

Research gave other, more fascinating hints. The term "basin" applies more to the land's geography than to its appearance. All streams drain inward, evaporating on dry valley floors or feeding saline lakes like Pyramid, Mono, or the Great Salt Lake itself. We owe the name "Great Basin" to John C. Frémont, who first recognized this unusual property. What Frémont did not know was that twelve thousand years ago, the land had been rich with forests and water. Two huge lakes, Lahontan in the west and Bonneville in the east, had filled many of its valleys, and Paleolithic tribesmen had roamed their shores hunting bison, camels, and mastodons. At its greatest extent, Lake Bonneville had covered more than twenty thousand square miles and reached depths of more than a thousand feet, pouring its fresh waters into the Pacific via the Snake River. As the climate dried out and the glaciers withdrew, the lake had fallen below its outlet and gradually shrunk to a mere fifteen hundred square miles, leaving behind vast stretches of salt flats and miles of its ancient beaches terraced against the flanks of neighboring mountains. Arid and barren today, the Great Basin was still haunted by vanished waters. To me Lake Bonneville had all the fantastic appeal of Ishmael's ocean, and when I gazed westward across its bed, I seemed to see in my mind's eye the same "ungraspable phantom of life."

Nor, despite the scorn of my outdoor friends, was I the only one drawn to the Great Basin. In those days of cold war the air force wanted to base two hundred MX missiles in the intermontane valleys. Each missile would be shuttled around a "racetrack loop" of twenty-three hardened silos spaced seven thousand feet apart. Theoretically, this would force the Russians to use forty-six hundred warheads to wipe out the system in a first strike. The resulting fireworks would make Hiroshima look like a flashbulb, but the air force thought that the deserts of Nevada and Utah, where atomic bombs had been tested since 1945, would be the most appropriate "national sacrifice area" in the event of war. They promoted the MX as "the most massive public works project ever undertaken," dwarfing the Alaska pipeline and the Panama Canal. Maps showed the system of roads and racetracks stretching halfway across Nevada. They looked weirdly anatomical, like a dissection of someone's lymphatic system.

Patriotic, conservative, and proud of its pioneer history, Utah had always welcomed big government projects. At that time it had more real wilderness than most states south of Alaska but less designated wilderness than New Jersey. Its conservationists formed an intense minority; they went out into the West Desert and found air force surveyors tying little orange ribbons to the sagebrush. Generals and deputy secretaries, sleek and convincing, had begun appearing on Salt Lake TV. People expected the bulldozers any day, and with my teaching contract soon to expire, I began to despair of seeing the West Desert before it was fenced off and paved.

But the chance finally came and, oddly enough, it was a fisherman who took me there.

Dave Hall, who worked for the Utah Division of Wildlife Resources, lived in the apartment above me and had brought from New Hampshire an everlasting itch for trout. Contemptuous of bait fishermen, he tied his own flies, swearing that to catch trout you had to think like one. He would cut open his first fish, tease out the contents of its stomach, select the matching fly, and wade back in with devastating effect. So closely did he identify with his quarry that he once tied flies with strands of his own beard. Friends assured me that he could catch trout in a rain puddle. I once asked him where he would go if he had the chance to fish anywhere in Utah, and he said, "I'd like to fish the Deeps."

"What Deeps?" I asked, thinking he meant some place like Jones Hole on the Green River, where lunkers thrive in the water of limestone springs. He certainly could not have meant the Great Salt Lake, which is barely fifty feet deep in the middle and salty enough to pickle the toughest trout.

"I mean the Deep Creek Mountains," he said, "in the West Desert. Dick Carter told me about them. They have a unique variety of cutthroat, but no one goes out there. It's a four-hour drive on dirt roads."

Dave explained that because the Deeps rise close to twelve thousand feet, they get a lot of snow. The trout of Lake Bonneville used to spawn in their streams, and when the lake began to shrink, they stayed behind, evolving into a distinct subspecies. When I suggested that maybe they should be protected, Dave said they were, but he had heard enough about them to want to drive out there just to take a look. These were mythic trout to him. He thought his new van would make it, and he wanted company. We could take the old Pony Express road around the south end of the salt desert, maybe stop at the Fish Springs bird refuge.

"How about next week?" I said. He had not known he was preaching to the converted. Something in the name sounded irresistibly wild and strange. I knew that before going anywhere else I would have to go into the Deeps.

Next day I called on Dick Carter at the Utah Wilderness Association. I found him sitting at a small desk overflowing with maps and documents describing lands that the Bureau of Land Management would be expected to donate for the MX. Living on handouts, Carter had built a vigorous coalition of preservationist groups. That day he looked tanned and disheveled, as if he had just walked in from the desert himself.

"The Deeps are pretty wild," he told me. "No campgrounds, no maintained trails. They're not on the way to anyplace else. They are heavily forested, but somehow they were allocated to BLM rather than to the Forest Service, so they have never been logged. The air force wants to build an MX base in the Snake Valley, just to the east. Plus, Atlas Minerals claims to have found uranium indicators in some of the alluvial fans. They got permits from BLM to drill up in those watersheds. But we went to the secretary of the interior and persuaded him to withdraw the area from development for three years pending reliable studies of its geology and ecology."

"What about the trout?" I asked.

"They are protected under the emergency withdrawal, along with other rare species," he said. "The Deeps are an island ecosystem. They preserve specimens of plants and animals that flourished in the Bonneville drainage twelve thousand years ago."

"How often have you been out there?" I asked.

"Couple of times," he said, looking wistfully at the heaps of documents. "Granite Creek and Trout Creek are the ones with the native trout. You can get more information from Cecil Garland, a rancher who lives in Callao. That's a small settlement at the base of the mountains." Carter leaned back in his chair and looked out the window, where the peaks of the Oquirrh Range just showed beyond the edge of a nearby office building. "If you go out there, take plenty of water," he said, "and extra gas. There are no services between here and there. No ranches either."

The trip began on the same interstate I had taken to get to the Arches. For twenty-five miles a stream of traffic carried us south along the level floor of Lake Bonneville, now buried by a siltation of suburbs. As we approached Point of the Mountain, a huge sandbar at the end of the valley, we could see the old beaches rising one above the other, as level and graded as railroad embankments. Today, instead of climbing through them into the Wasatch, we would follow them, more or less on the contour, for more than a hundred and fifty miles.

Dave Hall drove with his wife Becky, who did not share his fisherman's lust but felt the pull of the Deeps. I rode in back with another friend, Bob Condrat, who loved desert hiking and hated the MX missile. He had once worked for a defense contractor but had quit to take a job as a draftsman. Quiet and courteous, he had the slight air of melancholy common to activists in Republican Utah. He wore gold-rimmed glasses and a wonderful Old Testament beard. I could easily imagine him as a prospector in one of those classic westerns, wandering for months among the forlorn and bitten ranges with only his mandolin and his faithful burro for company.

At Lehi we turned off the interstate toward the south end of the Oquirrhs, which had bounded my view from Salt Lake. The irrigated farmlands soon fell behind, and the land turned a pale straw color. On the south-facing slopes we saw no trees but the dark green pom-poms of Utah juniper, which made the ground look wooly from a distance. Though it was dry as an oven, the air seemed to press down with a heavy, liquid weight. Near Vernon the irrigated fields of a sod farm stood out like bright green postage stamps. The pavement ended and gravel began drumming against the floor of the van. The last vehicle we saw was a tractor plowing a hundred-acre field under a dust plume five stories high. This was "dry farming," developed by Brigham Young, who must have thought that prayer would do for water. Sagebrush crowded along the shoulders, dull green and silvery, like weathered copper. Road dust drifted in through the windows, caking the insides of our nostrils. It had an astringent, earthy taste like potter's clay. With each mile westward the heat grew more intense. I could feel it sucking the moisture out of my pores and puckering my skin with a scaling of dried sweat.

Past the Onaqui Mountains, west of the Oquirrhs, the road ran out across a plain of buff-colored grass, and the mountains dribbled off into low hills that looked like melting scoops of ice cream. They sank to the desert floor in asymptotic curves; one had the sense of a landscape completely at rest. Though we could see for perhaps forty miles across this plain, hardly a trace of human life was visible—not a fence, not a windmill, not even the dust of a distant pickup. The only sign was the road itself, which, for all we knew, might have been laid yesterday, it was so level and smooth. There was not even a beer can or a plastic bag tossed by the side. At one point we stopped the car, and the silence came pouring in through the windows. It felt eerie and sinister, like scenes in movies about the aftermath of a nuclear war. We could stand it for only a few minutes, and then we had to get moving. Even the sound of the engine was reassuring.

We passed a crossroads with a sign for "Dugway." Bob said that most of the land to our right for the next thirty miles or so would be part of the Dugway Proving Grounds, a top secret installation the army used for testing nerve gas and other deadly weapons. A huge flock of sheep had recently been killed when a gas cloud had blown the wrong way. "They claimed the sheep died of natural causes," Bob said. "But who knows what goes on out here? It's too remote."

In fact, the Dugway Proving Grounds looked no different from any other part of the landscape. It did not even seem to be fenced. But on the map it showed as an ominous white space covering more than five hundred square miles. At its borders, marked "Danger—No Public Access," the thin red lines of the roads all disappeared. From what we could see, it looked like an ideal place for military research. No tourists would be passing by, and spies would have no place to hide in the miles of open desert. As for the environment, it was so bleak that no one would notice, or even care, if it were destroyed. Even the military had found a use for remoteness: it promised security, safety, and secrecy.

I told Bob that it looked like a good place for a missile system. "Maybe," he said, giving me a hard look, "but they won't be able to do it. They say they want to put in ten thousand miles of new roads and pour two million tons of concrete. They want something like a hundred billion gallons of water. Where are they going to get that much in a country like this? They'll never be able to build it, but they will try, and in the process they'll ruin a lot of land." He looked out the window over the short bleached grass toward the distant flats of the salt desert, where nothing moved to break the mineral stillness. "Besides," he said, "I think they like it out here. I learned about their mentality when I worked at China Lake, testing antiaircraft shells."

Ahead the Dugway Range rose out of the yellow sands of Lake Bonneville. Its peaks looked dark and hard, as if someone had gone over them with a blowtorch. Scorched earth, I thought, that was the military's trade. If they ever used the MX, large parts of two countries would end up looking like this.

We began climbing toward Dugway Pass, crossing the Bonneville terraces again. Scattered juniper trees began to appear, colored a dull bottle-green and rooted in flinty gravel. Looking east from the summit we could see the road winding toward us over the dun-colored plain; it looked as permanent as a finger mark on a dusty shelf. The Wasatch Range with its snowy peaks had long since vanished below the horizon, and with it our memories of aspen forests and streams overhung with wildflowers. To the west we could see the salt desert gleaming with porcelain brilliance against the blackened-aluminum ramparts of distant mountains.

We dropped down from the pass and over the Bonneville terraces. At that point I could not believe there had ever been water here. Heat rose from the road in waves, and the salt desert, shimmering with mirages, seemed to vibrate like metal under the sun. We had plenty of water with us, but I could still appreciate the desperate tales of the early explorers. Jedediah Smith, who had crossed the West Desert in 1827 with three other mountain men, told of drinking from brackish springs, stripping the flesh from their dead horses, and digging holes in the sand to cool their overheated bodies. "That kind of traveling is very tiresome to men in good health who can eat when and what they choose and drink as often as they desire," he wrote, "and to us worn down with hunger and fatigue and burning with thirst increased by the blazing sands it was almost insupportable . . . Our sleep was not repose, for tormented nature made us dream of things we had not and for the want of which it then seemed possible and even probable we might perish in the desert unheardof and unpitied."

Smith and his men crawled into Skull Valley, where they found a spring, and thence to the Great Salt Lake, "a most cheering view." But we were headed in the opposite direction. At this point the only life we saw, besides the ubiquitous bottle-green shrubs, were anthills about a foot high, spaced at thirty- to forty-foot intervals and surrounded by halos of baked clay, where the ants had removed every scrap of organic material. These anthills looked built to last. Bob said he thought they would survive the MX one way or another.

The road turned north around a clump of low buttes—the Black Rock Hills—and straightened out across a broad, flat valley. Ahead rose the Fish Springs Range, even more desolate than the Dugways, if that were possible. At their base I could make out a faint smear of green. Soon an aluminum sign appeared—"Fish Springs National Wildlife Refuge"—and suddenly the road was lined with high, waving reeds. Blue water—incongruous, wonderful—sparkled behind them. As we slowed in surprise, a brace of mallards exploded into flight; then a great blue heron took off, climbing with long, loping wingbeats into the desert sky. Even though Dave had mentioned this refuge, I was hardly prepared for water birds, particularly herons, which I had always associated with lakes and wetlands back East.

In the hour we spent on the refuge, we counted more than 30 species of water birds, gathered, it would seem, from all over the continent: snowy egrets standing like elegant hieroglyphs, white-faced ibis, black-crowned night herons, mergansers with their fancy crests, ducks of all kinds (including the blue-winged teal so well known in the prairie states), Canada geese, marsh hawks cutting and gliding above the reeds, gulls floating like white handkerchiefs against the black cliffs of the Fish Springs Range. At the one-room visitor center, we learned that out of the 166 species observed on the refuge since 1966, over a third are water or shorebirds, and at least 45 nest as well as visit. The refuge protects over ten thousand acres of marshland fed by artesian springs. Apparently sites like this are scattered all over the Great Basin—Ruby Lake in eastern Nevada, for instance, or Timpie Springs at the end of Skull Valley, whose ducks must have delighted Jed Smith and his men. When the birds began their northward migrations on the heels of the melting glaciers, the long shallow arms of Lake Bonneville promised food, safety, and breeding grounds. As the lake withdrew, the birds stuck to their ancient ways, hopping from marsh to marsh as we might cross a river on stepping stones. Like the Deep Creek trout, they too had survived, finding in remoteness the freedom to rest and breed in peace.

Still, as we wandered through the refuge, I could not shake off a sense of unreality. Despite the abundant water—some of the pools covered nearly a thousand acres—I saw very little vegetation besides the reeds and grasses. The mountains loomed beyond the pools like heaps of cinders, and the terraces belted along their flanks only reminded us of how much fresh water had vanished. The West Desert was a ghostly place, and Fish Springs seemed preternaturally moist and green, as if kept alive by a stubborn *genius loci*. Even the water was odd. We stopped at one of the springs, a deep well clogged with mats of yellow-green algae. The water was vivid blue, like Caribbean seawater, and it felt uncomfortably warm. Mindful of Jed Smith's ordeal, I took a sip and found it brackish and faintly sulfurous, like water in which you have boiled an egg. I dumped the rest back, and a cigar-shaped fish, black as a shoe, darted from one of the algae clumps. There were certainly no trout in these pools. I wondered if this were a Bonneville fish or some product of rapid evolution.

The road continued along the base of the mountains, and three miles later we swung around the north end into the Great Salt Lake Desert. Here we found hot springs welling up through the baked-clay floor. Sulfurous, briny, and rimmed by a bright-orange scum, they looked like suppurating sores. Between them the soil was glazed with salt; in fact we could have scooped up salt by the spoonful. And yet even here we found plants growing, spindly succulents in small clumps about a foot high, leaf-less and jointed, with the same weathered-copper color as sagebrush. Later I learned these were pickleweed, or *Allenrolfea occidentalis*, the most salt-tolerant of all desert plants. They grow on the fringes of saline basins and survive by sending a long taproot into the lower layers of soil, from which evaporating rainwater has leached the salts toward the surface. At the time, they reminded me of those fantastic "chemical gardens" we used to make by dropping seed crystals into syrupy solutions of sodium silicate, or "water glass." In the mineral waste of the salt desert they seemed to endure by taking on the characteristics of minerals themselves. They had found in a naturally polluted landscape some kind of rare opportunity, though to exploit it they had had to give up the features of most other plants, such as leaves and blossoms. They suggested to me that the key to survival might lie in a willingness to grow from within, to turn their creativity upon them-selves instead of attacking their environment, as human beings do. Perhaps to them remoteness meant life and freedom from competition.

Leaving the springs we got our first full view of the Deeps, an ordinary-looking range with brushy foothills and only one snowy peak in view. It was a bit of a disappointment, after so many miles of desert, not to see something more alpine and spectacular. The road cut south and west over a sagebrush plain, seeming to disappear into the base of the mountains. Two pronghorn antelope bounded off through the sage, raising puffs of dust. Far ahead I could make out a cluster of trees, the ranches of Callao. The mountains loomed nearer, rising from lumpy, scrubby foothills above the railroad-level terraces of Lake Bonneville. Once we entered the Deeps, we would have crossed the ancient lake bed, but instead of coming up for air, we would come up for water.

Callao had four or five working ranches, a few log cabins with caved-in roofs, several back lots full of rusting, antique machinery, and two pub-lic buildings—a schoolhouse and a whitewashed Mormon church. Cecil Garland's place was easy to find; it stood right on the main street and looked more prosperous than any of the others. His white adobe house was shaded by giant cottonwoods and surrounded by flower beds, vegetable gardens, fruit trees, corrals, and outbuildings. In the driveway were three pickup trucks and a tractor. In back were a radio tower, a machine shop, and a bunkerlike thing I took for a fallout shelter but later found out was a root cellar. On the front porch were some rocking chairs, a chest refrigerator, and a coffee table with several thin volumes of poetry. A rack of irrigation boots hung upside down on the wall.

Garland came out and waved us into his rockers, producing bottles of homemade root-beer. He looked about fifty, lanky and weatherbeaten, with a drooping gunfighter's mustache and a tan line across his forehead. He had grown up in North Carolina, he told us, dreamed of the West as a boy and finally bought a ranch in Montana. He had fought hard for the wilderness up there, but when his marriage broke up he had quit the state. No one knew where he had gone until Dick Carter, investigating the Deeps, had stumbled upon his place. Then the air force had decided to build the MX in his backyard.

"I came out here for the solitude," he said, "to live at peace with the land. I have a grazing allotment up there, just like everyone else, but I don't overdo it; I let the range recover and maintain itself. Mostly I feed my stock on hay grown with the Deep Creek water. If Atlas goes in there and starts mining, the erosion will silt up our streams. Besides, I seriously question if we should be mining uranium at all. I wonder about our sanity when we talk about defending ourselves with nuclear weapons. If we tear up the last 5 percent of our wilderness for that, we're nothing but a bunch of barbarians."

Garland showed us around. He ran beef cattle for cash income but grew all his own fruits and vegetables, kept bees, made cheese from his own milk, and raised his own poultry and eggs. He repaired the tractors himself. Once or twice a month he drove to Salt Lake to pick up supplies and speak out against the MX. He had even appeared on national TV. Callao, it seemed, was no longer so remote.

"You came out here just in time," he told us. "I'd go up Granite Creek. They don't allow cattle in there anymore, on account of the trout. Tom's Creek and the Basin are real pretty too, but some of my neighbors run stock up there. You'd have to bed down with the cows." He gave us a jar of honey and some pickled peppers out of his root cellar. "Take these," he said. "There's good water up there."

By the time we left Callao the lower slopes of the Deeps were streaked with shadow. We turned southwest and began climbing the Bonneville terraces for the last time, crossing alluvial fans where Atlas had found

uranium. Behind and below us Callao shrank into the landscape, as neat
and tiny as a model railroad town. Beyond it the salt desert spread to the
eastern horizon, plaster-white beneath the charcoal ranges. We crossed
Tom's Creek, where Jed Smith had slaked his thirst in 1827. We passed
an aqueduct, where Deep Creek water raced down a concrete trough
toward Callao. Five miles later we saw the mouth of Granite Creek opening like a dark slot in the mountain wall. A road came in from the right
and we took it, climbing steeply. At six thousand feet the road dropped
off the alluvial fan into the canyon. High granite walls rose up on either
side, shutting off the view. On our left we saw a line of trees. We could
hear the shouting of mountain water. A fresh, cool fragrance suddenly filled
the car. It was as if we had just walked from a hot street into an air-con-
ditioned home. I knew then what it really meant to say we were *in* the
mountains.

After we had gone about a mile, the road plunged into the creek, which
looked about two feet deep, and emerged on a gullied rocky slope, well
on its way to regaining the state of nature. We parked in the sagebrush
and ran down to the creek. When I touched the water, my arms tingled all
the way to my shoulders. Gratefully I washed off the dust and sweat that
caked my skin. The water was so cold and swift it felt almost abrasive,
but when I cupped a handful and drank it down, it tasted sweeter than
any water I could remember. I sat back on the bank, working my numbed
toes into the coarse granite sand, feeling clean at last but suddenly very
tired. I realized for the first time how much the desert had taken out of
us: not only our body moisture, but the very hope of finding water like
this, not bottled or piped or chlorinated, but living water open to the sky.

Dave, meanwhile, had been inspecting the creek for trout. "No luck,"
he reported. "Too many shadows. But the stream is perfect. Each of these
pools ought to have two or three frisky native cuts."

Becky smiled, "I'd like it here too."

And Bob said, "Yes—plenty of sweet water, no human beings."

At the head of the canyon, several miles to the west, we could see the
snowy summit of Ibapah Peak, twelve thousand feet high and our even-
tual goal. We strapped on our packs and followed the jeep road up through
an evergreen forest broken by sagebrush openings. The air cooled rapidly
as the shadows grew, and we breathed in thankfully its odors of crushed

herbs. After hiking a mile we had gained nearly a thousand feet, and we made camp in a small meadow where Becky found a spring. Mountain flowers grew plentifully—lupine, paintbrush, penstemon, all old friends. High cirrus clouds glowed pink as a full moon rose over the desert below. That night was one of the most peaceful I ever spent in the mountains.

Next morning we continued up the jeep trail, planning to leave our packs at a high camp. The summit of Ibapah, still almost a mile above us, appeared and disappeared beyond the trees. The canyon grew more and more lush, meadows of calf-deep grass alternating with sagey slopes and groves of aspen and fir. In many ways, the scenery reminded me of other mountains I knew, and yet there were curious differences. Many flowers seemed slightly off-color: the lupine were smaller and tinted with purple, the paintbrush were not red but candy-pink, the aspen looked whiter, their bark almost chalky. We found several huge anthills, one over six feet long and covered with brown pine needles, unlike anything we had ever seen. The ants seemed rather placid and were not much disturbed when poked with a stick. Dave said that the Deeps were known to harbor many odd types of insects and plants. He mentioned the giant stonefly, beloved by trout, an insect that normally occurs only in streams draining into the Pacific Ocean. Its presence here confirms that Lake Bonneville once had an outlet.

The jeep track ended in an aspen grove, where we left our packs and filled our water bottles. A steep, faint trail climbed through pine woods to a pass southwest of Ibapah. Near nine thousand feet the forest opened out to reveal the desert shimmering almost a vertical mile below. At ten thousand feet we encountered patches of snow and stopped for lunch in a grove of gnarly old pines. On some of these trees, the bark had been stripped by fire and the heartwood had bleached to amber. Rain and snow had eroded the softer portions, raising the grain in fantastic swirling patterns just like the lines on our contour maps. It felt very strange to see a human artifact thus imitated in the heart of the wilderness, almost as if the Deeps themselves were guiding us.

By now it was early afternoon, so we decided to strike out directly for the summit ridge, two thousand feet above us and nearly a mile to the north. The slope had steepened so much that the trees seemed to lean into it, like tottering candles. Thick snowbanks lay like slabs of frosting among the trees, filling the spongy soil with new water for Granite Creek. When the snowbanks began to converge, we had to start kicking steps, and we often sank up to our knees through the sun-softened crust. Two hours brought us to the ridge, exhilarated but out of breath. Ibapah was still seven hundred feet above us and more than half a mile away. We knew we could never climb it and get back to camp before dark, so we sat down to enjoy the view.

On the ridge, frost wedging had split the granite into vertical slabs, and the whole crest was studded with giant blocks. We might have been standing in the ruins of some ancient temple. The view was tremendous. To the west unknown ranges broke like dark storm waves against the horizon, their ravines glinting with snow. North and south the granite crest of the Deeps twisted away like a silver bracelet. At our feet the west slope plunged into wooded ravines from which long fingers of trees reached out toward the Goshute Valley, a thousand feet higher than Callao. To the east we could see the canyon of Granite Creek emptying into the desert, the salt basins gleaming like china, the scorched, rusty peaks of the Dugway Range, and the smoky blue shadows of higher, more distant ranges—the Stansburys with their pine forests, the Oquirrhs hiding Salt Lake, and the Wasatch with their summer snows and halo of midday clouds, promising water for the cities of the plain. In all that eastern view there was no sign of human life, not a road, not a building, not even a vapor trail in the sky.

It was then that the sense of remoteness hit me like the gut-cramping taste of cold spring water. Always before I had traveled in better-known wilderness areas, with maintained trails and rangers on patrol. If you got hurt, you could always count on someone coming along. But here we were completely cut off from the human world. It would be easy to die "unheardof and unpitied." Perhaps I should have been nervous, but I felt more exhilarated than afraid. Standing amid the ruined temple rocks with a vast landscape flowing away on all sides, I felt as if I had reached the center of the world. For this was the source of the creek we had climbed, the place where earth touched heaven and received the water of life.

From this enormous height, the Great Basin valleys looked as barren as they had from the air. Yet I now knew that this country harbored water birds, ingenious plants like the pickleweed, rare trout and insects, meadows of flowers, aspen forests, and sweet, unfailing streams. Their isolation had preserved them, but building a missile base would destroy that isolation forever. The generals who wanted to make this a national sacrifice area had probably never seen it except from the air. How could they know of its strange and abundant life?

And suppose they did know. What difference would it have made? Bob had said they liked the desert, and, as I looked at the glaring alkali flats below, I finally began to understand why. So many of their new weapons worked by spreading desolation, and down there, withered and burnt by solar radiation, the land itself seemed to affirm their ideals. It occurred to me how much the carnage of modern warfare had masked its environmental impacts, how much it expressed not only a hatred of human life, but a hatred of nature as well. Scorched earth was the best way to insure that no person or creature would rise up to challenge your will. The MX, which would desolate vast areas, seemed only a grotesque embodiment of this view.

To the generals, the Great Basin may have looked like their kind of country, but we knew now that this was an illusion. The birds of Fish Springs, the pickleweed thriving in salt pans, and the Deep Creek trout embodied a spirit of survival alien to the MX mentality. From the viewpoint of geologic time, their presence revealed that change and growth meant strength, not weakness. To adapt was not to surrender in disgrace, but to open the way to new and unexpected life. As Lake Bonneville had begun to recede, these creatures had kept faith with their origins, retreating to places where they could still find water, even as they had begun to evolve. Seen through the lens of planetary time, they all were changing, flowing like the water in their cells toward distant, unimaginable ends.

I looked down the valley of Granite Creek, whose waters we had carried back to the snowfields where they were born. Though I had not seen them, I knew that trout were idling in its pools, dappled with the shadows of aspen and fir. The whole course of the stream was visible, from the trickling snowpack through lush forest to the burning plain where it gave up its ghosts. I saw that stream in all phases of its life—as God might see my life or my country's life—under the aspect of eternity. No trout could have such a view. I tried to imagine them asking, in some flickering, trout-like way, where their creek began or whether it reached the sea. But as far as I could tell, they were just doing their best to fulfill the life they knew. They could not control the water that bore them or the process that carried them on through time, yet they seemed to accept both with what, in human terms, might be called an easy grace. Perhaps this was what had enabled them to evolve. They had survived by accepting the process without knowing its end.

As I gazed on Granite Creek, I finally saw what had drawn us into the Deeps. Without the desert they would have meant nothing special to us. Yet we had come to escape not only the blazing sands, but also the spiritual wastes of the MX mentality. We had felt, subconsciously, like the birds and the trout, retreating before the dryness of a nuclear age. Our coming, then, was a gesture of brotherhood, a homage to their spirit of survival. From them we learned that the deepest meaning of remoteness lay in its spiritual lessons. Like them, we too might survive if we learned to live by faith.

We glissaded the snowfields, then picked up our old trail and followed it down through the forest until it met the stream. All the way to our campsite, Dave looked for trout, but though we stopped at each perfect riffle and pool, we never saw one. Next morning we filled our bottles with Deep Creek water, packed up, and headed down the old jeep road. By noon we were back at the van. We poured in our extra gas and started away, losing the stream in the clatter of engine and gravel. At the canyon's mouth, the desert opened like a furnace, but we had soaked our T-shirts in the creek and wore them wet, a trick that gained us about twenty miles of coolness.

We drove north along the base of the Deeps toward Wendover, a border town on the interstate about eighty miles away. We could get gas there, and Dave wanted to check out the casino, explaining that every fisherman is a gambler at heart. We turned west around the north end of the Deeps and passed the cindery buttes of Gold Hill, where mining boomed in the early 1900s and the air force was planning an MX base for tomorrow. We met blacktop again on US 93, about sixty miles from the Deeps. After desert roads, a silent ride felt very strange, as if we were traveling down a tube under water.

Wendover turned out to be just a strip of casinos and truck stops. Above it water tanks sat like cakes on the barren hills. Beyond it I-80 stretched like a black tape across fifty miles of salt flats; looking along it, we could see diesel semis floating in the mirage. Wendover was a busy place. We drove up to the State Line Casino, which had a forty-foot statue of a cow-boy with a lucky grin and a waving mechanical arm. In the parking lot were cars from all over America. The velvet-black asphalt looked as if it had just been laid.

The casino was a low, rectangular building made of glass, aluminum, and prestressed concrete. Inside it was dark and moist; the air smelled of cigarettes, stale drinks, and nervous perspiration. Rows of middle-aged people in pastel doubleknits were feeding the slot machines, and when-ever someone hit a jackpot, all sorts of bells, whistles, and lights would go off. Beyond the slot machines were roulette wheels, dicing pits, and card tables watched by dealers with faces like porcelain dolls. Bob, Dave, and Becky wandered off into the crowd, but the place made my skin creep, and I left in a hurry.

In the parking lot, the heat and glare were intense. I unlocked the van and took out a bottle of Deep Creek water, then walked over to the edge of the blacktop. Beyond were only sunbitten rocks, gravel soil, and a few shreds of parched vegetation. Here the line between civilization and wilderness was sharp enough to be drawn with a pencil.

I stepped across. The rock underfoot was hot, but still cooler than the blacktop. I walked a few yards and then looked back at the casino. Inside were the American people, the ones the MX was supposed to defend. In the shimmering heat, Wendover itself looked like a mirage. I opened the bottle and took a long drink of Deep Creek water, still fresh and cool after so many desert miles. As I tilted the bottle, I caught sight of the Deeps themselves, like a line of blue crumbs on the far horizon. They looked like the shores of another America. Their remoteness filled me with hope.

CHAPTER EIGHT

A Home in the Winds

THE WORLD'S MOST BEAUTIFUL CAMPSITE

After the Deeps I found myself dreaming of water. A branch tapping against the bedroom window might sound like pebbles rolled in a stream. Birds chirping at dawn were small waves clapping. Cut grass smelled like the edges of waterfalls. "Come be immersed," John Muir had written to Emerson after their meeting in California. And Emerson had replied, "Solitude is a sublime mistress but an intolerable wife," as if he really knew. He had dreamed of becoming a transparent eyeball, but Muir was a vessel eager to be filled. I understood his thirst for remoteness now. He was a young adventurer, yearning to taste all things.

Muir had found the springs of adventure far back in storied ranges like those north and east of Salt Lake: the Uintas spread with moose pastures and trout-filled lakes, the Tetons mantled with summer ice. Mountains like these were the ultimate sources of life and character for every high western landscape from sandstone canyon to intermontane playa. Each place might possess a distinctive ecology, but all were linked by water. The Deeps had exposed this vital current, of which the elusive Snake Valley cutthroats formed a living signature. I wanted to meet trout in their native element now, and Dave Hall graciously shared some rudiments of the fly fisherman's art. But it was one thing to loft a fly and quite another to set it down on the live tip of a wave so that a trout looking up would see not a hooked feather but a tasty insect caught by the surface tension. Somewhere between the wrist and the leader's tip, as the line danced wave-like through the air, life entered into the fly through a miracle of art. The inevitable strike gave a tingling, almost sexual thrill. Muir had never known this particular form of grace, but he had experienced communion when-ever he bent to a mountain stream. "Drinking this champagne water is pure pleasure," he had exulted, "so is breathing the living air." His life had shown that adventure, pursued with imagination and resolve, might lead to a place that answered effortlessly to desire, a perfect place where one might feel as completely at home as the Deep Creek trout themselves.

Around this time a university colleague told me about the Wind River Mountains. They rose southeast of the Tetons, he said, a mere six-hour drive from Salt Lake City. He listed their virtues: all granite, deep lakes full of native cutthroats, lovely as the Sierra but twice as wild. He urged me to visit a place he called the world's most beautiful campsite, located just above Island Lake, at the entrance to Titcomb Basin. From there Frémont Peak on the Continental Divide was an easy climb; we could head off at dawn and be back before the afternoon storms.

So he pressed the case with an ardor like Muir's, but the name itself held just as much fascination. "Wind River Mountains" evoked potent images of the elements locked in dynamic tension. Wind was active, invis-ible, disturbing; water was passive, calm, and reflecting. Wind was a shap-ing, creative power, the spirit and breath of life. Water was clear, essential substance, that which can be formed. And mountains suggested grandeur and elevation, a place like an altar where heaven touched the earth. Combined, these words evoked all the mystery of creation, when the spirit of God was moving over the face of the waters—creating paradise, of course, and not just in mythic time, but here and now, in an actual place.

Others I knew had also heard of the Winds: Tom, a banjo player and engineer who had fought forest fires in Montana; Kim, his best friend, who worked in photography and video when he wasn't bike racing or rock climbing; Kathy, a hard-core skier and Fulbright scholar back from Algiers, where she had taught English while fending off Arab suitors. Three years of hiking and skiing together had made us feel clannish and native, though Kim was the only one born in Utah. By diverse paths we had all arrived at the place in life where the lure of freedom clashes most vividly with the yearning for home and roots. Kathy was longing for wildness after a year in the Old World; Tom liked his job but needed a mate; and Kim was fed up with hometown culture, about which he would hold forth pungently when we met at the Green Parrot Cafe for midnight margaritas. All of us craved experience and commitment, restlessly seeking rest as if unaware that restlessness itself had become a way of life.

For me the problem had crystallized into a choice between place and vocation. My three-year teaching contract was due to expire, and the only good offer had come from Carleton, an excellent college in southern Minnesota. To one in love with mountains, a life on the Plains was unthinkable, yet to stay in Utah would mean giving up a calling pursued through fifteen years of study and aspiration. I accepted the offer, but almost at once the water dreams returned. July brought hot, still days when every leaf on campus drooped with dust. Classes were finished; my books were packed; my office felt like a dead man's house. At night the trees outside would rustle like gravel shifting in creek beds. I thought of high meadows dappled with asters. I thought of clouds and the white noise of the wind.

It was Tom who finally took charge, declaring one night at the Parrot that he had heard enough sob stories. Next morning he packed us into his new Saab, loaded the stereo with country tunes, and drove up onto the wide, clay plains of Wyoming, where John C. Frémont had come exploring in 1842. All the ambitious lieutenant had noted were "artemisia barrens," and things had not changed much since then, just the occasional ranch house, stock tank, or magpie crouching over a road kill. But Kathy had a more enlightened view. "Open country!" she sighed, sticking her face out the window. "That's what the Chinese call wilderness." She breathed deeply, the wind tossing her short brown hair. "It's so fresh! In Algiers everything smells a thousand years old."

Tom laughed, "No place like home!" Bearded and blond, he steered the Saab like a yacht, leaning into the curves.

Beside him Kim drummed on the dash as Mary McCaslin moaned and twanged from the speakers. He was small and wiry, his dark beard and eyes set off by a blue work shirt. "Ah," he scoffed, "Slick City! You keep it. I'm getting out."

"Come on!" said Kathy, leaning forward. "Why?"

"There's nothing left," Kim teased. "Too many weekend climbers, too much pollution." He grinned into the rearview mirror. "Too many easterners."

"Well, " said Kathy, "I can't imagine a better place. Where would you go?"

"Anywhere that has TV!" Kim crowed. "Anywhere in America!" He punched up the stereo, flooding the car with mournful McCaslin:

> *Oh the wayward wind, it's a restless wind,*
> *It's a reckless wind that yearns to wander,*
> *And he was born the next of kin,*
> *The next of kin to the wayward wind.*

Five hours later the range hove into view, a jagged crest beyond scrubby foothills. At Pinedale the road turned northeast, climbing dusty moraines above the blue wedge of Frémont Lake. We parked at nine thousand feet and walked off into the high country, following Frémont's own route above the eponymous creek. Tom and Kim soon pulled ahead while Kathy lagged, snapping pictures. At Photographer's Point the cliffs dropped two thousand feet against a backdrop of castellated peaks, and we took turns posing before the postcard view. Kathy lay on her side, a wilderness odalisque in orange T-shirt and cleated boots.

Tom said, "You can put that on your wall back in Algiers."

"Oh, great!" Kim rolled his eyes. "She flies four thousand miles so she can walk into a calendar?"

Tom laughed. "Why not? This is America!"

Kathy took off her boots and rubbed her heels. Tom glanced at them, then took out moleskin. "Those look pretty ripe for only three miles," he said.

Kathy sighed. "I haven't worn boots in over a year. In Algiers you wear these flimsy cotton slippers."

We made camp after hiking another mile, then sipped mint tea in the dusk, warming ourselves with stories of Island Lake and the Great Divide. Next morning brought calm, rayless light of the sort that Muir had called "the clearest terrestrial manifestation of God." Wildflowers bloomed along the trail, red columbine, mountain bluebell, white cinquefoil. Most vivid of all were the deep pink blossoms of Parry primrose, which grew in every pocket of shade as if darkness were only a richer kind of soil. It was another great day for photographs, and Frémont appeared reassuringly from time to time, though it was still ten miles away by trail. Two climbers dressed in linen tunics and turquoise beads said they had gone up the day before from Indian Basin. "Took the snow gully all the way," they told us. "Piece of cake!"

Tom and Kim stopped at the halfway point, impatient for lunch, but I urged them to go another mile to Seneca Lake, which was up in the alpine zone. It proved to be more like two miles away, with a high ridge in between.

"Tallmadge," Kim growled, "that's the longest mile I ever hiked."

"Never mind," Kathy said. "Let's eat. My feet are suffering culture shock."

Seneca Lake was blue and rockbound, with Frémont looming splendidly beyond. But no one cared. Tom and Kim wanted to push on to camp. I offered Kathy my running shoes, but she said her boots needed breaking in. By the end of the lake she was limping, while the others had disappeared up ahead. It took us hours to reach Island Lake, and the glorious views in between offered scant relief. We stared at the Great Divide, which spread north and south from Frémont Peak like extended wings. The mountain looked ready to lift up from the earth. But we were not going to get there.

A white stripe on the far shore marked the stream from Titcomb Basin, though the valley's entrance was hidden by granite domes. The map showed no trail; we could only guess where Tom and Kim might have gone. Kathy said she was good for another mile, so we started picking our way down the lake. A path led north but soon petered out. Finally Kathy sat down. While she unlaced her boots, I climbed the nearest dome for a view. After struggling up a chimney clogged with chockstones and brush, I came out unexpectedly right above the stream. There was Tom's orange tent, pitched near a flume cascade that drained a series of terraced pools. The surrounding rock gleamed with glacial polish, and each crease or hollow held a green slip of meadow. In the distance, gray pinnacles thrust toward a flawless sky. I took one astonished breath, then another. Suddenly all fatigue was gone.

Kathy heard me shouting and struggled up. She gaped for a moment, then took off with a whoop. Kim looked up from a steaming pot as we burst into camp. "About time," he drawled. "My famous spaghetti's done."

"Where's Tom?" I panted.

"Inside the tent. He's got a headache."

"Look!" Kathy shouted, pointing into the flume. There was a tiny ledge and a nest the size of a tennis ball. A blue-brown bird was darting in and out, clipping the spray.

"What's the big deal?" Kim asked.

"It's a water ouzel!" I exclaimed. "John Muir's favorite bird!"

"Well!" Kim said, rubbing his eyes. "I guess this must be the place."

MISTAKE LAKE

That night I slept like a stone in one of my dreams. How easily the mind comes to rest on the white noise of a stream. Next morning brought Muir's calm, rayless light again, and with it the leisure to explore our camp. Above the tents, each pool held a perfect image of gray peaks under blue, enameled sky—icons of contemplative repose. Between them the water frothed in cataracts, making a beautiful, contained violence, like dissonance in a Mozart symphony. Wildflowers had taken root wherever soil had formed, even in joints no wider than my finger. It was thrilling to come upon a string of yellow daisies or white spring beauties running straight across the rock like a ribbon dropped from a maypole. Dozens of boulders lay strewn where the ice had left them, though they appeared to have been deliberately set out like abstract sculptures in a garden. Perhaps this impression came from their rougher texture and broken edges just slightly rounded, as if they formed a connecting link between Frémont's crest and the streamlined curves of water and bedrock below.

Whatever the cause, this place felt wonderfully peaceful. I sat for an hour or more gazing at the peaks or watching the ouzel dart through the waves. The stream made a right-angled bend around our camp, roaring through a trough formed by parallel joints in the rock. So clean were these angles and surfaces that the channel might have been cut by machine. The ouzel had built its nest facing east, just out of reach of the waves. No doubt, had it wished to, it could have admired Frémont Peak from its door. What a perfect home for a bird so devoted to motion and energy. No wonder John Muir had loved the water ouzel.

Meanwhile, the others had emerged. Kathy hobbled to one of the pools, shrieking as the cold water touched her heels. Tom lay in the sun nursing a sinus cold. Kim massaged his neck, which he had wrenched while lifting his pack. Neither of them wanted to try for Frémont. As for Kathy, the hike from Seneca Lake had rubbed the skin off her blisters, leaving red, oozing welts the size of pennies. This time she accepted my running shoes.

"I can't climb in these," she lamented, "but I don't want to stay here. What can we do?"

"Day trips," Kim shrugged.

"Let's go up the basin," I said. "Dave Hall says Mistake Lake is full of lunkers. It's only a mile or two."

"Two of *your* miles," Kim sneered. "I'll stay with Tom, maybe fish Island Lake. At least one of us ought to be able to catch some dinner."

"And if not," Tom smiled, "we can just eat my chicken stew."

So Kathy and I headed up Titcomb Basin, which soon opened into a classic U-shaped valley. At its head stood a ring of black peaks hung with glaciers. On its floor lay a chain of lakes, the lower, smaller ones deep blue and the upper ones, fed by melting ice, mint green. Between the lakes small meadows alternated with granite hummocks, among which erratic boulders and willow bushes were set in ways that suggested a perfect design, though we knew, intellectually, that time and chance had happened to them all. The sense of peace and loveliness deepened with every step. It seemed as if every feature that made our campsite beautiful had been repeated here on a grander scale. We had set up our tents at a focal point, where rays of beauty converged like sun through a burning glass. But now we seemed to be walking into the source.

In all my trips to the mountains I had never felt more alive, more full of grace. Was this what Muir had meant when he wrote, "The whole body seems to feel beauty when exposed to it as it feels the campfire or sunshine, entering not by the eyes alone, but equally through all one's flesh like radiant heat." What was it about this place that so attracted me? Some things I could easily recognize. There was, for instance, the replication of structure across scales—the edges of talus rocks, say, mirroring the summit crest as on the slopes of Katahdin. This gave a sense of order beneath the chaos of surface forms. There were also important contrasts between the rugged textures of crest or upper slope and the polished pavements or glassy lake surfaces—smooth, Euclidean forms balanced against complex, thrusting fractals. The whole landscape was charged with dynamic tension, a *coincidentia oppositorum* such as that sought after by mystics and poets like Coleridge, who had described it as the chief end of imagination. In the lower regions, scoured pavements and mirroring waters suggested a Taoist stance of alert passivity, while the Gothic spires at the headwall seemed to invite a romantic leap toward the infinite. Either way the place joined heaven and earth. You could drink the sky at your feet or reach out and touch it by climbing to the horizon. But there was no felt need for any action at all, other than merely to saunter at leisure while a clean, clear energy poured through your body like sunlight filling a room.

In this pleasant state I forgot all about jobs, lovers, impending moves, and everything else that had driven us into the Winds. Kathy walked buoyantly despite her heels, snapping photographs with childlike abandon. No matter where we turned, the landscape seemed to compose itself for a view. Each shot was framed by soaring verticals that were kept in harmonious bounds by the blue notes of water and sky. An erratic boulder, poised like a statue, drew as much light from reflections in the lake as it did from the circumambient air. So in drawing the landscape toward a single point, it made a wonderful place for the eye to rest. And the miracle was that the basin seemed to be full of such places, even to be composed wholly out of them, so that no matter where we looked we felt comfort , delight, and perfect poise, a sense that everything, including ourselves, was right.

By noon Mistake Lake came into view, wildly misnamed given the gorgeous setting. It was deep blue and completely rockbound, reflecting the black headwall towers and fleecy white cumuli that puffed along overhead. Next to shore the water was clear for twenty feet down, and the first thing I saw was a trout as big as my arm.

Only a fool would fish on an empty stomach, but trout have made fools of better men than me. Feigning composure, I threaded a line and tied on a daredevil, the small red and white wobbler I had never known to fail. The lure waltzed past the trout, who barely stirred. I tried again, putting some wrist into it. Two more casts, and the trout slid into the shadows. Kathy came up with a questioning look.

"A huge cutthroat," I panted. "He sneered at me!"

Kathy nodded slowly. "Why don't we have some lunch?" she said.

"Are you kidding? That's the biggest trout I ever saw!" But just then an even bigger one swam into view. I began hurling the lure, but the second fish went the way of the first.

Kathy cocked her head toward the packs. "I'll make some sandwiches," she said.

We ate, but I kept scanning the lake for rises. The landscape in all its glory had disappeared; all I could think of were fat trout sizzling in butter. When ripples appeared a short way off, I jumped up to cast but had no better luck than before. Then Kathy asked if she could try. I handed over the rod, grumbling something about beginner's luck. She made a few tentative casts, then squealed as another big trout swam into view. In a moment she too was hurling the lure, screaming at the fish. I went back to the packs to get some flies.

By the time I returned a breeze had risen, making it hard to cast. Kathy announced that her trout lust had burned out; she was going to take a nap. That was fine; I had noticed some good-looking rises upwind across the lake. Sure enough, an entire school of lunkers were idling like submarines just beneath the surface. But they ignored my half-dozen flies. Exasperated, I stooped to bait, fastening a piece of salami to a Mepps spinner in hopes it would trail an enticing, meaty scent. But not a fin stirred. Lust and embarrassment now gave way to rage. I tossed them cheese, even bits of bread. I longed for canned corn, so fatally attractive to trout that it's banned in Utah. For one crazy moment I even wished for a hand grenade. That would stun them into respect! But it was no use. These trout seemed happy and well-fed. Finally they swam off, flickering with contempt.

I slunk back to the packs, where Kathy lay sleeping in the shade of a boulder. Her frank, sunburnished face, nestled against the curve of her arm, looked full of generosity and peace. Maybe she had the right idea after all. I sat down beside her and leaned back against the rock. Why was it so important to catch these trout? I could admit to an ordinary fisherman's lust and even to competing with Kim, who would certainly make fun of our failures. But there was more. Eating wild foods had always possessed a sacramental appeal. In the Sierra I had eaten trout and wild onions, taking the life of the range into my body. It had felt like a sort of communion, a sharing for mutual transformation. Something comparable seemed to be called for after this morning, when Kathy and I had felt so completely at home. But of course these trout were the real natives, while we were tourists at best. Imagine them gliding along through a pure element that provided for every need. Like the pickerel of Walden Pond, they were living embodiments of the Winds.

Theirs was a world of the elements: wind, water, crystal, and light. What would it mean to call a place like this home, to live amid visionary splendors, miraculously fed, surrounded only by purity and sublimity? The trout had achieved a grace that we could only imagine. Battered by work and love, all four of us had lived like wanderers, propelled by great expectations from one place or person to the next. Our jealously guarded freedom masked a desperate urge to bond. Perhaps it was this that had made certain people, positions, or landscapes irresistible. Homeless by choice, we kept dreaming of home: a safe harbor, a place inviolate, a nest, a niche, somewhere we truly fit in. Indeed, we would know it, or him, or her, by the sense of a perfect fit. At last we'd relax, content just to be ourselves. Our spiritual and physical needs would be satisfied. We would no longer be tormented by desire.

Of course, such a home would always beckon, and it might never be the place where we actually lived. Think of John Muir, for whom Yosemite was home even while he was raising daughters and grapes in the Central Valley. Think of Sir Ernest Shackleton, so fatally drawn to Antarctica; he was never truly at home in England. And what about us? We lived uneasily in Salt Lake, earning money and sleeping in furnished rooms. I had changed my address eight times in the past six years. Perhaps that's why I felt so comfortable in the wilderness, carrying a monk's household on my back and leaving no trace but footprints or pressed grass.

Yet now, it seemed, we had found a home in the Winds. That afternoon I felt there was no place I would rather be—not Yosemite or the High Sierra, not Katahdin, the Deeps, or the Canyonlands. That the trout of Mistake Lake would not give themselves up was a minor annoyance. For one restful hour I savored a taste of perfection as sweet and pungent as wild strawberries. With such a place so near, how could one think of moving to Minnesota?

Back at camp it was late afternoon, and Tom was already cooking his chicken stew. Kim, squatting on a rock, called out, "Looks like you had the same luck as me."

I shrugged to hide my relief and went into the tent for a flask of bourbon. I wanted to party, like someone who's just bought a house. Kim held out his cup. "How was Mistake Lake?"

"Gorgeous," I said, pouring a slug, "And frustrating."

By the time I got to the part about trying bait, Kim was grinning sardonically. "You got it all wrong," he laughed. "Those trout live on freshwater shrimp. The only thing they'll take is a fly. Besides, they're not native cuts at all; they're stocked."

"Stocked?"

"Come on," Kim sneered. "I thought you were a naturalist. You think trout could migrate past all these waterfalls? They packed trout into all the high lakes starting back in the 1930s. This one got goldens instead of cuts by mistake, so it's called Mistake Lake." He drained his cup. "Looks like I'll have to go up there tomorrow."

"Suit yourself." The bourbon was working on me too. "It's so beautiful, you can't lose." And, thinking to salvage some dignity, I described the glories of Titcomb Basin.

But Kim was not impressed. "Of course it's beautiful," he said. "Don't you ever read *National Geographic*? It's a set piece. You point the camera, you shoot a calendar. Any fool can do it."

"Come on," said Kathy. "This place is powerful. I felt it too."

"Sure," said Kim. "I'm not saying you didn't. I'm saying you're taught to feel that way. I'm a photographer. I make images to sell, and people buy what they're taught to like. It's the same way with TV. I take what the crews bring in and turn it into the news. I guess you could say there's an element of reality, but real or not whatever goes on the air has to play well. Ninety percent of the raw footage gets tossed. There are really only a few basic stories anyway, only a few kinds of images I can use."

"He's bored," Tom put in with a smile.

"So you make the news replicate itself," I said. "It's a kind of mass education. Don't you feel any responsibility?"

"Oh sure," Kim said. "I wouldn't run anything that was untrue, I mean, made up or really distorted. But I don't set the editorial policy." He grinned.

"But what you do shapes people's sense of reality," I persisted. "You reinforce expectations and values. From that viewpoint, we can't trust our own desires."

"Yes," said Kathy. "it's like saying that life has to imitate art, instead of the other way around."

"Whatever," said Kim. "As long as it plays well."

After dinner Tom produced a deck of cards and a pan of popcorn, which rekindled the party mood. While he dealt, we discussed tomorrow's options. Kathy's heels had scabbed over but still felt very sore. Kim's neck hurt whenever he put on his pack. As for Tom, he had mainly napped in the tent. It looked as if we would have to stay put for another day.

We played hearts until well past dark. After Kim shot the moon twice, we all turned in. As I zipped up the tent, I noticed heat lightning flickering over Frémont.

The Perfection of Nature

Next morning, as I was dipping water for coffee, a weasel scampered down a spur that stuck out into the pool above camp. I was downwind, and the roaring water masked the crunch of my footsteps. The weasel flowed and darted over the rocks, eyes and nose bent to the ground. Halfway out the spur he saw me and ducked under a rock. No doubt he had hiding places all over the meadow. I sat down to watch, expecting him to pop up behind me and scurry away, but after a few moments his head reappeared, twisting back and forth like a conning tower. It was clear that he saw no avenue of escape from the bearded ogre squatting at his door. Apparently, swimming was out of the question. For several long minutes we stared at each other, the weasel twitching and sniffing in what seemed to be mounting alarm. Finally he began to warble, a wild, weird, hopeless piping sound, all the while staring me right in the eye. Whether this was a challenge, a spell, or a death song was hard to tell, but it did the trick. Spooked, and a bit ashamed, I turned away. A few moments later the weasel streaked from his hole and vanished into the meadow. I felt a glow of respect. Here was another creature truly at home who had defeated me with the intensity of its feelings.

Back at camp Kathy was contemplating a string of small yellow flowers that seemed to be growing right out of the rock. "JT," she said, "I want to stay here forever! This place has what the Chinese call *feng shui*, 'the perfection of nature.'" She closed her eyes and lifted her face to the sun.

"What's their sense of perfection?" I asked. "I woke up thinking about what Kim said last night."

Kathy laughed. "Relax. It's just culture. Kim has his attitudes, you have yours, the Algerians and the Chinese have theirs. I think the differences are fun, myself. Besides, we still have to live our own experience."

"So," I said, "tell me about feng shui."

Kathy assumed her most professorial look. "It has to do with balance and harmony," she said, "with all the elements present in due proportion—fire, air, water, metal, wood—and a proper balance between living and nonliving, rest and movement, the earthly and the celestial. When a place is feng shui, it has everything right. The great lines of earth energy come together. The Chinese have rules for designing houses and temples according to feng shui, so people will live in harmony with the world. But I think this place has it too. The ouzel nest is feng shui; so are these flowers, the mountains, the weasel you just saw. Everything! I'm calling this camp 'The Feng Shui Garden.' Look," she opened her notebook, "here's how they write it."

"What do those characters stand for?" I asked.

She smiled, "They stand for 'wind' and 'water.'"

After breakfast Kim announced that he would go to Mistake Lake. Tom's cold was flourishing, and Kathy said that she, too, wanted to rest in camp. I decided to spend the day around Island Lake, after spotting rises near the outlet. I wanted to catch some fish and sort out the conflicting perspectives offered by Kathy and Kim.

There was no doubt that our camp and its surroundings combined remoteness and wildness with a gardenlike sense of order and repose—not the formal geometry of western gardens, of course, but the studied asymmetry of Chinese or Japanese designs. Walking down the lakeshore, I felt a profound sense of arrangement in the small islands supporting a few twisted pines, in the pockets of soil cupped on the rolling pavements where pink and yellow wildflowers bloomed, in the terracing of cascades and pools. There was a feeling of cultivation in the short meadow grass, the trees and shrubs scaled to human dimensions, the boulders seldom higher than my waist. Cleanliness, too, seemed to prevail, for even the talus fields, dead branches, and whatever else might have been considered waste or debris seemed to add texture, accent, or color to the design. In larger views the grays, whites, and blues of the mineral world predominated, but up close the pinks, chrome yellows, reds, violets, and coppery greens of life would catch the eye. The openness of the landscape gave a sense of freedom and security; my gaze could rest as easily on a distant peak as on a nearby flower. And nothing ever seemed out of place. The land felt as if it had just been swept and washed.

As the morning wore on, I also became aware of a principle of movement, conveyed subtly by the diurnal changes in temperature and light and more forcefully by the sound of rushing water. The day began with a cool, white, dewy light that hardened into a hot, dry glare. The air warmed rapidly, though the ground retained its coolness till almost noon. By evening the earth had warmed but the air had cooled, so that all day one felt refreshing change. It was comforting, too, to camp by moving water, with which the mind retains an elemental sympathy. Attention floats on the rushing energies of the unconscious, riding on the river of the body—which, after all, is no fixed object but rather a stream of matter and energy squeezed into shape by chemistry and time. Like the yogi in meditation, the person who sits by moving water feels the mind descending into the body, pillowed by inner movements like breathing, heartbeat, or the flash of nerves. At such times the miracle of life presents itself. One feels peace like a river.

No wonder that over the centuries, in almost every culture, people have dreamed of finding a place where sensations like these would not only come spontaneously but endure forever. The paradise of the ancients lay remote from society, removed to a distant island or walled off in the midst of a desert. Inspired by the Hindus, perhaps, Dante had placed his earthly paradise on top of a mountain. There nature was perfectly ordered, manifesting both the harmony of a garden and the fecund exuberance of wilderness. The climb required dedication, suffering, and deep personal transformation, but to enter that place was to discover one's own true self, recognized by the perfect fit between human desire and the land's own native expression. Everything humans needed would be there—light, warmth, the water of life, the tangible presence of God. Under such circumstances it was no wonder that most ancient accounts left somewhat vague the question of how to get to paradise. Even Dante, on the cornice of Pride, had urged his readers not to dwell on the torments but on the summit reward. So every pilgrim dreams less of the journey than of the goal.

But for me, wandering in the alpine Eden of the Winds, remoteness no longer beckoned. That morning I felt as buoyant and strong as I ever had in my life. I fished every promising cove, but had no luck before the outlet stream. Here the lake plunged into rapids—not a great place to spin-cast, but I tried the daredevil anyway, and to my delight hooked a fifteen-inch cutthroat trout. Heart pounding, I wrestled him carefully toward the shallows, admiring the bright orange racing stripes beneath his panting gills. Surely this was a native trout! The Winds had given us beauty and now they were giving us life.

As I unhooked the trout, a cloud passed overhead, pushed by a scuff of wind. The land chilled and darkened for a moment. No doubt Mistake Lake was even colder. Now Kim would have to fish mighty hard to make good on his boast. I should have been happy enough with my own catch, but his sarcasm had rankled me all day.

There could be no doubt about the intensity of our desire, nor about the depth of our feeling response to the Winds. But the situation really was fraught with contradictions. If Kathy and I had found a home in the Winds, it was largely because sickness and injury had forced us to stay put. Had we climbed Frémont Peak and hiked out of Titcomb Basin as originally planned, we might never have fished Mistake Lake, met the weasel, or sat in the Feng Shui Garden. We would have blown right through, just as on every other trip. I realized with some amazement that in all these journeys I had never camped for more than two nights in the same place.

But if staying put had brought deeper intimacy, our sojourn still represented no more than a brief glimpse into the seasonal life of the range. Perhaps the clouds now building signaled a change in the weather. Would our camp feel like paradise under rain and sleet? It was spring now, in late July, but a month later the willows would start to turn. At this elevation winter would last nine months. Why hadn't we thought of that when all around us the climate had left its signatures: glaciers, permanent snowfields, lodgepoles broken by storms or twisted by heavy snow? We had come to the Winds at a perfect moment, at the height of spring when the seasonal forces had reached a balance that could not last. Even if we stayed for a week, we would still experience the Winds in the blink of an eye, and so it would be easy to think of them as perfect. Perhaps all dreams of an earthly paradise arise in such a way. We choose a single aspect, view, or state of nature and project it into eternity, where it then becomes a focal point for desire. Kim really had struck close to the truth, for this was akin to the photographic seeing that takes a momentary trace of a person or landscape and makes it stand for the whole living process. How can we know anything through a photograph? Is not seeing the world in blinks a kind of blindness?

But we had been looking at real landscapes, not photographs. We were moving through them, and being moved by desire. We were gazing not through a lens but through clean air. And yet we still chose what to look at and where to camp, reacting to the impressions of our senses according to inward criteria. No doubt these were universal to some degree, but they were also mediated by culture. Attraction to women, for instance, had a biological basis in sex overlain with cultural codes of gender and fashion. So too with landscapes. The fractal asymmetry of talus and ridge-line, the coincidence of opposites, the visual climaxes of peaks seemed archetypally beautiful. You could find them, with variations, in the art and mythology of disparate cultures. But a photogenic landscape like this engaged particular western aesthetic codes. John Ruskin, to take one example, had interpreted Gothic architecture in terms of the Alps, reflexively asserting that abrupt glacial landscapes typified spirituality and aspiration. Such ideas had influenced many Americans, including the architects of Yale's Gothic campus and the creators of our first national parks.

Similarly, nineteenth-century American landscape painters like Albert Bierstadt and Thomas Cole had believed that their task was to depict nature in such a way as to reveal its latent divinity. Twentieth-century photographers like Ansel Adams had continued this work, arguing that the goal was to produce an image of landscape more true than what could be seen with the naked eye. It had taken many trips to Yosemite before I had ever seen the High Sierras looking the way they did in an Ansel Adams print. Now I had to ask how much our love for the Winds came from a deep, essential response as opposed to the reflexes of a conditioned eye? How far could we trust such powerful feelings? There was just no way to tell.

I took my trout out of the lake, wrapped him in a wet T-shirt, and started back to camp. The mellow afternoon light poured over Frémont Peak like holy oil. And yet I was focused inward, churning with conflict. Ever since falling in love with Yosemite nine years before, I had been restlessly seeking another perfect landscape. Now one presented itself, but what did that mean? Perfection required a sense of fit, like a key that turns in a lock, yet both lock and key were tooled by culture and education. In short, perfection depended upon conventions. Suppose I had stumbled upon a place that felt like paradise, answering effortlessly to desire? Would that mean I was any closer to truth, to the sacred, the really real? Perhaps the divine would be hidden still deeper in such a case, for what disguise is more perfect than a surface that meets all expectations? The closer beings in nature appear to answer our needs, the farther we may be from appreciating their truth. And when the sense of perfection depends, even to the slightest degree, upon selection, abstraction, framing, or any other process by which part of the landscape is rendered invisible, then we collaborate in our own deception. Now I could understand Kim's cynicism. He had tasted the narcissism of the photographic eye. He knew we were wandering in a world of mirrors.

And yet, I still remembered moments of genuine encounter high in the alpine zone. They were the best things I had found on the Muir Trail. They had not been illusions! Something comparable could still happen here. Each day I was taking more of this place into my body, drinking its water, breathing its air. Now I had one fat trout in my pack as well. If the weather held tomorrow, perhaps we could still climb Frémont. Surely up there, exposed to the elements, we could find something hard enough to break these layered reflections.

Back at camp Kim had a golden trout even bigger than mine. He was justly proud and charmingly modest. "You were right," he said. "I fished all day but they wouldn't take my flies. I caught this one on a Mepps. Just dumb luck I guess."

Kathy stuffed the trout with rice, dried spinach, and herbs. We grilled and ate them, talking of trivial things. A cloud bank appeared in the west, its edges gilded by the sunset, and we watched the high slopes of Frémont catch the glow. Tom said his sinuses no longer ached; he'd be game for the peak if the weather held. Kim was eager to climb despite the pain in his neck. Kathy said she would try my running shoes. I kept quiet about the afternoon's dilemmas. This might be my last climb in the West, and I wanted companions.

CHAPTER NINE

The Great Divide

The tent zipper was frozen. I yanked it, cursing, and looked out to see a pink cloud bank in the west—red sky at morning. By the time I had assembled the stove, gray, ragged puffs were scudding toward the Divide. Tom heard the stove roar into life and crawled out, clutching two packs of Instant Ralston. He dumped them into a pot, stirred once or twice, then dove back in as the first squall hit.

For two hours rain lashed our perfect campsite. Every few seconds the tent would light up like a Chinese lantern, then shudder as thunder caromed off the walls of the basin. We ate in silence while rain flooded the meadows and lightning savaged the upper slopes. The mountains were living up to their name, but so what? Now that we were all set to go, the weather had turned. Only a fool would climb under such conditions. I had been caught in the open by lightning once on the Muir Trail, and it had felt like dodging artillery.

The cramped, stuffy tents offered dryness but little else. Tom and Kim started playing cards next door. Kathy and I tried conversation but soon exhausted our repertoire of hard-luck stories. Finally, when the rain let up, I made a dash for some nearby cliffs, where spalling granite had left a few dry niches. There I could sit with my legs drawn up. I tried recording three days of reflection, but words brought no relief. The pen felt hot in my numbed hand; the line of ink looked like the track of a burning iron.

I was angry at the weather, at life, at the thought of moving to Minnesota despite the door that stood open there. It was no good thinking about all of this anymore. I just wanted to get up on that mountain.

The summit was visible from camp. Oddly it had remained clear during most of the storm. The map showed a ridge leading south and west from the peak. Halfway up, at twelve thousand feet, a bulge in the contour line suggested a saddle. Accessible from a couloir on the east side—perhaps the "snow gully" that the climbers had mentioned—it might give us a view of oncoming weather and a place from which we could safely retreat. But the route above would be totally exposed. Although the climb looked technically easy—no steeper, really, than a flight of stairs—there would be no place to hide and no path or handrail to speed the descent. The rain was letting up, and the clouds were brightening to the north as the storm's black, oily mass moved south beyond Mount Lester. In the west a patch of blue sky had appeared. Had a front moved through, or was this just an interval between squalls, something my climbing friends would call a "sucker hole?" There was no way to tell. But if we could reach the saddle, we might get a wider view. Then if the weather held, we could try for the peak.

I folded the map and hurried back to camp, where the others embraced this plan with comic eagerness. After three hours huddled in tents they were ready for any ordeal, so long as it promised movement and fresh air. We packed lunch and set off for Indian Basin. Almost at once the rain picked up again. Kim growled, "Whose idea was this?" But no one suggested that we go back.

The trail led to a high valley rimmed by crags where dull lakes, strewn with boulders, glinted beneath the overcast. The wind tore at our ponchos, but we had warmed to the climb. I could feel my breath deepening with the altitude, my heartbeat driving like a drum. Each step seemed to push the ground away. Soon the southwest ridge appeared. There was the snowfield dropping off to the east. Tom took the lead, angling across talus broken by outcrops and patches of ice. It was tricky work, spider-dancing over the rocks, but the clouds kept brightening, and blue patches were already gusting past the summit. As we reached the snow, the sun came out, and the rocks began to steam.

We stopped for gorp, shedding ponchos. Our sweaty clothes were soon steaming like the rocks.

"Let's get it on," Kim said. "We've got the sun."

I took the lead, kicking steps in the granular snow. The hot sun cooked my back as cold chips sprayed my naked shins. This was the best part of adventure, persevering to the point where nature turns to serve your desire. I had always felt a deep biological thrill in navigating extreme environments, where mechanical forces grind all matter back to simple, archaic forms. Life glories in defying the spirit of gravity, but there's a psychological thrill as well. To reach the heart of remoteness demands skill and knowledge combined with endurance and strength of will, an ascetic rejection of all those habits of heart, mind, and body that civilization offers in trade for our self-reliance.

It may seem strange to link asceticism and adventure. The first "ascetics" were early Christians who sought enlightenment by fasting and praying in the desert. But today's wilderness pilgrims also delight in excursions that toughen the body and strip the mind. There's an athletic pleasure in strenuous physical action that goes beyond a simple release of endorphins. And darker, more intricate satisfactions may also accrue. I loved watching people react to my stories and slides, particularly if danger was involved. An encounter that seemed routine to me would often catch the breath of parents or friends. I savored the idea that ascetic practice could lift me above the common herd, that struggle and suffering could purify desire, and that nature, like the god pursued by the mystics, would respond affirmatively to such devotion.

It was only years later that I recognized hedonism under this cowl of renunciation. The more I traveled in search of experience, the more I craved exotic places and vivid sensations. I began to judge trips by their distance, their hardship, their visionary extremes, unaware that the yen for adventure itself had taken precedence over any particular landscape. Even this trip to the Winds had been conceived, deep down, as a door that would open onto a limitless future of expeditions. The perfect campsite would call again and again, yet I would inevitably set out from it as I had today, into the world of the elements. Adventure could promise but would never provide a home.

Signs had been offered, of course. That spring the legendary Fred Beckey, pioneer climber of the Wasatch canyons, had given a slide show at the university. I had used his guidebook to the North Cascades and remembered with awe the tone and detail of his route descriptions. The more challenging were accompanied by diagrams as intricate as the score for a Bach partita. I was eager to meet the author of such designs, yet in public Beckey had appeared ill at ease. Of medium height, tanned and wiry, with thin hair and grizzled beard, he spoke in short bursts, rocking forward on the balls of his feet as if he were testing a foothold. Something fierce and insatiable in his manner clashed with the poised magnificence of the slides, to which he offered terse, mainly technical commentary. I had never seen such splendid pictures of mountains. One or two would have been rapture enough, yet Beckey had dozens. Bright and precise as snowflakes, they finally began to drift over me in a blizzard of pure sublimity. Beckey breathed mountains; his adventures were more extreme than anything I could imagine attempting. It did not occur to me that such connoisseurship could ever advance to a dangerous frustration, nor that beauty and risk might become a kind of addiction.

Nor did it occur to me that morning on Frémont Peak, where nature had turned to serve our desire. Each step was bringing us closer to the horizon. Near the top of the snowfield, I could reach out and almost touch the granite walls that rose toward Frémont's shoulder. Ahead, grass and flowers were waving against the blue. Fulfillment seemed imminent. Nothing would be denied! As we stepped off the snow and onto rough grass, a warm wind came gusting up from the west. In another moment, we stood looking down on the world's most beautiful campsite.

Kim laid a hand on my shoulder. "This is sweet!"

Tom sat down, mopping his brow. Kathy was scampering from one viewpoint to the next, snapping photos. Kim shook his head. She caught him and wrinkled her nose. "Pooh on you! My Nikon is hungry."

"Happy calendar," said Kim. Then, "Who brought the food?"

We lunched on the grass, propped against sun-warmed boulders. Our alp was the size of a small backyard, cut off to the west by cliffs, to the east by the snow we had climbed, and to the north by a giant staircase leading to Frémont. Save for the mountain, we enjoyed unobstructed views. Directly west lay the peaks of Titcomb Basin, glinting at noon like shattered pewter. Below them the lakes spread out in rich, organic curves. We watched them glitter in the sun, drinking in the view. Two marmots waddled toward us out of the rocks, their whiskers twitching. Kim threw an apricot, which they sniffed and ignored, then a salami wrapper, which they devoured. Salt must have been scarce up here. I tossed a peanut, and a marmot dove for it.

"So," Kim said, "is he feng shui or just a greedy pig?"

"He's overweight," Tom said. "He doesn't hike enough."

"Why should he?" Kathy laughed. "He's got it all right here: a beautiful home with a garden, a mate, a priceless view, and traveling gods to feed him." She snapped a picture of the marmot. "I think I'll stay," she added.

"Sounds good to me," said Tom, stretching out.

"Wait!" I said. "We're halfway up. We can't stop now."

"You guys don't have to stop," Kathy said. "I'll be fine here. My feet are happy." She looked at the three of us. "Really," she said, "if the weather gets bad I'll just go down."

Kim and I looked at each other. It was hard to tell whether he wanted the peak for its own sake or just to keep up with me. With big wall climbs and hundred-mile bike races under his belt he certainly had nothing to prove.

"You got us into this," he grinned.

It was true. I wanted to stand on the Great Divide again, looking into the future. I wanted the mountain to help me decide what to do with my life. And I wanted companions, adventurers like myself. Another storm was building in the north, flanked by cumuli and outflung cirrus. The weather was moving southeast, but with luck the mountain might stay clear for a few more hours.

"What do you think the odds of making it are?" I asked.

"That depends," Kim laughed. "How fast can you climb?"

But I was not taking that bait. "Look," I said. "It will be safer if we stick together. We'll just agree on a crump time. If the weather turns, we can always bail out." I turned to Tom. "How's your cold?"

Tom's eyes looked watery, his face swollen. But he just shrugged, "Compared to what?"

"Okay," I said. "We'll stop every half hour to reassess."

We started up the talus above the saddle. After five minutes I was breathing hard. Kim passed me without looking back and soon scrambled out of earshot. So much for half-hour check-ins. Tom came behind, laboring with his cold. All I could see of Kathy was a dab of red flannel against a boulder. Like our perfect camp, she was disappearing into the landscape.

I turned back to the mountain. With two thousand vertical feet to go, we had to keep moving, yet we were already strung out on the exposed face, as if we were racing each other instead of the weather. The wind seemed to increase with every step. I realized how much I hated talus, so broken and tricky and vicious to knees and ankles. What were we doing here, anyway? I had instigated the climb, despite Tom's reluctance and poor health. Yet no one had suggested we turn back. It would have been shameful to stop halfway up, to admit a preference for flowers, views, and repose instead of the challenges of altitude and exposure. But Kathy had not felt ashamed. It was only the men, it seemed, who needed the peak.

It struck me that many great wilderness writers had also been single men. What had driven Thoreau, Muir, and Abbey to embrace the beauty of nature, remote from society and the company of women? I recalled the rapturous tones in which Muir had described the landscapes and creatures of the Sierra. He loved a nature charged with divinity, the way a mystic would love his god. I had long wondered about Muir's unrelenting enthusiasm. You would think he had never had a moment of pain or doubt. Now I realized that he had written with the passion of a young man for whom everything pales before his heart's desire.

Thoreau, too, had gloried in all the sensations aroused by the Walden woods: the taste of water, the feel of swamp mud between his toes, the hooting of loons and locomotives, the resiny smell of newly split pine. The clink of an arrowhead disturbed by his hoe delighted him more, he said, than oratorios. Generations of readers, struggling with depression, had come away from *Walden* believing that their emotional needs could be satisfied by nature.

As for Abbey, who could forget his delicious, lyrical descriptions, not only of sweet things like the cliffrose and canyon wren, but also of buzzards, scorpions, flash floods, and poison springs. Beautiful or cruel, Abbey praised whatever gave vivid sensation. He imagined the desert as fascinating but unattainable, like a princess out of the old romances. He had launched a raft onto the "silt-rich bosom of the Colorado" and floated through Glen Canyon with a "sense of achievement and joy" as profound as a young man's first sexual encounter.

These men all spoke with prophetic voices that dazzled me with their certainty and poise. But the light of such constant rapture cast a shadow.

I could sense beneath Muir's enthusiasm an aching loneliness. In letters to his confidante, Mrs. Carr, he had confessed his doubts about the naturalist's life he had chosen over a promising industrial career. He had worried about finding a mate and a place in society. He and his wilderness brethren were all misfits who had disdained to compete for success in the usual masculine ways. The shadow side of their work revealed the pain of difference and exclusion. No wonder they had longed to give themselves to an ideal. Such a gesture would not only purify desire but grant a measure of absolution, like Goethe's Faust giving himself at last to Helen of Troy. How could you be excluded if you were wed to the absolute?

But these men had experienced rejection in more personal ways. Muir had been beaten and overworked by a Calvinist father who believed that salvation came only through suffering and labor. Thoreau's only brother had died, and Elizabeth Sewell had rejected his marriage proposal because her father saw no future in the profession of letters. Textual hints suggest that Abbey first went to the desert to heal from a broken love: his list of the world's delights includes "the silk of a girl's thigh," and later he carves her initials on an aspen tree. All these men, it seemed, had been driven to nature by wounds. I could imagine how people like them might have seen the land as a promise of beauty, wholeness, and power. For the land allows itself to be loved without resisting. Unlike human beings, it never argues. It asks for nothing. And because its creatures speak with their whole being, they are without guile; they hide nothing. How easily, then, does the land receive our dreams. To proud, shy men who have been deeply wounded, it may be easier to love a tree or a stone than a woman.

But such a turn could not explain the intensity and persistence of their devotions, so eloquently conveyed by their books. Nor could it fully explain what we were doing on Frémont that day, toiling upward with wind at our backs and gray clouds racing toward us. The big storm was moving down from the north; outstretched cirrus had already reached Dinwoody and Gannet peaks. We had been climbing for an hour on talus that now gave way to slabs, where friction climbing was required. This would have been a good place to turn back, but I hardly gave it a thought. I could not imagine having to tell people back in Salt Lake that I had given up Frémont Peak. So I kept on, head down in the wind, staring at the rock underfoot and grasping at friction holds with numbing hands. What was I trying to prove? And to whom? What kind of story was I aspiring to join?

Adventure entered the western mind through the old romances, where knights set forth in response to a challenge or summons. They went out alone, leaving the center of civilization, and entered a wilderness peopled with adversaries: wizards, monsters, seductive women, or renegade warriors. Each chance encounter posed a test; the knights prevailed through character and skill, fulfilling the expectations of chivalry. They endured great suffering and loneliness, but upon return they received the highest honor their culture could bestow: they became part of its mythology. For each adventure affirmed their culture's ideals. The knights fought not for themselves alone, but for society. They all set forth as representative men.

The explorers and nature writers whose works I loved had also set out with social concerns in mind. They were not simply trying to escape; they wanted to change our view of the world. Thoreau went to Walden, in part, to test nature's power to focus and resolve societal contradictions. Muir sought alternatives to Calvinism and the industrial mind. For Abbey, the desert affirmed anarchic ideals in an age of war, mass culture, and materialism. While all three men rejected contemporary norms, their adventures and stories affirmed the noblest values of culture. They never really left civilization; they carried it with them. It was a mighty burden, but it made them heroes.

We read of knights in shining armor but seldom think of armor as a burden. In the tales it appears as a badge of heroism, but how awkward and sweaty it must have been in real life, hampering movement and hastening fatigue. What armor, besides rain gear and wool, were we carrying as we toiled up Frémont? The nature writers had gone out armed with science, woodcraft, and the power of words. They had survived elemental encounters and returned as storytellers. But their arms had exacted a price. For in confronting the Other with knowledge, skill, and imagination, it is quite possible to return undefeated and so miss the experience of transformation.

Thoreau was the only one of these men who had embraced initiation. Once Muir had undergone conversion during his first summer in the Sierra, he had returned to the same themes in both his traveling and his art. In effect he had written the same book over and over; only the characters and the settings had changed. As for Abbey, the hero of *Desert Solitaire* had left Arches the same way he had entered, driving through a snowstorm with ideas, politics, and verbal style intact. He appeared to have fought the land to a draw. Indeed, all he could think of was coming back, as if "Abbey's Road" had only led round in a circle.

In the old romances, too, the knights had set out again and again. Adventure was supposed to confirm identity, but one adventure never seemed enough. You might think that Lancelot would have been satisfied to win the title of best knight of the world, but in the romances he never rests. Instead he becomes identified with restlessness, endlessly questing as "knight-errant." For most of his career he lives alone, a single, heroic man in the wilderness. One may speculate on his wound—not the physical ones from which he so quickly recovers, but the spiritual one that drove him to seek adventure. T. H. White imagined that it was ugliness, depicting Lancelot as a misfit who hoped to win acceptance by making his life a work of art. Whatever the case—and how can we know, since Lancelot, like the hero of any narrative, is only a fiction—that shining armor could work just as much to cover an inner wound as to guard against wounds from without. A brilliant perfection of style could keep a person from healing and thereby work to perpetuate itself. So the spirit of romance condemns its devotees to a life of eternal return.

It seemed that I too had been trying to prove myself over and over, always looking toward the next range, across the next valley, craving remoteness. I wanted to fall in love with the perfect place, but I feared such a fall the way a mountaineer fears gravity. For to fall would mean losing control and plunging into a world of dark, ambiguous relationships that would expose all carefully guarded wounds. But it would be even worse to cease from adventure and exploration, for that would mean abandoning the story I wanted my life to be writing. It would mean stepping away from the pilgrim's path mapped out by the nature writers who had followed the spirit of romance. For so many years I had dreamed of the West and the Great Divide at the heart of remoteness. I still wanted a godlike view that would clarify all my relationships. And so, despite the manifest irony of this endeavor and the increasing danger of the storm, I kept on, straining for a glimpse of Kim at the edge of the sky.

By now the clouds had begun to coalesce, squeezing the blue into jagged strips. My legs throbbed in the cold; the wind felt like coarse sand driving against them. Time and again I would feel a cramp starting and pause to massage a calf or thigh, but I dared not stop for more than a moment. The summit was only a few hundred feet above. I knew that the danger was growing with every step, for we would have to come back this way, heading into the storm, but I repressed the thought. Up ahead Kim gave a shout. I saw him silhouetted against the sky, arms flung wide. Then he disappeared. Tom was laboring through talus three hundred feet below. I put my head down, pushing the mountain away. Each step now took two breaths. My lungs ached; my legs were quivering like bowstrings. And then, all at once, I stood on the Great Divide.

The summit was a file of blocks no more than five feet wide. The wind, driving eastward, moaned and whistled between them. I found Kim crouched in a crevice.

"Nice work!" I panted.

"Where's Tom?" His eyes were wide and a little dull.

"He's coming," I said. "He was about ten minutes behind."

Kim shivered. "We've got to get out of here."

I opened the pack and pulled out a bag of gorp. As I tore it open, I began to shake uncontrollably. Kim helped me pull on a sweater, gloves, and a windbreaker.

"Jesus!" I gasped as the shaking subsided.

"Take a look," said Kim. "Then let's get the hell out of here!"

I climbed the nearest block, bracing against the wind. The east face dropped six hundred feet to the Upper Frémont Glacier, a square mile of white ice melting toward Minnesota. To the north and south the spine of the Winds twisted off in a welter of peaks and canyons. To the west lay the green pools of Titcomb Basin and the blue wedge of Frémont Lake thrusting into the desert. From this enormous height I could see no movement save for the streaming clouds. It was an epic view, more spectacular than anything else I had seen in the West. So it registered to the objective eye. But the tearing wind, which grew colder with every blast, had thrown my mind into fear and confusion. There was no power here for me. Staring into that vast landscape streaked with sunlight and shadow, I felt a dizzying shift in perspective. One moment the mountains appeared to be thrusting upward, serene, sublime, an architecture of aspiration. The next they appeared as heaps of ruins, passive victims gnawed by ice, vulnerable in their stone rigidity. I saw glaciers eating into the West, chewing the delectable mountains into soil that would be carried east toward the Plains, a land of water, flatness, and smug prosperity. I did not want to go there! Yet the sky over Utah held only violent darkness. This was not the radiant land out of which Harry Yount had appeared to be striding in that old photograph taken on Berthoud Pass. Like him I now stood looking east into the face of civilization. But I had come lured by the spirit of romance, from which the mountains were now cutting me off. They were not going to give me what I wanted. They had let me down. Worse, they were driving me down.

Tom came up, puffing and flushed. I pulled out his parka and handed him gorp and water. He grinned broadly, then wolfed the food. He snapped a picture of Kim and me, then peeked over the edge at the glacier below. He whistled softly. "Wow," he murmured. "Intense!"

Kim chuckled, "You could ski it."

"Next time," said Tom, glancing at the clouds. "Five minutes and I'm out of here. Whose idea was this?"

"Never mind," I said. "Remember, on the way out your body's a machine."

"Yeah?" said Tom, "well, mine needs a valve job. If we make it back, you owe me a margarita."

We jumped off the summit into the wind, which immediately made us squint and weep. Gusts whipped our clothes and knocked us off balance, making the tricky rock even more difficult. In my lust for the peak I had forgotten that going down always requires more care than going up. Now we were cold and tired, more prone to misstep where even the slightest injury could be fatal. The storms were beginning to merge. Rain plumes were already sweeping the Green River desert. We descended as fast as we could, but it felt like trying to run down a broken staircase. The tendons in my knees began to ache. I kept one eye on the ground and one on the sky, repressing the thought that it might already be too late.

Soon the talus ended, and we came to the slabs, which proved even tougher to descend. On the way up we had relied on small ledges and friction holds, but on the way down we had to slide. A slip might have sent us rolling for hundreds of feet. Downclimbing backward, though safer, would have taken too long. The slope was such that I could see only a few yards ahead, and I somehow veered off into a zone of small cliffs that forced me to rockclimb. I yelled at the others to contour northward, and by the time I had worked my way back onto the face, they were far below. Now I was all alone with the sky closing in. Everything around looked deathly cold and gray.

Then I caught sight of a polemonium, the same flower that grows on high passes along the John Muir Trail. A spike of blooms, hand-high and bluer than African violets, sprang from a cluster of green, resilient leaves. It was rooted in sand on a ledge more than twelve thousand feet above the sea, at the upper limit of life. Its blue cut through my pain like a shout of joy. I felt welcomed, embraced by the living world. I laughed out loud. Then I sat down and wept.

The sky was ink dark now. There was no blue anywhere but in that flower. What grace had brought it here to thrive in the world of the elements? At this altitude most other plants grew less than two inches high and took on the colors of weathered rock. Somehow its blue seemed incredibly rich, like a jewel falling out of a long-forgotten drawer. I thought of all the wild and beautiful places I had been, of all my journeys in search of the mythic West. Each had enriched me in deep, unexpected ways. But I had always moved on, never stopping to build a lasting relation with any place. Even though I had tried to walk lightly on the land, I had always taken something away, be it photographs, memories, knowledge, or even wisdom. I had taken as if I deserved these things, without any thought of making a return. I had hoarded experience, living on memories and dreams. But here was a being that gave of its beauty freely, abundantly, without calculation. It belonged here, and it was not going down. Gazing upon it, I realized that I too would have to be rooted to grow. I would have to give up my dream of the West, even though I had no idea what could possibly replace it. I would move to Minnesota, though how I could live there was difficult to imagine. I would have to make some return for the gifts all these journeys had given. What form that might take was as dark to me as the sky. Yet the flower before me glowed with grace and forgiveness.

I ran down to the saddle, where Tom and Kim were waiting.

"Was that you laughing up there?" Kim asked.

"Yes," I said, panting. "That was me. I stopped for a flower."

Kim rolled his eyes. "First, he takes me up a peak in a storm. Then he gets lost on the cliffs. Then, just when we're about to escape, he stops for a flower. I will never understand these guys from the East."

"Me neither," Tom laughed, "but who cares? We're outta here!" He jumped onto the snowfield. "Check out my skateboard glissade!"

We leapt after him, sliding dizzily in the snow. Halfway down I looked back to see gray cumuli crowding the summit. A peal of thunder boomed out of Titcomb Basin.

"We're leaving!" Kim shouted. "We're leaving!"

Ten minutes later we skidded off the snow, which had taken an hour to climb. Thunder crashed behind us, echoing across the basin. We struck out for the shore of the largest lake, where we spotted Kathy striding along in her poncho. She stopped when she heard our shouts. "Hi, guys!" she called. "Did you get what you wanted?"

Before we could answer another crash shook the air. We looked back to see the south face completely socked in. Lightning was striking the ridge we had come down less than an hour before. Somewhere up there was my polemonium, blooming.

The whole basin now began shaking with flashes and detonations. We turned and hurried off down the trail. Rain came over the ridge as a driving mist that soon increased to a downpour. Back at camp we cooked and ate in the tents. The next day we hiked fourteen miles out of the Winds and drove six hours back to Salt Lake City.

CHAPTER TEN

Moving to Minnesota

A SPECIAL PLACE

Salt Lake was hot, hotter than I had ever known it. After being shut up for a week, my apartment felt like a sauna. The night after our return from the Winds, I lay awake listening to the rattle of dry leaves, tasting dust. Toward dawn I fell asleep and dreamed of water. In the morning my skin felt as if it had been painted with varnish.

I spent the next weeks in farewell, cutting ties. My colleagues were impressed by the "plum job" I had found, but what did they know? Only those who had hiked with me could understand the feelings that throbbed beneath the cheerful, busy facade I presented during a flurry of last-minute research, errands, and meetings. I climbed the Pfeifferhorn once more to savor its views of blue remoteness, but the sight no longer held any dream of the future. Instead a strong, high wind blew out of the Great Basin while Salt Lake sprawled below in a haze of smog, complacent beneath its evil exhalations.

During the last week I packed all I owned into the smallest truck that U-Haul had to offer. Besides some thirty cartons of books and files, there were only three chairs, two suitcases, a box of dishes, and my camping gear. My landlady, compassionate, insisted I take the recliner from her furnished apartment, in which I had sat so many nights grading papers. I hitched the Volkswagen behind, gathered a few vegetables from the garden, shook hands with Tom, Kim, Kathy, Dave, and Becky. Everyone promised to keep in touch, but who were we kidding? This Utah life was over, and all of us would go on to new adventures. I climbed in and started the engine. It was only when the interstate plunged into Parley's Canyon that all the week's pent-up feelings began to flow. Perhaps it was the spectacle of so much raw debris, or maybe the howl of the engine straining against the grade, but by the time I had reached the top, I was sobbing through clenched teeth and pounding the steering wheel. It was all I could do to stay in the lane. Fortunately there were few other cars heading east at this hour. By the time I reached Wyoming, the fit had passed. My face felt as raw as sandpaper. My hands, stiff and swollen, seemed welded to the wheel.

Leaving Utah was worse than leaving Connecticut, for it meant giving up a dream as well as a place. The future lay east, but with no dream for guidance, how could I get there? I felt like a man struck blind who gropes with extended hands, not yet having learned how to move by listening. A cloud bank followed me all across Wyoming, and by sundown the underglow had made it look like a slab of meat. I drove mechanically, fuelled by bad coffee, into the endless dark of the Great Plains. At every stop the wind came rushing eastward, rattling the dry grass and chicory by the roadside, cooling my back where it had sweated against the truck's cracked vinyl upholstery. Overhead, stars glinted like motes of dust. In my dazed condition I felt the wind could have picked me up like a tumbleweed. By midnight the road had crossed the hundredth meridian and reached the Missouri at Chamberlain, South Dakota. I drove across the bridge into a solid wall of humidity.

Next morning the road cut its way through grain for hundreds of miles. It seemed to be floating in a sea of corn broken only by the occasional blue-green of oats or the yellow of stiff, shaved wheat. I rolled down the windows to keep from dissolving in sweat. The land was all fenced and planted; after Wyoming's open range, the manicured farms seemed tame, even claustrophobic. How different this journey was from the last time I had crossed the Plains, full of desire that had seemed so young and strong. Then the great distances had beckoned; now my mind was a fist of disappointment.

It was afternoon when I crossed the Minnesota border and turned northeast on secondary roads, slowing for small, well-kept towns embroidered with fruit trees and flower beds. Here were gardens thick with squash and tomatoes, raspberry patches, orchards laden with early apples. The road passed lakes where people fished from motorboats or canoes. I saw red-winged blackbirds darting among cattails, while great blue herons posed in the shallows like Giacometti statues. On the horizon white cumuli were gathering into thunderheads, promising rain. I thought of my asparagus beds back home in Connecticut, my apple trees that had gone unpruned for years. I thought of Lake Waramaug and its glacial rock. I thought of water.

Approaching Northfield, the land grew lumpy, low rounded hills and hollows filled with marshes or lakes. After the Plains even a small hill could kindle hope, but these offered scant relief. A Chamber of Commerce sign proclaimed Northfield "A Special Place." What did they know? It was getting dark. The air felt close, heavy with moisture; the sky had turned an ominous, murky green. I found the restaurant where I had been interviewed and ordered a hamburger and a pitcher of beer. Thunder grumbled outside as rain skittered against the glass. By the time I was halfway through the pitcher, the wind had risen to a howl, and the rain was roaring like gravel in a chute. Every few seconds the windows flashed and the building shook. Somewhere a siren went off. I thought of arriving in Salt Lake three years before, of huddling in a tent high in the Winds, of leaping off Frémont's shoulder onto the snow. But here there was no place to escape.

I drank until the storm moved on, then drove to the unfurnished house I had signed up to rent from the college. I locked the truck and carried my pack inside. The place smelled of plaster, fresh paint, and attic dust. My footsteps echoed on the bare wood floors. I rolled out a foam pad and a sleeping bag. What is a house, I thought, but a slightly more permanent tent?

PRAIRIE AND WOOD

Next morning the streets were dry. I walked around town, admiring the white Victorian homes set out like wedding cakes on their deep green lawns and shaded by elms as venerable as those of New Haven. Along Division Street, in the center of town, antique storefronts alternated with 1950s brick and aluminum. I discovered the Ideal Café, which opened for breakfast at 5:00 A.M. and carried local poetry on the menus. I discovered Jacobsen's dry goods store, which carried button-down shirts and size 50 overalls. Beyond the town square, with its fountain designed by a local sculptor, the Cannon River ran brown and full past the Malto-Meal plant, from which a sweet, farinaceous odor came wafting over the town.

Northfield seemed like a wholesome place. Apart from two colleges, Carleton and St. Olaf, its main claim to fame was defeating the gang of Jesse James, who had once tried to rob the bank. Although the town celebrated this victory each fall with a carnival and an art show, there did not seem to have been a lot of action since then. When I turned on public radio in the morning, I would sometimes hear creepy organ music and Garrison Keillor reading police reports from the *Northfield News*: "Keys were locked in a car! . . . *Kids* were running in the street! . . . *Trash cans* were mysteriously overturned!"

My new colleagues were trim, lively people with clothes from the L. L. Bean catalog and degrees from places like Chicago, Stanford, and Yale. They came from all over the country—two had even grown up in Utah— and they all had landed, like me, in this small, elite institution surrounded by cornfields. The students proved equally cosmopolitan. Here was a "college" in the original sense: a gathering of people committed to living and learning together. Though some of us would remain here longer than others, we all faced the task of creating a community.

For me that meant learning to stay in one place. I worked till midnight on weekdays and explored the countryside on weekends, striving to orient myself in what seemed largely featureless terrain. Beyond the town's thick trees, the land rolled off in billows of corn and oats toward horizons broken only by the occasional feed mixer or silo. My geologist colleagues described the land as "low-relief, hummocky terrain" found at the edge of continental glaciers, where the ice had kneaded the land like bread as it moved back and forth in response to small changes in climate. To one enamored of geologic time, there was some comfort in contemplating the grandeur of Pleistocene ice and the huge beasts that had roamed these steppes when people first came into North America. I noticed the granite boulders that farmers had dragged from their fields; they had originated hundreds of miles to the north in the Canadian Shield, where the earth's original crust was exposed. Apart from such erratics, the land hardly spoke in dramatic gestures. Rock was exposed mainly in roadcuts, where I found white layers of Saint Peter Sandstone, the remains of an Ordovician beach, or the younger Decorah Shale, studded with fossil cephalopods. These strata had lain undisturbed for five hundred million years, suggesting only the heartland's endless, cratonic sleep. This landscape, I thought, had nothing to beckon adventurers.

Not surprisingly, wilderness also proved to be scarce. This was farm country, and every arable square foot had been put to use. Outside of town the trees grew only in shelterbelts, along creek bottoms, or in ravines where the land was too steep to plow. As for the fields, they looked as tidy as lawns, industrial monocultures rolled out like carpet beneath the sky. I remembered the Illinois cornfield into which I had ventured years before on the way to California; it had felt like walking into a factory. The only thing wild in such landscapes was the sky, which could build John Muir's "cloud mountains" and generate storms of extraordinary violence.

When I shared these impressions with my colleagues, they urged me to visit McKnight Prairie, a forty-acre tract that had been donated to the college. It had been grazed, they said, but never plowed, and many of its native plants remained. I drove out the next afternoon, threading a maze of gravel roads to a low hill surrounded by corn. There was no sign, and the place did not look promising. I started toward the highest point, wading through milkweed, goldenrod, and a blue-green grass that spread from the roadsides like matted hair. The going got easier on the slopes, where the plants grew shorter as the soil dried out. Climbing felt, oddly, like coming ashore. On top I found a quite different community: short, bristly grasses that grew in tufts, dried clumps of flowers with spiny stalks, prostrate hairy-leafed plants that spread in rosettes like alpine species, and even some bright-colored lichen on slabs of bedrock. The air felt cooler up here; the wind blew steadily out of the west as if it had been traveling unimpeded for hundreds of miles. Surely this was the same wind that Shelley, my student from Kansas, had written of years before on the top of Mount Katahdin. I could imagine it starting out from the cirques of the Wind River Range and rushing over a thousand miles of sandy-colored grass. Now this remnant of prairie rose like an island awash in alien corn. But the wind had not changed. It still brought messages from the distant mountains.

I drove back to town thinking only of the West. I was not ready to understand the prairie; to me it was just a low hill with a strange, archaic feel. Back home, work seemed to intensify as fall descended upon the campus.

By early October the lawns were sprinkled with frost, and the morning wind carried odors of straw and spices. All over town the trees had begun to turn, first the sugar maples, whose tops caught an orange that crept like flames through their massed, green foliage, then the poplars and cottonwoods that turned yellow all at once as if touched with a magic wand. I strolled through the neighborhoods, snapping close-ups of leaves, branches, and tree crowns that shone through my lens like Byzantine mosaics. Outside of town the colors were just as rich: brown corduroy of a plowed field, agate red of sumac leaves. In Utah fall had brought only coolness and desiccation; the trees had cast off their leaves like dull, brown paper. But here brightness and fragrance both fell from the air.

Soon it was frosting every night. The maples' lights went out in little more than a week. Each tree stood against the sky like a twist of wire, rattling in the gusts that blew from the pewter clouds. By November the first snow had buried the leaves. For a while work kept the cold and darkness at bay. I did not go to the prairie but stayed indoors, and the day after turning in grades, I flew to Utah for a week of skiing and partying. My friends offered welcome and reassurance. "Remember," they said, "the first trip back is really part of your move. The first year in a new place is always pathological." But in moments of solitude, I still felt like a ghost. We were moving on, like graduates, into new lives that would not include one another. At week's end, as the plane took off from Salt Lake, I looked for the Wasatch, but they were hidden by clouds. The pain came back, an ache rather than a pang; it lay deeper now, buried by three months of work and a carpet of dead leaves. I did not see the mountains again. When the clouds finally opened over Nebraska, the high plains were already dusted with snow. As the plane began its descent toward Minnesota, I found myself wanting winter. I just wanted to gather in and go numb.

THE WINTER ART

In Minnesota, darkness and cold arrive together. By Christmas the nights are sixteen hours long, and temperatures can drop to thirty below. Add wind, and you experience polar conditions. But people adapt. I bought a down parka and insulated overpants for the walk to school, but any exposed part soon felt the bitter effects. After three or four blocks, my beard would be caked with ice, my cheeks would sting, and the bridge of my nose would ache. I felt, at times, like some kind of arctic explorer, even though certain colleagues went jogging in ski hats and long johns at ten below. No doubt there was some ascetic virtue in this, suggesting the survival of the fittest, but my goal that year was to build an indoor life.

As winter deepened, the office and classroom windows grew layers of frost that eventually shut off all view of the outside world. Students walked to class through the steam tunnels, whose walls they had painted with tropical murals. Yet the season was full of wonder in its extremes. The snow came early and stayed, building in layers whose properties changed with depth or temperature. I could imagine the same process giving rise over thousands of years to ice caps and continental glaciers. The snow would arrive on a day of overcast when the sky clamped down like a lid, trapping enough heat to keep the air at a comfortable zero to ten above; it drifted in billows like Utah powder, filling the fields and hollows, burying fences like whipped cream. Each passing front would be followed by clearing skies and a cold so hard and glassy that I sometimes thought the air itself might shatter. Wind often came with the cold, whirling the snow from the eaves across streets and lawns, grinding its delicate crystals into a hard, abrasive powder that stung like sand. At twenty degrees below zero, snow ceased to feel like a form of water and became an alien, mineral substance. In town it squeaked underfoot like styrofoam. Out in the country it scythed across the roads in evil-looking swirls, driven relentlessly by the wind.

Winter seemed to epitomize that elemental world I had found in the highest parts of the mountains, where all things were reduced to their fundamental expression. At night the air was so clear I could make out the colors of stars. The darkness seemed depthless, abyssal. I felt the naked hostility of outer space, as if God's finger were pressing down on the earth, squeezing the biosphere to a thin film. To survive, life had to gather itself in, wrap itself in husks, hunker down to den in the earth. The long, long nights seemed to fill the world with darkness. Even on bright days the sunlight hardly warmed; it felt like the pitiless glitter dancing in a crystal. At times I felt the only thing moving was wind.

In such a season one is prone to depression. I threw myself into work and the life of the campus. I held long office hours and invited my students for meals. Since most felt uprooted themselves, they welcomed the chance to sit in a real living room and eat home-cooked food. I had decorated the walls with photographs of Utah, so the talk soon ranged beyond English literature to tales of the Canyonlands, the Winds, or Katahdin. The students listened excitedly as I described my wilderness course. Could not something like that be offered at Carleton? They had plenty of ideas about where to go: the Bighorn Mountains, the Black Hills, or the Boundary Waters Canoe Area. At first I demurred. The mountains were just too far away, and who could think of launching canoes with January howling outside? But the students persisted, and before long I was immersed in the nature writers once more.

To notice some things, one must have a mind of winter. Most of the writers I knew had written of other seasons and dwelt on landscapes remote from this one. The only midwestern writer among them was Aldo Leopold, who had loved the prairie and so seemed a logical choice for Carleton. His *Sand County Almanac* opened with January and a curious skunk track in the snow. The book had never seemed personally significant, yet now it spoke to my sense of winter exile. Leopold, too, had been educated at Yale and inspired by dreams of the West. He had gone to work for the Forest Service, managing game in the forests of Arizona and New Mexico. It was a job well suited to a hunter, whose sense of manhood was bound up with a strenuous outdoor life, a utilitarian conservationist in the mold of Pinchot and Roosevelt. But Leopold's western adventures had led to unlooked-for conversions. The sight of a strange, green fire in the eyes of a dying wolf had opened his own eyes to the limitations of scientific management, particularly as it concerned the relationships between predators and prey. The spectacle of mountains denuded by unchecked deer herds had made him realize that once people killed the wolves, they would have to take over the job of controlling the deer. He had begun to ponder the complex, communal relations that govern natural systems. He thought they might have ethical implications.

Leopold had intended to stay in the West forever. He had even married into a prominent New Mexico ranching family. But one day a spring snow storm had caught him in the mountains unprepared. Trapped for three days, he had struggled out with a serious kidney infection. After a sixteen-month convalescence he was able to return to work, but only at desk jobs, never out on the range. Eventually the Forest Service had transferred him to a laboratory in Madison, Wisconsin. There, surrounded by remnant prairie, second-growth woods, and abandoned farms, he had developed a naturalist's microscopic eye and an almost clairvoyant talent for reading the land. There, too, he had produced his limpid, profound, and deceptively simple essays, each of which, as I now perceived, contained the distilled wisdom of a life.

A Sand County Almanac was unlike any other book on my list, for it contained both adventure stories, descriptive sketches, and philosophical disquisitions. It ranged over the continent, while centering on the Midwest. Intensely romantic, its narrator nevertheless shunned grandeur in every form. He preferred small things like field mice and burr oaks to vistas of castellated peaks. For him beauty lay as much in process as in presence: the mating dance of woodcocks, the blaze of November blackberries, the elegant wing-folding of plovers returning in May. Leopold was fascinated by the aesthetics of change, even as he engaged by necessity with the challenge of staying in one place. Eventually he left the Forest Service to take a professorship at the University of Wisconsin, and shortly thereafter he and his family bought an abandoned farm near the town of Portage. "It is here," he later wrote, "that we seek—and still find—our meat from God."

Certainly Leopold's meat was no adventurer's manna, nor fast food either. It came with patience, learning, and sitting still, as he watched for hints in the January snow: a spot of blood, a faint trickle of water, rabbit hairs, a forked sumac next to a boulder. It came, too, with a practice of seasonal rituals whereby Leopold and his family participated in the life of the land. Many other nature writers had seemed content to observe, but Leopold engaged with the land. He planted hardwoods, pine trees, and prairie perennials, seeking to restore the original flora. He spread ash from his fireplace beneath his apple trees. He banded chickadees and greeted returning geese. He looked for spring on his hands and knees in the mud and found *Draba*, "the smallest flower that blows." Such activities grew over time into a systematic practice of personal ecology, where even the simplest acts—eating food, splitting firewood, or drawing water—eventually took on sacramental value. So Leopold could warn, only half in jest, that "there are two spiritual dangers in not owning a farm." I realized, with growing excitement, how this practice must have informed both his teaching and his writing while these, in turn, must have strengthened his faith in the practice itself.

Leopold's personal ecology had matured in the Midwest, but it had originated in the transformative experiences of his youth. The phases of his life, and the wisdom he had harvested from each, were all linked together in his book by stories. Reading him suggested that storytelling itself might hold the key to integrating a love of adventure and wilderness with a sense of community and a prophetic teaching vocation. Leopold's stories were of two kinds: memoirs of adventure in remote parts of the continent, and sketches of his current life in the Midwest. The former, describing moments of transformation, resembled conversion narratives; the latter, illustrating his personal ecology, seemed more like parables. At first I responded most strongly to his western stories, which were vivid, elegiac, and sweet with the same nostalgia I felt for the Deeps and the Winds. I was surprised when he warned that it was "a point of wisdom never to revisit a wilderness"; after reading his lovely account of canoeing the Colorado Delta, I could not imagine why he had stayed in Wisconsin. But without some distance in space and time he might not have been able to write about those green lagoons; the gifts that he had received from the land would have rested with him, inert. But by writing the story of that Edenic voyage, he had passed its gifts along, thus fulfilling the sort of obligation that I had sensed when coming down Frémont Peak. By sharing the story he had made the place more real, not only to his readers, but to himself. So he would not need to go back. And the loss of those green lagoons to cantaloupe fields would seem, if no less tragic, at least less futile or insignificant.

In contrast, Leopold's sketches showed how he strove to enact in his current life the wisdom he had gained from transforming journeys. It was as if he had carried all those significant places with him and brought them to bear on his Sand County farm. If staying put had narrowed his sphere of action to unprepossessing landscapes, it had also deepened the meaning of even the simplest gesture. Leopold, too, had heard of the Book of Nature, but for him it was more than Emerson's code or Muir's sacred history. It presented itself, initially, as the traces of recent biological activity; reading it meant interpreting scat, tracks, and everything else that hunters call "reading sign." These markings not only revealed who had done what and when, but also hinted at the web of relations that bound land and creatures together. These relations, invisible in themselves, extended downward into the soil's microbiota and backward into the evolutionary past. So reading the Book of Nature meant learning to see the unseen in space and in time.

As a settler Leopold had added his own words to the Book of Nature, writing, as he put it, with axe in hand. He was aware of the responsibility such actions imposed. As a hunter, he killed for meat. As a gardener, he harvested apples and fertilized the trees; he cut birch saplings that interfered with his pines. For better or worse, each choice left a mark. In a world where one creature's meat was another's death, there could be no moral purity. Yet the land's integrity and coherence were vivid, unmistakable facts. Each individual transaction—catastrophe for one, harvest or feast for another—contributed to the flow of meaning and energy through the system. Leopold often seemed unsure about how to judge his own actions. But rather than worry, he chose to honor in stories and parables the creatures with whom his own life was enmeshed.

By pursuing the craft of a storyteller, Leopold seemed to be trying to imitate natural systems, where nothing is lost and destruction promotes new growth. For narrative, like soil building, always requires transformation. Writing of pine trees, Leopold had found himself thinking of institutions. The pine needles fall, like the farewell addresses of public servants, and are "filed in the duff to increase the wisdom of the stand. It is this accumulated wisdom that hushes the footsteps of whoever walks under pines." He might have added, but was content to imply, that it takes a year or more for such wisdom to be released, either by composting bacteria or by the storyteller's imagination. And such transformation takes place in the dark, under snow, in the soil below dreams or memory. It is slow, secretive, unheroic work. How few poets have sung the virtues of compost! And yet what finally sustains the land and everything on it? The humility of a storyteller returning gifts corresponds to the humble processes whereby last summer's wreckage is transformed into the humus of tomorrow. In this way, as Leopold saw, our humanity grows from the earth.

Storytelling was the art that helped people get through winter. The Ojibway in their bark lodges had woven myths against the outer darkness, creating culture in a circle of firelight. I could feel the same warmth coalesce in my living room, where students sat on the floor eating popcorn and telling of climbs in Wyoming or canoe trips in northern Ontario. We, too, were imitating nature, creating niches in one another's minds and turning experience into wisdom by means of story. All this stirred memory and desire in the dead of winter. It helped us to keep faith that we would hear once again the laughter of moving water.

LIVING WITH BIOLOGICAL TIME

In late February I began to dream again. I would find myself in the Arctic, walking down wide yellow valleys stitched by crinkled streams, or driving for hours through forests of black spruce to a put-in point on a nameless lake whose waters, I knew, flowed into Hudson's Bay. Sometimes I would dream of maps, my eye ranging over white space dotted with Eskimo names toward the pink-rimmed, indented coastlines of the far north.

Outside, November's snow still lay packed against the elms and maples. But one day the air warmed into the low twenties, just enough to create patches of thaw around anything dark that stood in the sun. For a brief hour I caught a new scent in the air, the flavorless sweetness of liquid water. Then winter clamped down again with new blizzards, and the dreams returned, insistent with color and restless movement, as if I were traveling with a migrating herd.

One morning in March, as I stood over the kitchen sink, I caught the red flash of a cardinal. He streaked into view, perched for a moment on a standing twig, then sped off before I could take a breath. What was this bright spot of life blown suddenly into view? He looked so vivid against the drab, bleached yard, the old barn with its peeling boards, the slatternly, matted grass. A horizontal perch was too much trouble to find; he was moving so fast a vertical one would do. His image hummed in my mind like a bowstring, and later, as I sat writing at my empty desk, the pale, cold, anointing sunlight of early spring came groping through steel-wool clouds as if it wanted to finger each brittle leaf, and blue sky appeared overhead for the first time in weeks.

Soon the air was full of the smell of water. By afternoon the streets would be damp and glistening. In less than a week most of the snow had disappeared, though remnants lingered in every north-facing shadow. Spring's advent seemed as impetuous as fall's collapse into winter. By April the land wore an air of taut expectancy. One day, beneath a bush, I found dozens of ladybugs swarming in the sun; the next I discovered the campus woods bursting with wildflowers: pale trout lilies with mottled leaves, creamy bloodroot whose broken stems would stain my fingers orange, or the lavender hepatica, lover of limey soils. When I checked the flowerbeds around my house, I discovered sharp, rolled shoots of hostas stabbing through papery leaves. I recalled the Zen admonition that wild or tame, no flower blooms without the whole spring behind it.

As soon as I could, I drove out to the prairie to see what was going on. As I approached, its winter-shorn profile suggested a sleeping buffalo. Surrounded by unplowed fields, it looked even more like an island in time. Elk had once grazed here, and black bear had foraged for tubers and pocket gophers. Now I found every grass hummock bristling with shoots. Flowers had sprung up: yellow puccoons like clumps of scrambled eggs, pink downy tufts of prairie smoke, the prairie violet with its divided leaves. I walked bent down, for things seemed to be happening near the ground, and before long I was crawling, looking for spring on hands and knees, as Leopold had advised. I found pasque flowers with hairy stems and lavender blossoms that cupped the sun like parabolic mirrors to focus its warmth on the swelling ovaries. I found a badger hole with a violet growing beside it. And nearby, in a patch of sand, I found the *Draba* that Leopold had loved. A hair-thin stem lifted its cluster of white, pinhead blooms from a rosette of furry leaves no bigger than grains of barley. If I had not read Leopold, I might have stepped on it, unknowing. Yet now I could appreciate the poetry and grace in its tiny form, unique expressions of the prairie's own winter art. I could feel the wind wrestling with it as I crouched, nodding in sympathy. Beneath the soil, I sensed the presence of roots, the strength and richness that grew over time with the humble practice of staying in one place. It occurred to me how wrong I had been to look for a home in some landscape that answered effortlessly to desire. For home is not a place one finds, but a place one makes. One grows a home like skin, like a body, or like a body of friends. Home coevolves with community, as species in ecosystems do. And growing a home takes time, which is most wisely reckoned not in a sequence of dramatic gestures but in breathing cycles like the seasons. So roots push down in pulses, and the soil adds new layers each year, making the unseen more joyously visible each spring, building our faith.

Meanwhile, in the bare fields that stretched away from the prairie on all sides, every low place had filled with water. The migrating flocks had begun to arrive even before the last snowbanks had melted. Now whole companies of sandpipers, dowitchers, and stilts patrolled the shallower pools, probing the muddy edges in search of worms. Over the larger pools and lakes the ducks blew in like leaves: green-headed mallards, shovelers, canvasbacks, and blue-winged teal. Each small depression, so inauspicious in fall and winter, now became a chalice brimful of life. It was as if the earth had opened itself like a hand to catch some of the laughter and movement that fell so extravagantly from the sky. I watched, enchanted, as great blue herons came gliding in. I watched gulls in their sail-white plumage pitch and veer. Over the brown, warm fields I saw hawks riding thermals, climbing toward light on extended wings. And above and beyond all these came great chevrons of Canada geese, filling the air with their strenuous, throaty cries.

To stand on the prairie with geese overhead was to feel the power of biological time. I remembered the childhood thrill of hearing the first honks sounding over Lake Waramaug, when I rushed outside barefoot to wave at the flocks coming in. I waved at them now, though I must have appeared as no more than a tiny speck, prairie-colored, thousands of feet below. I felt the power of spring in the soil, thrusting upward from winter roots grown strong from the composted debris of the past. It gave me something to stand on while contemplating these pulsing rivers of life. The geese beat north, surfing the western wind, strung out against the sky like the notes of a song. I thought of Leopold's "wild poem" and the call of stories. How could the geese find strength for such an immense migration?

I pictured them in their winter feeding grounds down South, where the waters rarely froze. As the days lengthened, the migratory urge must have come on like the tingling restlessness of sexual desire. I could imagine them lifting into the sky, seized by a thirst for remoteness. Somewhere, deep in their memory or in their genes, they carried an image of Arctic breeding grounds. To arrive there would no doubt have felt like coming home. What would they find but a niche of cleanliness, vast solitude, eternal light, and the affirmation of epic journeys meant to end in conception?

And yet a goose's career does not end with breeding. They mate for life and return again and again. Why should the tundra be more precious to them than the bayous of Mississippi or the Minnesota lakes where they rest along the way? They seem to live in many places at once. Perhaps in summer they dream of the southern feeding grounds, just as in winter they dream of journeys and Arctic light. They do not stay in one single place very long. Indeed it would be more accurate to say, as a theologian might, that their home is the journey itself. Perhaps, then, home is less a place than an action. The geese enact a home in their long migration, stitching remote places into an ecological web that spans the continent. Home grows for them in time and space, configured both by the cycle of seasons and the ancient flyway that follows the Mississippi Valley.

To lead such a migratory life would require much more than knowledge and skill. As Leopold said, a goose who leaves the bayous must believe in ice-free lakes and sloughs a thousand miles to the north. A goose stakes all, in a consummate act of faith. To live a migratory life means to live on the edge of certainty. You must imitate wind in the intensity of your desire, but you must also hold steadfastly to the goal. You need something to home in on. So not only faith but hope is required. Perhaps that's one function of the strenuous cries that Leopold likened to poetry or music. Perhaps the geese call out to encourage each other.

And what about us, who also need hope and faith when nothing moves but wind and the mind? We too need teachers and storytellers to strengthen us. Surrounded by tragic darkness and the mineral sublimities of ice, how easy it is to brood upon wreckage, dissolution, or exile. The mind sinks relentlessly toward bitterness. But storytelling can redeem our past by making return for its gifts, for place is a space with a story, and by sharing the story you make the place your own. The present, too, is enriched by story, which creates community whenever two or three gather in magic circles of listening. From such circles peace grows naturally, like flowers that bloom with the whole spring behind them. And finally, stories can open the future by building our faith, for telling a story is both the last step of an old journey and the first step of a new one. In story, experience and dream coincide, completing a spiritual movement in our life that reflects the great circles of biological time. So we engage the comedy of survival with its promise of resurrection. So each spring, the prairie blooms from its roots, and the wild geese return, glorifying and praising God.

That was the key to living in Minnesota. Although I had left the mountains behind in a geographic sense, I still loved them and could always return. Indeed, I had carried them with me in images and stories that made them more real with each telling. Each place I had loved was becoming one of my homes, a node in a web of places spanning the continent and knit together by stories. I could follow the stories back anytime and discover exactly where I was. I was learning, gradually, to inhabit North America.

Back on campus the term came rapidly to an end. I heard that my nature writers course had been approved. As I sat grading papers, looking north through the pine trees outside the office, I thought of the geese in their country of endless lakes. That's where the wilderness lay in Minnesota. I thought of my father's canoeing stories and the dreams that had come just before the late winter thaw. In the back of my mind I heard the rustle of water and a faint echo of strenuous cries.

CHAPTER ELEVEN

In the Mazes of Quetico

Northwest of Lake Superior, in Ontario's Quetico Provincial Park, there is a lake called Kahshahpiwi. To get there you have to paddle five days from the nearest road and pack your gear over a dozen portages, six of which are among the longest and swampiest anywhere. On the fourth day you start at a lake with the ominous name of Silence and begin working your way through a chain of nameless ponds, gradually losing patience and dry clothes, until at last you slide your canoe into a bay crooked like a bent finger. Choked with rushes and lily pads, it does not look promising, but soon you round a point and Kahshahpiwi unrolls at last, like a long temple corridor paved with blue stone.

I have a good view of the lake from where I sit now, on the tip of an island not far from its center. Kahshahpiwi is narrow here, barely a quarter of a mile wide, and it lies in a trough between high, forested ridges. At regular intervals the bedrock swells into bluffs a hundred feet high that plunge straight down to the water. Up close they reveal the striations of glaciers; from a distance they look like the stumps of ruined columns. The water is exceptionally clear, with no trace of the tannin that turns some lakes the color of tea.

Canoeists talk a lot about Kahshahpiwi, and most emphasize the difficulty of access, the beauty of the scenery, the depth and clarity of the water, or the good fishing. But many will also mention the abandoned fire tower on the western ridge, which you can reach by climbing up from an old ranger cabin on the shore. Apparently this is the only place in Quetico where you can get an overview of the country, and for that reason, I suppose, many consider it the climax of their trip.

This fire tower has also attracted us—myself, that is, and four students from the Wilderness Field Station operated by the Associated Colleges of the Midwest near Ely, Minnesota. They are taking my course on American wilderness literature, and after a week and a half of classes, they are out for a ten-day field trip. Their assignment is to imitate the life of travel, observation, and meditation described by our nature writers while keeping what Thoreau called "a meteorological journal of the mind." Quetico is supposed to act as an intellectual and psychological laboratory, and the trip is meant to be more than just a vacation. But so far no one seems to be writing much, and after five straight days of canoeing, tempers are getting short all around. No one objected when I proposed that we stop for a day on Kahshahpiwi to write, relax, and visit the fire tower.

This morning, after a breakfast of wild blueberry pancakes, we dispersed with our journals to different parts of the island. The students looked preoccupied, with what I suspect were quite personal questions. Two, Cindi and Jon, have extensive outdoor experience, while the others, Sarah and Chris, are making their first canoe trip. Quiet, strong, and immensely competent in the woods, Cindi has emerged as a sort of mainstay, tireless on portages and cheerful in any weather. She has a naturalist's eye and a real affection for wildlife. Jon, on the other hand, is quite concerned about the spiritual aspects of wilderness travel. A serious vegetarian and an aspiring writer, he canoes in a purple long john shirt and cut-off fatigues, with his Dionysian curls held back by a rolled bandanna, but his rustic appearance and easy manner belie an intense, almost driven intellect.

Cindi and Jon have clearly won the admiration of the novices. Sarah, who is stylish and suburban, feels out of place and worries about slowing us down on portages. We have been kidding her about her "designer equipment," all of which bears the Eddie Bauer label, and about her remarkable talent for looking well groomed under any conditions. For her this trip is a rite of initiation, but she has kept her sense of humor and so far has been writing more than anyone else. Chris, the other novice, is also a child of suburbia. He seems to have memorized every Beatles song and

Monty Python comedy routine, not to mention a large number of recent TV commercials, and he keeps us entertained with a stream of media chatter. Yet he often notices things the others miss, like the gray water spiders that spin hidden webs among shoreline rocks. He is quick, surprisingly intuitive, and enthusiastic about everything.

Fortunately this island has enough solitude for all of us. So while the students are off collecting their thoughts, I've decided to collect some of mine. My journeys out West revealed a good deal about how mountaineering relates to literary and philosophical traditions, but even after five trips to Quetico, I am not sure what to think about canoeing.

First of all, it is easy to feel out of place and even disoriented here. The arts of mountain travel do not seem as effective in canoe country. Second, my slides of canoe trips never seem adequate to the memories. Everyone agrees that each lake, portage, or campsite has a distinctive character, but it never seems to come out on film. How then do I recognize it while traveling, and what is the best way to respond? Finally, I wonder if it really makes sense to speak of spiritual values in canoeing. The mountains have always drawn people on vision quests, but no such imagery clings to the lakes of Quetico. Canoeing is a much humbler form of travel than mountaineering; its literature consists of a few Indian myths, a handful of voyageurs' songs, and the vignettes of a small group of nature writers. Who ever heard of a mystic in a canoe? It seems quixotic to look for spiritual dimensions here, and yet the possibility nags me like a child's riddle.

Well, the sun is already lifting above the trees, and mare's tail clouds are breezing in from the west. If these questions have any answers at all, Kahshahpiwi ought to provide some clues. With its granite bluffs and glaciated shores, it reminds me more of the mountains than any other lake in Quetico. Today it seems pristine, fresh, vibrant, and cleansed, charged with the energy of light and wind.

I certainly never expected to find such a place up here, and the long interstate journey north from Minneapolis did nothing to prepare for it. The first time I made that drive, I had watched eagerly for signs of approaching wilderness, but the canoe country seemed to lack borders as clear as the foothills that mark the gates of the mountains. I and my companions had noticed only a gradual change in the vegetation from grassland to hardwoods to northern mixed forest. The towns grew scattered, and the farms thinned out—derelict pastures invaded by sumac and juniper, gray sagging barns with rusty tin roofs. The road sometimes crossed a brushed-in stream or passed a lakeshore clotted with cabins, but otherwise it just bored through featureless woods. I did not know I had entered canoe country until the road turned suddenly to dirt and ended, ten miles later, at the opening of a lake. It felt like being jolted awake in a strange house. This, I knew, was the jumping-off place. Yet though I could see far across the water, I had no idea which way to go in order to begin a journey.

But we launched canoes all the same, and the first thing I learned was that travel in Quetico depends on finding the campsites and portages. They are the only fixed points on a journey, and they are easy to miss. Camping requires a place close to shore with enough dry, level ground for a couple of tents. But surprisingly few such places exist in these tangled, rocky woods. There may be only two or three on a given lake, and they are not shown on the topo maps. If you have not been told where they are, you may have to hunt for hours before settling down for the night.

It is much the same with portages, which connect lakes by the shortest and most practical routes. They are not visible from a distance, and without maps you could never tell where they were. On a lake with twenty-two inlets (not an extravagant number for Quetico), only three or four may lead to portages, while the others may end surrounded by hills or marshes. You soon learn to travel in small, straight lines from point to point, avoiding broad, open water and referring constantly to your maps. You cannot afford to lose track of your position, for all lakes look pretty much the same from a canoe; islands blend into the shoreline, bays remain hidden until you round a point, and portages and campsites appear only when you are just about to land, as faint anomalies in the forest wall. So canoe travel keeps you constantly on the alert. Once you misjudge a position, you're lost.

I've often wondered what you could do if something happened to your maps. In the mountains it would be easy to circle back to the trail, but here there are no trails apart from the portages, and those lead only to other lakes, thus leaving you, so to speak, in the same boat. You could try retracing your steps, but you leave no tracks on a lake, and everything looks different when seen from the other side. You could take a compass bearing and strike out across country, but bushwhacking with a canoe is not much fun, particularly over terrain as wet and tangled as this. You could abandon your canoe and try walking out, but you'd soon hit another lake—maybe one of the long, narrow ones—and have to hike twenty miles around to gain one mile on your bearing. In the mountains it would be easy to climb for an overview of the country, but Quetico has no summits or landmarks on which to take a bearing. As a last resort you might try going downstream until you struck a road or a dam, but here the land is so flat that the water, when it flows at all, may flow in any conceivable direction. Quetico is a vast system of baffles, chambers, and catchbasins: it has no slope, no axis, and no geometry. Everything is contorted, looped, knotted, and twisted together. A cup of water poured in at one end might take a thousand years to get to the other side.

Consider also the sense of progress you get in the mountains, where your trip proceeds by a series of minor climaxes. Passes and river crossings add up to a good story organized by adventures and culminating at a point from which you can see the whole world spread out like a map. With the vast geometry of the landscape converging upon the peak where you stand, you feel a wonderful power and a weightlessness in your limbs, as if you could go on hiking and climbing forever.

But no such ecstasies reward the canoeist, whose path twists and turns on itself, following crooked streams, or threads its way among islands scattered like rocky crumbs on the flat, deceptive lakes. Nowhere does the journey culminate in a godlike view, nor does it resolve into adventures shaped by topography. Instead it unfolds gradually, almost organically. The canoeist remains connected to home by a long thin thread of memory but feels little progress while traveling. If the mountains present themselves dramatically, as a setting for heroic action, the canoe country presents itself problematically, as a maze where all journeys proceed by feints and starts, and all progress occurs by indirection.

Fortunately, aerial photography has given us excellent maps that clearly indicate where the portages ought to be. When we get there, we find them trodden bare from centuries of use. Who first discovered them? No doubt it was the Indians who came into this country soon after the ice had melted. Think how many thousands of hours they must have spent poking into every channel and inlet, looking for the shortest distance between lakes. How could they know if the trees on shore were hiding only a low rock ridge or three miles of black spruce and alder? Those native explorers must have paid close attention, remembering every detail of every lake, until they were able to perfect in their minds a map of this country as precise as the ones we carried.

In those days every traveler needed a guide, someone who had explored until the land was imprinted in his nerves. No maps existed apart from human beings, and to pass on their knowledge the guides would have to go with the young people on initiatory journeys. We have found their markings on certain cliffs, dull figures of moose, canoes, or human hands, in rusty pigment, protected by overhangs, and hardly visible at thirty yards. Even today you have to know precisely where to look for them. As with campsites, you still need someone to tell you where they are.

For thousands of years there was only one way to thread the mazes of Quetico: build a relationship with the old people as you learned the land by heart. My students and I have done neither. Instead we have used our maps to cheat the maze. Because they present an artificial view of the land (as it might be seen from the top of a mountain), they enable us to navigate without relying on memory. Hence they give us only a shallow sense of location. Our journey remains undisciplined; though we move freely, like tourists, we gain no strength. No wonder we still feel dependent and vulnerable: we know instinctively that without maps we would be lost.

I now see why we have been drawn to the fire tower. The view would validate the imagery of our maps, thus reducing our sense of helpless dependency. It would give us a feeling of accomplishment by revealing the shape of our journey in a moment. It would provide our trip with an obvious climax, thus making it easier to turn into a story. Best of all, it would imitate the summit experience of mountaineering and thereby disengage us momentarily from this probing and inconclusive mode of travel by canoe. But of course all this would provide only a false sense of security. Rather than bringing us closer to the land, it would actually increase our distance from it.

The sun is high now, and the mare's tails have stretched clear across the sky. Beneath them, small gray puffs have appeared in the west. Time to think about getting some lunch. I put the journal away, stretch around, and am startled to see Jon squatting barefoot on a rock. He laughs, "I've been watching for fifteen minutes. You were really concentrating."

"How did your writing go?" I stammer.

"Pretty well," he says. "I got some good stuff about rocks. They must go deep into the earth, much deeper than the lakes. This is the Canadian Shield, four billion years old. There were mountains here once. This rock we're sitting on must have been inside a mountain."

"Does it remind you of places out West?"

"Partly, but the country up here is more mixed. The land and water sort of penetrate into each other. I always feel as if I'm walking *on* the mountains, but here I feel kind of sucked in. The whole place is like one giant sponge."

"What are the others up to?"

"Making lunch. They still want to go to the fire tower."

"Don't you?"

"I don't think so," he says. "This is a very beautiful lake, very pure. It bugs me that someone would put up a steel tower here. That's not what I came for."

"Perhaps we shouldn't go," I suggest.

"No," he says. "I know how I feel, but I wouldn't want to speak for the others."

He's right, of course. We have been running the trip along more or less democratic lines.

As we start for camp, he says, "You ought to try taking off your shoes. This moss feels really good on the feet."

Back at camp we find the others busily gooping peanut butter on rounds of Cindi's homemade pita bread. Chris says he is "written out" and wants to take off for the fire tower right after lunch. "I've checked out this whole island," he says. "I feel like climbing something." Cindi and Sarah nod. When neither Jon nor I join in, Chris adds, "Besides, you're the only one who really knows where we are, because you've got the maps. It would be nice if the rest of us could see where we're going. We could see everything from up there. It could be the high point of the trip."

Jon cannot restrain himself. "It's ugly," he says. "It doesn't belong here. It isn't natural."

"Neither is this," says Chris, striking one of the canoes, which booms like a barrel.

Jon glances at me, then backs off with a shrug. It appears that we will stick to the original plan. The sandwiches come around; I pick off spots of mold and wash down the bread with instant lemonade. Meanwhile, the wind picks up and the puffs at the far end of the lake begin massing into a squall. By the time we have finished, barely half an hour later, the lake has taken on a sullen, oily hue and the wind comes sweet with the smell of rain. Even Chris has to agree that this is no time to be launching canoes.

We stash our firewood under the upturned boats and string a tarp over the packs and life jackets. Visibly disappointed, the students retreat to their tents, and soon I can hear the fluffing of sleeping bags, the flap of journal pages, and the grunts of someone getting a back rub. I am less disappointed than they are but still not eager to spend the afternoon in a tent. Besides, Chris's statement reminds me of one of the morning's questions. I decide to stay out under the tarp and watch the rain.

Chris had said, "You're the one who really knows where we are." In what sense is that true? Certainly not because of the maps, which now seem at best a cheap expedient. Certainly not because of my memory, which is only five journeys old. I wonder what it means to *be* somewhere in Quetico. How do we sense the character of its places, which are so memorable yet so difficult to photograph? If we can't see ahead, how do we know where we are? And while we travel, how do we tell one place from another?

Predictably the rain hits long before the answers. Driving like spray through every chink in the forest, it shrinks my visible world to a radius of thirty yards. It even drifts in under the tarp, threatening to soak my journal. No point in sitting here, where it's almost as wet as outside. I wriggle into parka and rain pants. If I can't get any writing done, I might as well go for a walk.

Once out from under the tarp, I notice that while the rain has obscured everything at a distance, it has heightened the colors and textures of everything nearby. A colleague who had lived in Japan once told me that his hosts preferred to walk in their gardens after a rain, explaining that water brought out the hidden character of things. This rain, which denies us the fire tower, seems to have turned our wilderness into a garden. As I walk, I am forced to experience everything up close for the first time.

On its shoreward arm our island is rocky but thick with woods. The trees are jack pine, red pine, spruce, and fir, and the ground is covered with sphagnum, star moss, blueberries, and wintergreen. Today every pine needle carries a drop of silver. The moss underfoot compresses soundlessly, like down. As I start to climb, the litter of twigs and pine cone scales creaks softly to my step, as rich and scratchy as Harris tweed. Dead leaves shine like polished leather. The seamless bark of a young balsam fir wraps tightly around its trunk. I touch it, and it feels as smooth as an apple skin, almost satiny, certainly alive. How could I have missed all these textures? On top of the island, fringing bare rock, the lichens grow bunched like cauliflower. I press them down and they spring back with wonderful resiliency. Two hours of sun would dry them to a crisp, but now I can work my fingers deep into them, feeling the gritty soil beneath and the obdurate, depthless bedrock they eat. A clean smell of earth comes up from the lichens, like the scent of an April garden. I close my eyes and feel the rain trickling down my fingers and into the soil. Suddenly the whole place seems to be pulsating! I open my eyes, and the world jumps back, quivering just a few yards away. There is water everywhere, streaming down twigs and branches, braiding the tree trunks, dancing in every crease of exposed rock. My parka and hands are soaked. The moss underfoot has swollen like a sponge. In fact, the whole country *is* a sponge! I can hardly tell land from water anymore. Things are getting mixed, ambiguous. Time to get up and go. But where to? I seem to be *in* the land rather than on it, more like a swimming fish than a human being. Maybe the shore, where land and water are more distinct, would give me a better perspective.

With all my senses so strongly engaged, it is hard to contemplate this powerful place. Because I cannot actually see it, that is, comprehend it in a single view, I have trouble conceptualizing it. I could not know, or recognize, it by visual signs alone. But mountain places appeal very strongly to vision: we easily recognize them from pictures, because we usually remember them as scenes. Our culture has evolved a scheme of aesthetic categories for landscapes, and because some mountain ranges (like the Winds or the High Sierras) fit more closely than others, we think of them as inherently more attractive. Their landscapes tend to be self-composing and therefore easy to capture on film. But Quetico places like this island forest may be harder to photograph because we experience them largely through senses other than sight.

The distinctive spirit of a place can enter in many ways: through touch, for instance, or smell. Remember the silky rush of water against your skin, the chafing of stone against your palm, the lumpy ground massaging your back as you fall asleep after paddling all day. Think of the smells that surround and penetrate before you're even aware of them: the Christmas fragrance of balsam fir, the pepper of woodsmoke that stays in your sweater for days, or the oily scent of fish on your hands long after you've cleaned them. I love the stink of swamps as we push our way through; it's a blend of mud, fart, and rotting vegetables. And who can forget his companions after he's smelled them reeking of sweat, old woolens, insect repellent, and squashed mosquitoes?

Tastes linger too: the frosty tartness of wild blueberries, the delicate snowy flavor of smallmouth bass caught less than an hour before. Something about wild foods invites us to eat with ceremony, as if we were taking into our bodies the condensed essences of their native ground. What sweetness the blueberry sucks from the ancient rocks of Quetico! And the white meat of the bass, as fresh as spring water or wilderness air, allows us to take on some of its pure, darting life and commune—not just in fancy—with the deepest waters of Kahshahpiwi, where it grew.

I move through the dripping forest toward the shore, comforted by the swish and slap of rain-slickened branches. It is a sound I know, and so loud as to deafen me to almost everything else. But here is a good flat rock where I can stand and listen for the hiss of raindrops striking the lake or the clop and chuckle of small waves breaking. I think of all the other sounds that water makes in this country: the ploosh of paddles dipping to their stroke, the rustle of water under the bow, the snore of rapids a long way off, the tap and tink of droplets in wet woods, or the sound of a lake at night, in dead calm, which is not a single sound but a magnification of every sound, as if the water had gradually tightened into one enormous resonant membrane.

It is easy to be overwhelmed by your sensations here, and because you experience places through all your senses, it is not easy to tell where one place begins and another ends; you feel only a rising or lessening intensity of character. In the mountains you can know a place by the way it is framed, but here is no landscape in the usual sense, no scenery to label picturesque or sublime.

In Quetico the sense of place seems to depend as much upon internal as upon external factors. It is, for example, as much a matter of time as of space. Take this island, which has become real to me only because I have spent time in its textured and dripping woods. No one told us about it, and if it had not been for the rain, we would all have run off to the fire tower. No doubt others have passed it by, even on sunnier days. Seen from a distance, it looks like nothing special, but known with the intimacy of touch and smell, it leaps into vivid life.

I realize, therefore, that sensing a place in Quetico begins when you engage yourself with a part of the land. The deeper your investment of time and attention, the stronger the place will become. Conversely, the same spot might have a different character for someone else, or even for you, should you ever return. For where you are cannot be separated from who you are, and going from one place to another involves a process of growth. To travel is to be changed. Perhaps this is another reason why the land resists tourism and photography: because it cannot be known easily or quickly, it is hard to package or anthologize. It is too complicated and spreads too far. To know it you have to let it absorb you, entering, like a symbiotic microbe, into the tissues of a larger, more intricate being.

I walk back toward camp, reaching every now and then for a hand-ful of blueberries. (Man shall not live by truth alone.) I wonder what the students are doing. Though the rain has stopped, clouds still hide the shore, and the wind has churned the lake into jagged waves the color of wet cement. Chris will be disappointed, but now I am glad we won't be climbing the fire tower. It seems not only a cheat but an actual threat to the intimacy we ought to be seeking. I imagine it standing against the sky with a kind of imperial insolence, stark and aggressive, like the watch-towers along the Iron Curtain. But the threat here is more subtle. Jon was right to suspect the fire tower; it would seduce us into accepting a superficial knowledge of the land. Instead of a living relation, it would give us a visual image, falsely separating the place from the person. Thus while making us feel in control, it would actually leave us weaker and more dependent.

Back at camp I find a crackling driftwood fire, built by Sarah using one match and a roll of birchbark. Jon stirs a pot of macaroni and cheese made with five kinds of vegetable pasta. Cindi has been watching gulls all afternoon, correlating their behavior with the phases of the storm. Chris comes in with a bucket of blueberries. "I found the lunker!" he grins, showing me one as big as the end of my thumb. "I came out to talk with you but you were gone, so I went for a walk. I got some great sensations for the journal."

"Sorry about the rain," I say, not meaning it.

"Couldn't we go up the fire tower tomorrow?" Sarah asks.

"Why not?" says Chris, turning to me. "It's on our way, isn't it?"

I turn to Jon, who shrugs, "I'm easy." And Cindi says, "If we get off early, I wouldn't mind." What now? I do not want these people seduced into tourism; it would go against everything I am trying to teach them. And yet if I step in to prevent them from going, I risk splitting the group and alienating the beginners. The moment lengthens uncomfortably. Finally I say, "Let's get up early and see how we feel. We can decide when we get under way."

This seems to work for everyone but me, and we gather around the fire as Jon loads our plates with steaming, adhesive macaroni. Cindi tells a few mountain stories, and Chris winds up with vignettes from Monty Python. By the time we have finished, it is well after dark, and all we can hear is the sigh of wind and the clatter of wavelets on the shore. Chris goes off to wash the dishes, while the others crawl into their tents. I stay up to douse the fire and check the canoes and gear. When I finish, Chris has still not returned. I eventually find him at the south end of the island, watching stars appear and disappear through the streaming clouds.

"I'm going to be sorry to leave this place," he says. "I had a great walk this afternoon. It was the best day yet."

Later, when everyone is in bed, I lie awake wondering what will happen tomorrow. If the group insists on climbing the fire tower, perhaps I can use it as a scene of instruction. The moment of greatest temptation might be the best time to reveal this afternoon's ideas. But if I am going to criticize my students for wanting that artificial view, I'll have to present a good argument for the virtues of canoeing. I know how to thread the mazes of Quetico and how to appreciate the character of its places.

But what spiritual values inhere in canoeing, and how can I get them across? Outside, rain taps like fingers on the tent. The wind smells of water and broken evergreens. The hard ground kneads my back as I fall asleep, still wondering.

Next morning the sun is out and the lake is calm. We will have easy paddling to the south end, where a mile-long portage will take us away from Kahshahpiwi. As people mill about the campsite, cleaning up and packing their gear, I sense a real change in the mood of the group. Surprisingly, no one seems in much of a hurry, except for the gulls who want to scavenge our camp. They float a few yards offshore, fluffing their wings and squawking in our direction.

As we launch canoes, a gentle breeze rises from the north, blowing our way. The woods smell fragrant and newly washed. It feels good to be moving again, after a whole day in one place. Chris and Sarah take the lead, with Jon in his purple shirt duffing between them. Cindi and I follow, carrying the rest of the gear. Our paddles knife through the waves, and the canoes leap forward, trailing a wake that fizzes, swirls, and closes without a trace. Our island drops away to the stern, and fifteen minutes later I can hardly distinguish it from the dark, crowding forest of the shore.

As I relax into the rhythm of paddling, my mind drifts back to the last unanswered question. The fire tower is still a few miles away, and perhaps before we get there I can find something to tell my students. If canoeing has spiritual virtues, they must be quite different from those of mountaineering, and it would be foolish to seek one in country appropriate for the other. Yet this, apparently, is what we have been trying to do. Perhaps I can distinguish these two modes of travel in terms of the elements that most define them: rock for the mountains, and for the canoe country, water.

The mountains present themselves as a series of obstacles, where you travel by fixed landmarks and focus your mind on tangible goals. You struggle against the massive impenetrability of rock, forcing a way upward against gravity. Success requires an inflexible, almost crystalline strength of will. Often you have to take desperate risks, but the mountains promise immediate rewards. You gain strength from overcoming your mental and physical limitations, and the summit euphoria frees you from all self-doubt. Moreover, your identity is confirmed through opposition to something monumental. Mountaineering thus appeals to the romantic and the young, for whom self-definition is a primary concern. It is fitting that their symbol should be a high peak standing in splendid isolation, enduring with the intense, geometric fixity of rock.

Canoe country, on the other hand, presents itself as a maze. Though it has plenty of rock, its dominant element is water, which penetrates it on every level to link all animate and inanimate beings. This water runs in the sap of ferns, the resin of white pines, the urine of wolves, the juice of blueberries, the blood of herons, the slime of earthworms, and the sweat of human beings. It gathers in deep lake basins, braids into rivers and creeks, or stretches to hairline seeps that quicken the joints of the bedrock. It floats your canoe and makes travel possible, but by seeking its own level it withholds any sense of direction. Because of water the land presents itself as a series of choices and thereby forces you to create your own journey. It does not pose challenges but questions, and in so doing it absorbs you, almost without your knowing.

Successful canoeing requires you to give up the aims and skills of a mountaineer. In the first place, you must learn to travel without a goal, for Quetico has no center and promises no summit views. Borne on water, you move in a horizontal plane, probing the maze with close attention but always returning by kinked and knotted paths to the point where you first launched canoes. You must also renounce the desire for trophies, since Quetico has no passes or secondary peaks, and its places elude your efforts to capture them on film. Finally, you must give up the pleasures of storytelling, since travel here is very much a continuous process not easily broken into episodes. A canoe trip does not advance so much as it grows, unfolding gradually, like a bud, or pushing on like a root that follows a crack in the rock. Where is the heroism in such a process? Where does it climax? In Quetico the land is hardly dramatic and will not let you define yourself by struggle, aggression, or mythmaking.

Yet I have found that this practice of renunciation provides appropriate rewards. Though goalless travel may cause disorientation, it also frees your mind to receive unpredictable gifts. I remember, for instance, an extraordinary thing that happened on the way to Kahshahpiwi. We had come to a portage in the pouring rain and were standing, soaked and discouraged, under dripping trees. Too tired to speak, we just stared at the gray lake, waiting for the rain to go away. Suddenly two minks came slithering down the slope beside us, darted twice around my legs before realizing I wasn't a tree, stopped and stared up with what seemed the most flabbergasted expressions, and then streaked off into the bushes. I had never seen wild animals playing before. They were beautiful with their bright black eyes and amber fur slickened to dark points by the rain. If we had not been standing utterly still, worn out and discouraged and wet to the skin, they would never have come so close. We looked at one another and broke into smiles. The minks were gone. Who could have found them by seeking?

Another reward of travel by canoe is an increasing familiarity with the land and a corresponding sense of inner strength. The more time and attention you give, the more you begin to feel at home. You can spend a day on an island and leave with no remorse, for you carry its character impressed in your memory. The more you engage with the land, the more willing you are to let it change you, and the less eager you are to emerge with the same thoughts and feelings you had when you went in. Quetico purifies you, as a wetland cleanses the waters migrating through it. Canoeing teaches you to love deeply and let go, to accept disorientation as an opportunity to learn. Rather than confirming your self-image, it affirms your capacity to grow. It strengthens the gentle virtues of poise, self-effacement, intimacy, and faith.

The mountains draw you with their sublime landscapes, promising heroism and the power of godlike vision. You measure yourself against eternal rock, and you succeed by the energy of your aspiration. But here to be strong is to bend and flow, to launch yourself on this fluid medium with a willingness to set off in any direction. For there are numberless ways to thread the mazes of Quetico, and you will succeed only by imitating water, which overcomes all things by not resisting.

The end of canoeing as a spiritual discipline is to turn you from an explorer into a guide. In the beginning you chafe against disorientation, but as you extend yourself into the country, learning the campsites and portages, a map of the maze begins to grow in your memory. It is marked with vivid places, but when you bring others here you may find that they see things differently. All you can do is to show them the way through. It is not important that they should all reach the same place, or that you should try always to control what they learn. They have their own journeys to make. Your job is to build their faith in the process of journeying itself, to put them in touch with Quetico and withdraw. You must believe that the land will teach them as it has taught you, and that one day they too will mature into guides, stewards, and preservers of all things linked by water.

So I realize, with something like a laugh, that I should no longer worry about whether or not we climb the fire tower. I will neither forbid nor encourage it, since the process of decision is part of my students' personal growth. As young people, they have every reason to think in terms of a summit experience, just as I, a young teacher, have been all too eager to control what they learn. I watch them pulling rhythmically to their strokes, tanned and strong after a week on the trail, and suddenly I feel a great rush of affection. It's wonderful to be together here, on Kahshahpiwi Lake, with a brisk north wind and the August sunlight tossing up from the waves.

As we round a point, a queer white shape appears in the woods, and I soon realize it's the abandoned ranger cabin. Though the fire tower is not visible, the trail starts there, and this morning we could have the place all to ourselves. Soon the cabin comes into plain view. And then an extraordinary thing happens. As we approach, still close to shore, the lead canoe shows no inclination to turn. We pass the cabin, and no one says anything. The only sound is water rustling under the bow. Ahead the shore begins narrowing toward the portage. The wind brings a Christmas fragrance of balsam fir.

CHAPTER TWELVE

Meeting the Tree of Life

A pine cone sits on my desk in southern Ohio. It is not large—less than two inches long—and it has no decorative value. I have seen other pine cones handsomely displayed, singly or arranged with flowers, nested in Christmas wreaths or heaped in baskets on end tables. Foxtail pines from the High Sierra, ponderosa pines from the Rockies, or pinyon pines from the Canyonlands all grow beautiful cones in the familiar beehive shape. Up close, their radiating scales have the carved elegance of Scandinavian furniture.

But this cone of mine has neither symmetry nor grace. In fact *cone* is hardly the proper word; it looks more like an oversized cashew. Pick it up, and it feels surprisingly heavy. Drop it, and it clatters like a stone. The bumpy, irregular scales overlap like shingles, and you would be hard put to pry them apart, even with a knife. This cone has a clenched, impenetrable look, as if it had no interest in promoting the future.

Such cones belong to the jack pine, a prolific and weedy tree that grows across North America in a broad band stretching from northern Alberta to Nova Scotia, between Hudson Bay and central Minnesota. The jack pine thrives in the poorest soil—rock outcrops, sandy moraine—and it tolerates extremes of heat, cold, and drought that discourage more popular trees. Loggers have little use for it, except occasionally for pulp. If you drive through a northern town, you will not see it growing in many front yards. It lives on the edge of society, a fact suggested by its common name.

The cone on my desk came from a jack pine that grows on a rock over-looking the northwest arm of Horse Lake, two miles from the Canadian border, in the Boundary Waters Canoe Area of Minnesota. How I came by it is a story of unlooked-for transformation, about learning to teach and seeing the unseen.

The first time I encountered jack pines, I was not impressed. It was near the end of that first year at Carleton, when I was still wrestling with my love for the mythic West. Despite all I had discovered about the power of season change, the eloquence of the prairie, and the valor of migrating geese, I still found it hard to think of Minnesota as some kind of promised land. The tallest thing in sight was always a grain elevator, and what passed for "wilderness" was a two-section county park where the land was too steep to plow. I had not yet discovered Quetico or gone north, except in my dreams. But two colleagues who had grown up in the West understood my confusion. They invited me on their next trip to the Boundary Waters.

I remember putting in at Basswood Lake, near Ely, and paddling north toward Canada. Jack pines were growing on the shores. Here and there a statelier white or red pine would tower above them. The border lakes were intricate, rockbound, and clean as those in the mountains, but with no commanding summits it was the tall pines that drew the eye. Along with occasional rocky bluffs, they provided the only sublimity one could find in this country. The white pines were smooth and dark, with feathery needles and haunting, irregular crowns that suggested a character both ancient and oriental. The reds were more rugged and western in appearance, with long, stiff needles and coarse, brick-red bark that broke off like pieces of jigsaw puzzle. The red pine looked like an American tree. With the white pine, it dominated the open, virgin forests of the border lakes.

The jack pines were far less interesting. We found them crowding the rocky bluffs as we slowed toward portages, scrawny trees seldom a foot in diameter, with shaggy bark that curled and broke like weathered shingles. Threadbare twigs dangled from the branches, a cluster of small, coarse needles at each end. We noticed the odd cones that clung to the twigs like lumps of dough. Some were green, some tan, and some bleached to a driftwood gray. It was no fun camping under jack pines, for the sharp needles pierced our tent floors and our clothes. We found ourselves looking for campsites in white or red pine groves, where the ground was soft underfoot and we could look out on evening waters framed by massive pillars and brush-stroke foliage, serene as the view from a Japanese temple door.

That was the lake country: beautiful, surely, but not the mountains I loved. Ever since hiking the Muir Trail, I had dreamed of achieving an integrated professional life that would combine literature and wilderness travel with teaching. So far I had succeeded pretty well. But this country of prairie, woods, and lakes was challenging that dream.

In those days I saw the experience of great literature and the experience of great places as all of a piece. I had chosen to teach for the same reasons that everyone does: because the material, books and mountains, had changed my life. In the giddy, confusing years of the 1960s, I had been drawn to literature because I loved words and hungered for wisdom. The visionary poets of the twentieth century had inspired me with their prophetic certainty. They spoke the truths my generation needed to thread our way through the mazes of sex and politics, the clashing horrors of Vietnam, the cloying idolatry of drugs, the seductions of cults and patriotism. Reading them felt like cupping my hands in a snowmelt stream.

Then, too, I had shared an Edenic view of university life. So many of us had believed that the campus embodied a nobler set of values than the culture at large. College had seemed like a perfect community, dedicated to truth, wisdom, and personal fulfillment. Knowledge and insight counted for more than wealth. Passion and creativity were valued above status and power. Politics was ennobled by virtuous ideals. Best of all, there was a place for everyone. It was up to the campus, then, to set an example for society as a whole. To participate in the academic life was an act of public service.

Our government, of course, had viewed public service differently. The army had looked like the start of a long dry spell. But grace comes in curious ways. A two-day pass was good for a lot in California and often supplied enough "tonic of wildness" to offset the numbing effects of a week's training. I remember lying awake in the barracks as images from those weekend encounters returned: a necklace of blue surf boiling around a rock, the flint-black silhouettes of cormorants skimming the waves, mint-blue anemones in tide pools, dark, hieroglyphic cypresses spun from the rock.

It was the portentous quality of images like these that had first drawn me to the work of the nature writers. Reading them I had discovered that writing was not just a means of expression; it was also a way of seeing the unseen. Poems and stories could reveal the hidden web of ecological, historical, and spiritual relations that give each place its distinctive character. A conversation had begun in my mind between the poetry and the land, and before long I had begun traveling farther and wider, up the coast to the redwood forests of Gary Snyder and inland to John Muir's Yosemite. By summer's end I knew why Jeffers had written of the Big Sur crying out for tragedy like all beautiful places, and why Muir had named the Sierra the Range of Light.

Back in graduate school after hiking the Muir Trail, I had been surprised to find that no one had heard of the nature writers, so I made them the focus of my research. As for teaching, I had conceived of it as an improvisational performing art. My goal was to capture my students' imagination through a combination of wit, empathy, awesome knowledge, and sheer entertainment. Nor was I much of a naturalist in those days; I saw wilderness as a scene for heroic action. So my classes had focused on the literature of adventure, writers like Muir, Clarence King, and John McPhee, with an admixture of natural history and vision quests as represented by Abbey, Thoreau, and Annie Dillard. I could not imagine taking students anywhere but into the mountains. In literature and in landscape, I was devoted to the sublime.

All this I pondered in the fading light as my colleagues and I drove south away from the Boundary Waters. That canoe trip had been like no other journey. Even though it had had no center, no peak experience, no culminating vision, it had made an undeniable impression, like my first excursions along the Big Sur coast. There was, after all, some sublimity in these virgin woods. Perhaps I could make do with the Boundary Waters in some way or other. As we sped into farm country at last, I composed my mind to remember the tall pines. When jack pines appeared, silhouetted against the burning dusk, I put them out of my mind.

Inevitably I became a naturalist, for the essence of the canoe country lies in its details. I took my first Carleton class to Horse Lake because it was convenient: five portages in, with two neighboring campsites shaded by red and white pines. The approach could not have appeared less promising: five miles of slow paddling down a twisted, muskeg stream lined with anorexic spruce and thickets of alder. The water was dark as molasses and frothed over rapids like so much root beer. Yet here and there, a cluster of jack pines would appear on a rock, and we would catch the flutelike call of a white-throated sparrow. Steering close to shore, we often struck sweet gale bushes, releasing a startling fragrance of camphor. We saw mink weaving among the rocks, dark and sinuous as the stream itself. On portages we found red knots of bunchberries shining like buttons. And then the woods would open onto a new lake with its own distinctive character—light, scent, color, and shoreline texture all accentuating the spirit of the place.

Travel here was intimate and absorbing, without drama yet subtly transforming. Each time I returned, I became more attuned to small things: the canoe-like shape of a spruce needle, the coralline branching of reindeer moss, the snap of a dragonfly catching a mosquito. I learned that small herbaceous plants like trillium and wild sarsaparilla come up each year from the same root, leaving annual rings that show they are often older than the trees above them. They flourish in old soil with a thick layer of duff, but they cannot compete in disturbed areas, where raspberry, fireweed, and poison ivy take over. I learned that loons, sleek as torpedoes in water, can hardly move on land. Once I chanced upon one of their shallow nests, built in some reeds less than a handsbreadth from the lake. In it were two eggs the size of avocados, colored the same dull green as an army jeep. I got out of there fast, for the parents were surely close by. Loons mate for life and spend their winters along the Florida coast, not unlike some rich Minnesota farmers. I loved them for their constancy, their beauty, their heroic journeys. They come north to breed, each pair claiming a lake and defending it with their wild, ecstatic cries that shimmer long afterward in your mind, like some sound equivalent of the northern lights.

Returning to the same place again and again was a new experience for me. All my previous trips had been explorations; in fact, I had never taken a class to the same place twice. Therefore the details had often escaped me. I had been satisfied to encounter the landscape as scenery that presented itself in the most blatant, romantic terms. But getting to know a place is a slow process, like making friends, and each time I went to the Boundary Waters I discovered a deeper layer of detail. The accumulation of chance encounters led me gradually toward an ecological view, with a new feeling for subtlety and a deeper sense of participation.

Not surprisingly my taste in literature began to change. I drifted away from prophetic and visionary writers toward those who celebrated relationship and community. I began to prefer the understated, laconic sketches of Leopold and the brief epiphanies of Snyder, both of which seemed to mirror the ways in which the land presented itself. The land does not speak, yet it hides nothing; to be there is to listen, to become involved. So too with writers like these. The sense of beauty depended on coming to see relationships between imagery, allusions, point of view, and the character of the speaker. Here was an aesthetic of nuance, not the alpine sublimity of high peaks, but the variety and intricacy of moss, the dipping sine curve of a woodpecker in flight, the artless art of symbiosis enabling lichen to feed on rock. The beauty of these texts, like that of the Boundary Waters itself, was always just coming into view. It was easy to miss, like a mink disappearing. Reading these texts and reading the land required the same poised alertness and imagination.

This ecological sense also began to influence my teaching. In canoe country, everyone depends on everyone else. One ankle sprained on a portage means the end of the trip, no matter whose ankle it is. To launch canoes, therefore, is to begin a study in ethics. A canoe trip is not like a military campaign; the leader is not the boss, but rather the guide who facilitates the adventure. I found that, despite my familiarity with the place and experience in dealing with emergencies, I was no more likely to spot a moose than the greenhorn (or sophomore) in the bow. Nor could I, in my role as guide, take credit for any such sightings. This may be bear and wolf country, but the animals appear by grace; they are not found by seeking. All learning comes as a gift to the prepared mind. The best memories of these trips always turned out to be things I had least expected.

I soon noticed similar processes at work in my classes back home. Try as I might, I could not control what my students learned. As a young teacher, I had prepared assiduously, arriving with sheaves of notes and a clutch of books, well-scuffed, which I would pile conspicuously on the floor. (I had seen this done in graduate school, with its culture of "esoter-rorism.") After some brief opening remarks, I would try to lead the class through a series of key insights. My students, however, proved much less compliant than those of Socrates. They were always running off on a tangent or seizing on wacky ideas that had no place in my lesson plan. I would nod politely, glance at my watch, and then wrench the discussion back to its formal course. This worked only about half the time. I began to sympathize with my middle-aged colleagues, who stood around the coffee maker complaining that their students were getting more sullen and ignorant by the year.

After several canoe trips, however, I began to think there might be a better way. I realized that my students were bringing to literature the same beginner's mind that all of us brought to the woods. Each kind of expertise, after all, imposes its own limits on the imagination. So I began to experiment. I arranged the chairs in a circle, which encouraged open discussion. I came to class without books, which forced me to listen to what the students were saying, as if we were all encountering these texts for the first time. Initially it was an act, but it got results. Discussions took off. I no longer left class exhausted. Instead of bringing notes, I began to take them. Gradually the act became a genuine style. I found myself changing from a performer and impresario to a plain member and citizen of the learning community. As a teacher, I had gained strength by giving up control.

I suppose it was natural to begin seeing my whole career in ecological terms as well. In fanciful moments, I imagined a kind of "professional succession," beginning with the waste lands of the army. First came the brushed-in heaths of graduate school, where big minds lumbered among the lush growth, browsing on new ideas. This soon gave way to deciduous thickets of temporary jobs, where we all struggled to publish, designing new courses and jostling for a place. Over time the real work made itself known: nature writing and wilderness travel emerged like evergreen saplings under the pale, leggy birches of freshman English. This was the mixed, transitional woods of assistant professorship, tough going if you were on foot, yet evolving steadily toward the light-filled climax of tenure, where everyone would be guaranteed a place in the sun. In the white pine forests of the border lakes, the air was sweet and quiet as a church. You could sit down anywhere and feel at home. I wanted my life to be like this too. I wanted to realize the dream of a community where the order and decency of human relationships mirrored the beauty of nature itself.

Blithe as this vision was, I did not see it just as a dream of the 1960s. It had been preached, in one form or another, by all the great nature writers. Even Leopold had used the harmony and integrity of nature as a standard against which to measure both social and individual character. He had written that one of the banes of an ecological education was to live alone in a world of wounds. People abused the land because they had not come to love it. They could not love it until they had learned to see the unseen. The role of the teacher, therefore, whether enacted in class, in print, or in the woods, was vital to healing both society and the earth. I felt very good about what I was doing. My life seemed all of a piece.

But being made a little lower than the angels, we cannot imagine paradise without overlooking some vital component. In this case, it was the jack pine. Five years after moving to Minnesota, I discovered that despite my newfound reverence for detail, I had not been paying close enough attention. That summer I was teaching my course at the A. C. M. Field Station near Ely, and one evening I heard a visiting scientist named Bud Heinselman lecture on forest fire. I was astonished by his perspective. To my untutored eye, this country had always seemed wonderfully lush and green. Yet, incredibly, its character has evolved through periodic destruction by fire. Despite the abundance of surface water in lakes, swamps, and streams, the land dries out in August, and fires are ignited by "dry lightning" from thunderstorms that move on before dropping their rain. Fires sweep along the ground, destroying the duff and leaving a mineral soil enriched with ash. It kills the tall pines, though some may survive on the edges to seed in a new generation. The versatile aspens send up clones from underground roots that survive periodic burns; what appears as a grove may in fact be a single plant of great antiquity. The aspen saplings provide abundant food for deer, moose, and beaver, all of which multiply after a fire. Since fires bring on lush growths of blueberry and raspberry, bears increase as well. The Ojibway, who lived here before us, were known to set fires to increase the berry crop. The old growth forests of tall pine may be pleasant and admirable, but they do not support much wildlife, since they offer so little food. This was not the paradise of which we have heard, where all creatures thrive in the abundance of the Lord.

Because of fire, what we humans perceive as a timeless, enduring wilderness is really no more than a wave in the stream of life. The pattern of succession, so evident in clear-cut and burnt-over areas, does not actually lead to a stable, perennial state. In the Boundary Waters, a "climax community" does not exist. What we think of as climax forest is only a forest waiting to be burned. The longer the wait, the greater the accumulation of fuel and the fiercer the holocaust when it finally comes. Core out the oldest trees in a stand, and you are likely to find thin bands of charcoal; these trees stood on the edge of an ancient burn. You can find the same sort of evidence by sampling the sediments in lakes and bogs: a paper-thin layer of ash appears like a colored leaf in a book. Using these methods, Heinselman and his team had compiled a history of fires reaching back more than three hundred years. Their findings revealed a mosaic of overlapping burns at irregular intervals and of varying size. They concluded that a given area can expect to burn about once a century under natural conditions.

This fire cycle is invisible to us, because its period exceeds the span of a human life. But all species who live here must shape their lives to its curve. Heinselman took the jack pine as an example. The persistent cones are sealed by a heat-sensitive resin. When a fire comes through, the cone opens to release its seeds, whose internal chemistry has been activated by heat. (Foresters attempting to raise jack pines found they had to bake the seeds before they would sprout.) The seeds land on a mineral soil enriched with ash and open to the sun. They cannot get started if they land on shady duff. The species *needs* fire in order to reproduce. Every stand marks a place that was once burnt to the ground.

After hearing all this, we had to see for ourselves. I stuck one of the stubby cones on my knife and held it over the stove. At first nothing happened. The cone blackened and started to smoke. Then suddenly it began to arch like a worm. It was alive! I yanked it away, but it continued to bend. The scales opened like spreading fingers, slowing as it cooled. I tapped it on the table, and several seeds fell out. They were shiny black and smaller than the head of a pin. Each bore a long translucent wing. I tossed one into the air and watched it drift away, spinning like a fan. We opened several other cones, and even the oldest and grayest held glistening seeds, each one ready to catch the wind. I believe that my affection for jack pines dates from that moment when I first beheld its seeds. Such frail tokens upon which to set all one's hope! Yet the numberless, scraggy stands showed that the species knew how to survive, and not just survive, but prevail.

That fall I stood for tenure and was denied. Four days before Christmas, the dean and the president called me in and told me that my time at the college was up. I had not, in their view, demonstrated "the qualities of mind necessary to sustain a permanent teaching position." They did not wish to discuss the decision; I had the right to request a written explanation from the dean.

It was early morning, the shortest day of the year. I walked blinking into the pale light. My lungs felt as if they were stuffed with wool. The campus buildings, so comfortable and familiar, were shimmering as if seen through a heat flicker. The air tasted of dust and ash. My body felt weightless and disoriented, as if I were falling through space.

To some this may seem like an extreme reaction. It certainly was for me. I had never expected anything like this to happen. It was a disaster far worse than being plucked out of graduate school by the draft. I had lost not just a job, but a whole career. Incredible as it may seem, teaching experience counts for little in academia; professors, like fashion models, grow less attractive with age. But that was not all. I had thought I was paying close attention, both to my department and to the college administration. Yet now it appeared that I had grossly misread the signs.

For about two weeks I lived in shock. At night I would lie awake, heat rolling off my body in waves. My thoughts raced back and forth through my six years at the college, throwing old fears into sudden, lurid relief or magnifying the already monstrous silhouettes of my enemies. No place was safe. The air stung with betrayal. When I awoke at dawn, my sheets would be damp and clinging.

Word got out after New Year's, when classes resumed. My students and colleagues were outraged. They urged me to appeal—what else was there to do? Gradually my shock settled into a hard and glowing rage. I spent hours conferring with my supporters. I filed the appeal, and thereby obtained some of the documents from my review. I requested an explanation from the dean. His letter described a person I hardly recognized. So all my free time went into building a case. It was exacting, lawyerly work, comforting in a way, though I had little hope for success. The documents hinted at some reasons for the decision—suspicion of my teaching methods, my wilderness trips, and my practice of nature writing—but since tenure reviews are confidential, I knew the real reasons would always be hidden.

Meanwhile I forgot all about the Boundary Waters and the jack pine. Life went on, not the life I had known as a member and citizen of this idealized community, but a kind of internal, psychic exile. On the surface everything looked the same: I taught my classes, dozed through department meetings, and ate my hamburger in the student union. But underneath, all my relationships had gone into suspense. Everything I had taken for granted was now called into question. To the college, I was both a nonperson and a cause celebre. I belonged and did not belong. This was an anguishing condition, but it had the virtue of turning me into an observer.

Almost immediately my enemies began to reveal themselves by their behavior. Certain members of my department greeted me with the same bland courtesy they had affected for six years, as if nothing extraordinary had happened. Others became effusive, suddenly interested in my research and my plans. One of these was a man who had come up to me after the departmental review, clasped my hand, and congratulated me on winning their endorsement for tenure; shortly thereafter, he had written a lethal report to the Dean. Others, less subtle, expressed their regrets and then made a point of avoiding me. That winter was strewn with such brittle, inauthentic encounters, the scorched debris of an ideal professional life.

At the same time, however, I received all kinds of unlooked-for support. The students wrote angry editorials and launched a petition drive. My friends in the English Department released the confidential letters they had submitted for my review. Other professors, some only distant acquaintances, called me to say they had protested the decision. Letters came in from faraway parts of the country. Even the janitor in my building, who drove the bus for canoe trips, stopped by the office every day, just to check in. One morning he told me about the time he and his wife had come home to find their farmhouse in flames. Nothing was insured; they lost all they had. But people came from all over with offers of food, clothing, a place to stay. It gave them hope, he said. And two years later, they had jobs in town, a snug new house, and a baby girl.

Meanwhile, as I say, I had forgotten the jack pine, for my intellect was consumed with the legalities of my appeal. Yet as the winter wore on, I became aware of a growing clarity in my emotional life. I began to realize that every relationship based on some calculus of power—anything from professional envy or ambition to campus politics to private social agendas—had begun to wither the moment I was fired. But those based on a free gift of love—straight talk, a favor, a moment of affirmation, a small forgiveness—bloomed and flourished more vigorously than before. Some, indeed, had sprung up from roots of which I was not even aware. And so, broken and poor in spirit, I began to feel spiritually enriched, as if a table were being spread for me in full view of my enemies.

The appeal process required a formal hearing that was finally scheduled for May. I have only the dimmest memories of the first weeks of my nature writers course, which had been planned in happier times. I did not really expect to win tenure from the appeal, since the hearing board could only ask the president to reconsider. But I did hope the faculty would condemn the decision and the process by which it had been reached as a violation of principles in which we all supposedly believed. I hoped, in short, for a moral victory.

Spring came late, and the board rejected my appeal—for lack, as the chairman said, of a "smoking gun." Thus the community declared itself. I no longer had a future here, nor anywhere in my chosen vocation.

A few days later, my class left for the Boundary Waters. Throughout the long drive I sat quietly on the bus, numb with the ache of impending exile. We followed winter as it retreated north. Five hours into the trip, we crossed the Laurentian Divide, beyond which all the streams flow toward Hudson Bay. Up here the woods were budding, open, and full of light. The aspen crowns were barely misted with green. As we approached our jumping-off place, I noticed jack pines clustering, dark and shaggy, among the smooth, chalky trunks of the aspen. I noticed them the next morning, as we launched canoes onto the twisting muskeg stream that led to Horse Lake. We camped in our old places under the tall pines. While the students bustled about, exploring, gathering wood, savoring the excitement of adventure, I sat looking out on the water, as if fixing the place in my mind would somehow undo the decree of banishment. My throat was full of loss. I envied the students their youth, their freshness, their eagerness for the future.

Next afternoon we dispersed to various parts of the lake for journal writing and meditation. Two students, who knew me from other courses, asked me to come along with them. I was grateful to be asked. No doubt they had sensed my mood.

We canoed to the northwest shore of the lake, where a high bluff plunged to the water. On top a cluster of jack pines offered the only shade. We climbed up to them and sat down in the dry moss, lichen, and needle duff, looking out over the lake. The shores were quilted with aspens and ever-greens: cedar, white spruce, and balsam fir. Here and there, a white pine spread its lone, oriental flag above them. I thought how pristine the country looked, and yet it was ripe for a conflagration. It was hard to imagine fire on such a fresh, clear day, with spring winds rippling the ice-cold water.

We sat making small talk for a while. Then one of the students asked, "What are you going to do?" It was not an unusual question. I had heard it often that spring, from my aging colleagues trapped in the English Department, from students seeking letters of recommendation. I usually said something flippant like "get another job." I did not want to own my grief. But here in the woods the question caught me off guard. I experienced a hot flash of anxiety, followed by one of those extraordinary moments when time slows down and everything seems brilliantly clear, as if seen through a microscope. "What are you going to do?" It was not just a question of what to do next, but of what to do now. What are you going to do now, right now, right here? It meant this moment. It meant every moment when someone else consents to listen. What are you going to do with the gift of their attention? It meant every moment of life. What are you going to do with it? Where will you take your stand?

I looked off to the far shore where aspens danced, glittering with hope. I felt the coarse, tindery duff beside me, laced with the nodding shadows of jack pine boughs. I saw the clenched, bulbous cones overhead, ready for lightning. They knew what to expect from that guileless sky.

And so I told those students everything, everything I have just told you. And as I did so, I felt myself stretching and cracking open, and from behind the charred crust of my anger I felt winged words falling into the wind, spinning away to take root God knows where. I realized that this was true teaching at last: the act of bearing witness, to own a truth you have lived beyond all pretense. I realized, too, that the tenure review had come as a gift, for it had clarified all my relationships. It had opened my eyes to the spiritual dimension of life, the network of love that sustains us through times of despair and empowers us to transmute suffering into wisdom. This world is unseen, like harmony in music or the complex ecology of the Boundary Waters, yet it determines the character of our life. It leaves a signature in each work of our nature writers, just as the fire cycle leaves its mark in the jack pine cone. With each winged seed, the jack pine speaks with its whole being the wisdom of centuries of evolutionary time. It has learned to ride into the future on the energy of its own destruction.

Across the lake a stiff wind had arisen, scuffing the aspen groves to white and darkening the water as it approached. Soon our canoe began bumping against the shore. Other canoes were already heading back toward camp. From this height, they looked like grains of rice.

We got up and brushed the lichens and twigs from our clothes. It was time to move on. As the students ran down to grab the canoe, I stayed a moment under the jack pines. I reached up and plucked a cone, savoring its gnarled surface, the thought of its winged and hidden life. In my hand it felt strangely warm. I heard the students calling and started down. I put the pine cone in my pocket. Here it is.

Suggestions for Further Reading

Nature writing has experienced an extraordinary renascence over the past two decades, to the point where it is arguably the most vital genre in American literature. Many fine anthologies are available. *The Norton Book of Nature Writing* (New York: Norton, 1990), edited by Robert Finch and John Elder, offers a large and comprehensive selection from the past two centuries of British and American prose. Thomas J. Lyon's *This Incomperable Lande* (Boston: Houghton Mifflin, 1990) includes extended selections from classic American works, along with an outstanding critical introduction. *Being in the World: An Environmental Reader for Writers*, edited by Scott Slovic and Terrell Dixon (New York: Macmillan, 1993), contains a wide and varied selection, with a preponderance of contemporary work and multicultural representation, all cross-indexed thematically and rhetorically, with excellent notes and study questions. Lorraine Anderson's *Sisters of the Earth* (New York: Vintage, 1991) is a comprehensive anthology of women's writing about nature. Stephen Trimble's *Words from the Land* (Reno: University of Nevada Press, 1995) combines extended contemporary selections with a fascinating introduction based on conversations with the authors about their writing practice. Other useful collections of current nature writing include *On Nature*, edited by Daniel Halpern (*Antaeus* 57 [autumn 1986], San Francisco: North Point Press, 1987) and *On Nature's Terms*, edited by Thomas J. Lyon and Peter Stine (College Station: Texas A&M University Press, 1992).

For those interested in criticism on nature writing, the most useful omnibus work is the two-volume *American Nature Writing*, edited by John Elder (New York: Scribner's Reference, 1996), which has up-to-date articles on general topics as well as individual writers. Lawrence Buell's *The Environmental Imagination* (Cambridge: Harvard University Press, 1995) offers an erudite, sophisticated treatment of ecocentric thinking and representation in American literature; although Thoreau is its center of gravity, the book ranges widely, treats fiction as well as nonfiction, and deals extensively with writing by women, Native Americans, and other cultural groups. Other synoptic commentaries include John Elder's *Imagining the Earth: Poetry and the Vision of Nature* (Athens: University of Georgia Press, 1997), John P. O'Grady's *Pilgrims to the Wild* (Salt Lake City: University of Utah Press, 1993), Sherman Paul's *For Love of the World: Essays on Nature Writers* (Iowa City: University of Iowa Press, 1992), and Scott Slovic's *Seeking Awareness in American Nature Writing* (Salt Lake City: University of Utah Press, 1992). Peter Fritzell's *Nature Writing and America: Essays upon a Cultural Type* (Ames: Iowa State University Press, 1990) applies deconstructionist methods to the genre. John Cooley's *Earthly Words* (Ann Arbor: University of Michigan Press, 1994) offers a selection of recent essays on nine major writers. Edward Lueders's valuable *Writing Natural History: Dialogues with Authors* (Salt Lake City: University of Utah Press, 1989) presents current writers' views on the craft in their own words. Critical and theoretical approaches are surveyed in *The Ecocriticism Reader*, edited by Cheryll Glotfelty and Harold Fromm (Athens: University of Georgia Press, 1995).

On wilderness in American culture and thought, see Roderick Nash's *Wilderness and the American Mind* (New Haven: Yale University Press, 1973) and Max Oelschlaeger's *The Idea of Wilderness: From Prehistory to Ecology* (New Haven: Yale University Press, 1991). On the John Muir Trail, see Hal Roth, *Pathway in the Sky* (Berkeley: Howell-North, 1965) and Francis Farquhar, *History of the Sierra Nevada* (Berkeley: University of California Press, 1965). Mitchell Thomashow's *Ecological Identity: Becoming a Reflective Environmentalist* (Cambridge: MIT Press, 1995) is a lucid, wise, and comprehensive discussion of how experience of the natural world can affect our sense of self and how this process of personal and professional identity formation can be brought to bear on education. For ideas and models of teaching environmental literature with an outdoor emphasis, see Frederick Waage's anthology *Teaching Environmental Literature* (New York: Modern Language Association, 1985).

The critical literature on Emerson is immense. For a recent synthesis of views and a good bibliography, see Michael Branch's article on Emerson in *American Nature Writing* (above). Standard biographies include Gay Wilson Allen's *Waldo Emerson: A Biography* (New York: Viking, 1981) and Robert D. Richardson's *Emerson: The Mind on Fire* (Berkeley: University of California Press, 1995). Synoptic commentaries include Lawrence Buell's *Literary Transcendentalism* (Ithaca: Cornell University Press, 1973), Barbara Packer's *Emerson's Fall: A New Interpretation of the Major Essays* (New York: Continuum, 1982), and Sherman Paul's *Emerson's Angle of Vision: Man and Nature in American Experience* (Cambridge: Harvard University Press, 1952).

Thoreau criticism is also a major industry. Excellent biographies include Walter Harding's *The Days of Henry Thoreau* (New York: Alfred A. Knopf, 1965) and Robert D. Richardson's *Thoreau: A Life of the Mind* (Berkeley: University of California Press, 1986). Fine comprehensive studies include Sherman Paul's *The Shores of America: Thoreau's Inward Exploration* (Urbana: University of Illinois Press, 1958) and Joel Porte's *Emerson and Thoreau: Transcendentalists in Conflict* (Middletown: Wesleyan University Press, 1966). John Hildebidle's *Thoreau: A Naturalist's Liberty* (Cambridge: Harvard University Press, 1983) discusses Thoreau's affinities with the traditions of scientific and literary natural history. William Howarth's *Thoreau in the Mountains* (New York: Farrar Straus Giroux, 1982) includes a useful commentary on the ascent of Katahdin. For critical readings of "Ktaadn," see Ronald Wesley Hoag's "The Mark on the Wilderness: Thoreau's Contact with Katahdin" (*Texas Studies in Literature and Language*, 24 [1982]) and my "'Ktaadn': Thoreau in the Wilderness of Words" (*Emerson Society Quarterly*, 31:3 [1985]). For an excellent literary, historical, and geographic guide to Thoreau's northern travels, see J. Parker Huber's *The Wildest Country: A Guide to Thoreau's Maine* (Boston: Appalachian Mountain Club, 1981).

Several noteworthy biographies of Muir are available, including Linnie Marsh Wolfe's *Son of the Wilderness* (New York: Alfred A. Knopf, 1949), Stephen Fox's *John Muir and His Legacy: The American Conservation Movement* (Boston: Little, Brown, 1981), and Frederick Turner's *Rediscovering America: John Muir in His Time and Ours* (New York: Viking, 1985). Thomas J. Lyon's article on Muir in *American Nature Writing* (above) offers an up-to-date commentary with bibliography. Michael Cohen's *The Pathless Way* (Madison: University of Wisconsin Press, 1984) is a learned and highly personal response to Muir's life and work from the perspective of a college teacher and sometime Sierra park ranger. For commentary on *My First Summer in the Sierra*, see Paul's *For Love of the World* (above) and my article "John Muir and the Poetics of Natural Conversion" (*North Dakota Quarterly* 59:2 [spring 1991]).

The current biography of Edward Abbey is James Bishop Jr.'s worshipful *Epitaph for a Desert Anarchist: The Life and Legacy of Edward Abbey* (New York: Atheneum/Macmillan, 1994). For a comprehensive study of Abbey's works, see Ann Ronald's *The New West of Edward Abbey* (Reno: University of Nevada Press, 1982). Other useful commentaries include those in Scott Slovic's *Seeking Awareness* (above) and the essays collected by James Hepworth and Gregory McNamee in *Resist Much, Obey Little: Some Notes on Edward Abbey* (Tucson: Harbinger House, 1989). For synoptic commentary and bibliography on Barry Lopez, see my article in *American Nature Writing* (above). Other useful treatments are those by Scott Slovic in *Seeking Awareness* (above) and Sherman Paul in *For Love of the World* (above). For a naturalist's view of southern Utah, see Ann Zwinger's *Wind in the Rock* (New York: Harper and Row, 1978). For the human and natural history of the Salt Lake Valley and the Great Basin, see Dale Morgan's *The Great Salt Lake* (Albuquerque: University of New Mexico Press, 1947) and Stephen Trimble's *The Sagebrush Ocean* (Reno: University of Nevada Press, 1989). C. L. Rawlins's vivid *Sky's Witness: A Year in the Wind River Range* (New York: Henry Holt, 1994) will be of interest to anyone who wants to go into the Winds.

The life and work of Aldo Leopold are treated comprehensively in Susan Flader's *Thinking Like a Mountain* (Columbia: University of Missouri Press, 1974). J. Baird Callicott's centenary collection *Companion to* A Sand County Almanac: *Interpretive and Critical Essays* (Madison: University of Wisconsin Press, 1987) is still the best source for Leopold criticism. For human and natural history of the prairie, see John Madson's *Where the Sky Began: Land of the Tallgrass Prairie* (Boston: Houghton Mifflin, 1982). For the human and natural history of the Boundary Waters and Quetico, see R. Newell Searle's *Saving Quetico-Superior: A Land Set Apart* (St. Paul: Minnesota Historical Society, 1977), Clifford and Isabel Ahlgren's *Lob Trees in the Wilderness* (Minneapolis: University of Minnesota Press, 1984), and Shan Walshe's *Plants of Quetico and the Ontario Shield* (Toronto: University of Toronto Press, 1980).

About the Book

Meeting the Tree of Life describes a young teacher's coming of age through wilderness adventures framed by his study of nature writing. Tallmadge's path begins with a discovery of Big Sur and the High Sierra during an Army tour in the late 1960s and leads through New England's mountains and universities to the New West of Utah and Wyoming. There, under the spell of romantics like Henry Thoreau, John Muir, and Edward Abbey, he searches for an Edenic landscape in which to enact his vocation. He turns first to the mountains, whose clean, enduring rock, and sublime geometry promise a godlike view of the world, and then to the deserts, whose austerity and remoteness offer the strength to live without institutions. But each place thwarts and then transforms the author's desire, revealing unexpected dimensions to the landscape's power and grace. When his path forces him out of the West, Tallmadge discovers in Minnesota's canoe country a "spirituality of water" that embodies goalless travel and living by faith. And the cone of the humble jack pine (Tallmadge's "tree of life"), which needs fire to release its seeds, shows him what true teaching and personal survival really mean.

John Tallmadge is a professor of literature and environmental studies at the Union Institute Graduate School in Cincinnati, Ohio.